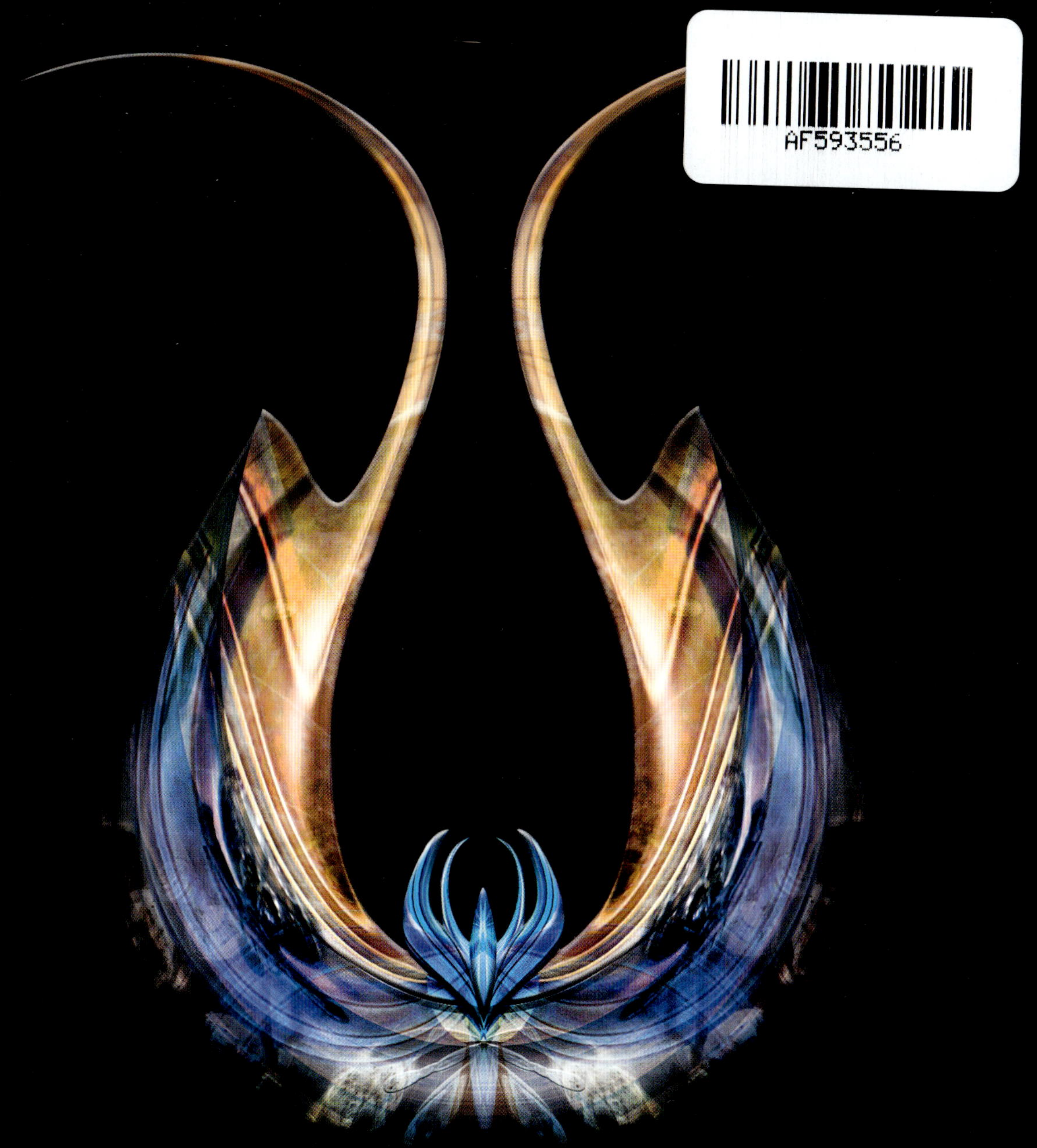

FINE ART PHOTOSHOP

Exploring the World of Photographic Art

Ella Putney Carlson

Amherst Media, Inc. ■ Buffalo, NY

I'd like to dedicate this book to my husband, Rob, who always supports my insanity without question; and to Alison Miniter, the best challenger, instigator, and collaborator I could possibly imagine. —Ella Putney Carlson

All photographs by the author unless otherwise noted.

Published by:
Amherst Media, Inc., P.O. Box 538, Buffalo, N.Y. 14213
www.AmherstMedia.com

Publisher: Craig Alesse
Senior Editor/Production Manager: Michelle Perkins
Editors: Barbara A. Lynch-Johnt and Beth Alesse
Acquisitions Editor: Harvey Goldstein
Associate Publisher: Kate Neaverth
Editorial Assistance from: Ray Bakos, Rebecca Rudell, Jen Sexton
Business Manager: Adam Richards

ISBN-13: 978-1-68203-200-8
Library of Congress Control Number: 2016952155

Printed in The United States of America.
10 9 8 7 6 5 4 3 2 1

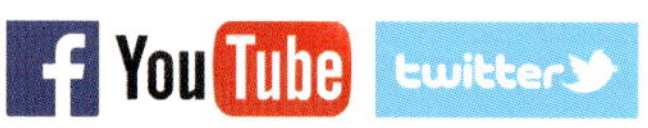

www.facebook.com/AmherstMediaInc
www.youtube.com/AmherstMedia
www.twitter.com/AmherstMedia

Contents

Detritus Series

Alien Series

Tea Reconsidered Series

Collaboration and Beyond Series

About the Author

Ella Putney Carlson

Ella Putney Carlson is a photographic illustrator and educator. She has her MFA from the New Hampshire Institute of Art, and she has earned the professional photography degrees of Master Photographer, Master Artist, Craftsman, and Certified Professional Photographer. She has also earned her educational associate degree from the American Society of Photographers. She has earned multiple Kodak Gallery Awards, Fuji Masterpiece Awards, and Courts of Honor awards.

She has been teaching at the University of Mass, Lowell, since 1999. In addition, she teaches workshops in Photoshop and Corel Painter for state and regional professional photography groups. She has also taught at New Hampshire Institute of Art, Middlesex Community College and DeCordova Museum, and her art has been exhibited in various galleries and museums.

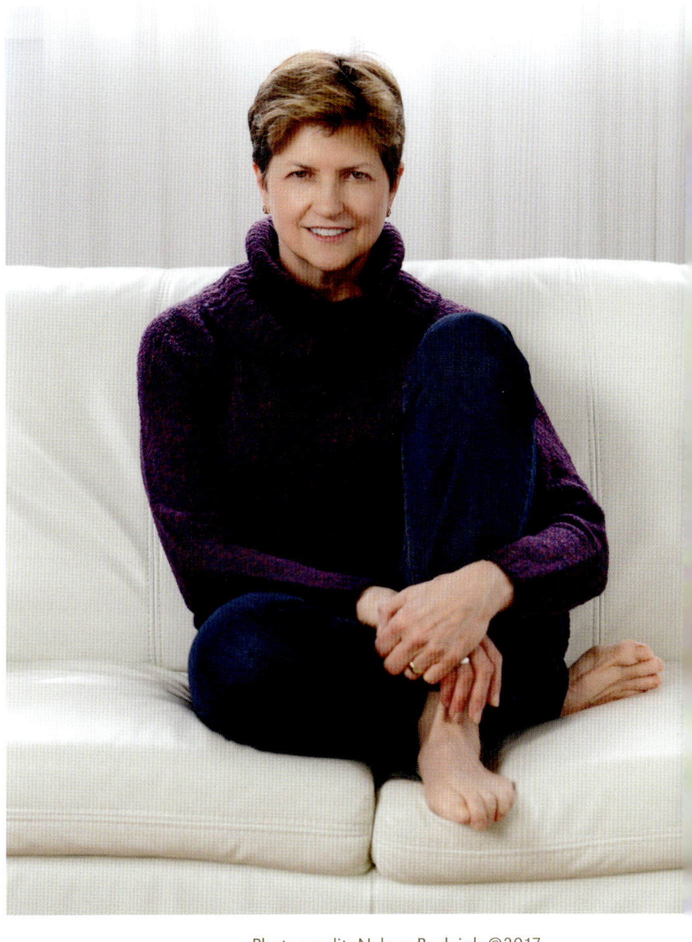

Photo credit: Nylora Bruleigh ©2017

Credits:
M.Photog., M. Artist, Cr., CPP, EA-ASP
International Award-Winning Photographer
PPA Photographer of the Year, Diamond (2015–2016)
PPA Photographer of the Year (2015, 2014, 2013, 2011, 2010, 2008, 2007)
MA Photographic Excellence Award (2017, 2016, 2014, 2011, 2010)
NH Photographer of the Year (2009)

More about Ella Putney Carlson:
www.ellaputneycarlson.com
twitter.com/ellacarlson
www.facebook.com/Ella-Putney-Carlson-Art-271461129552384

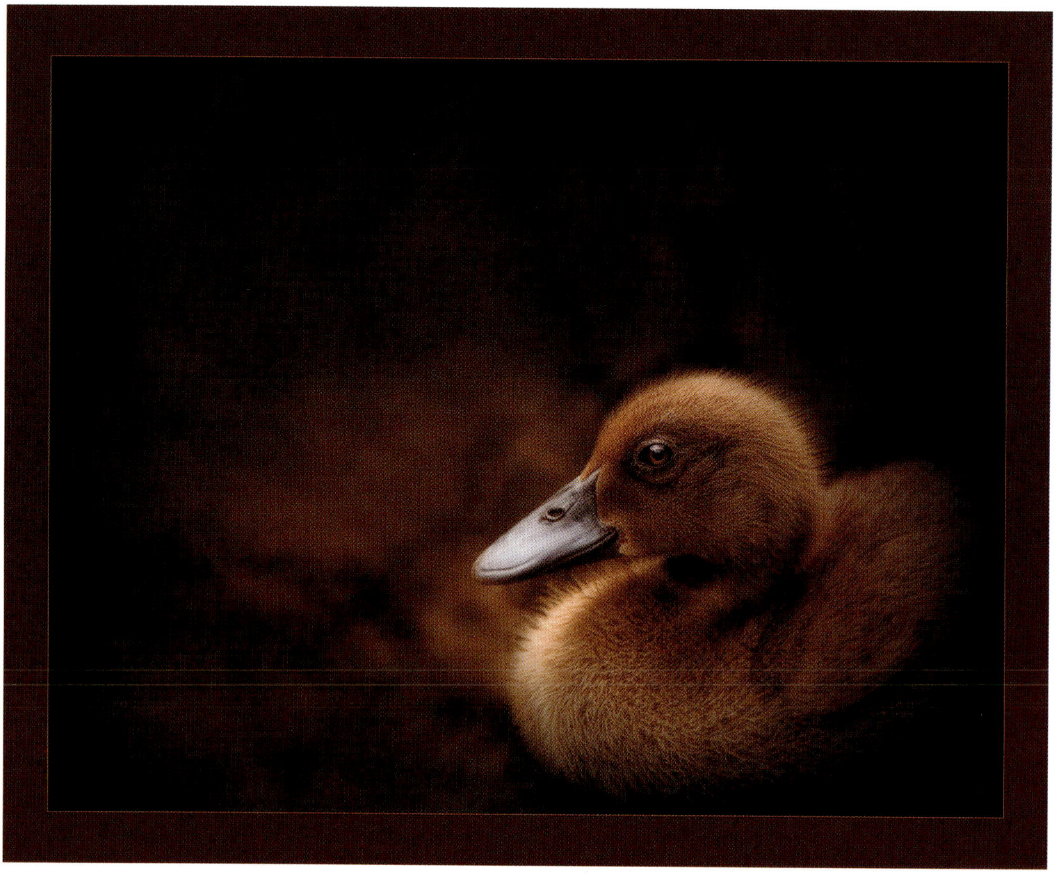

Create An Image That Speaks

"I wish I could be in your head." I've heard it many times, as have many of my colleagues who create imagery that is unexpected or somewhat unique.

My head is a pretty harrowing place at times. The truth is that, in addition to those wonderful moments of creative clarity, nearly all artists are often worried. We're afraid that we are going to lose our ability to see things in original, interesting or captivating ways. We're afraid there won't be a market for what we do. Writers and artists all know that the blank page is the scariest of things to behold. As an artist whose medium is photography, I may start with a captured image, but that is just the first mark on my canvas. From there, I have to use what I know about digital processing, as well as all that goes into a successful composition, to create something that speaks to me and, I hope, to others as well.

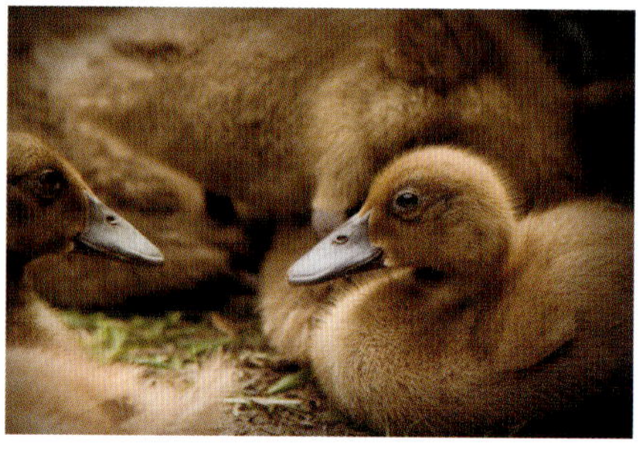

Self-Challenge

One of the creative tools I use to hone those skills is self-challenge. This image, *The Donald*, began with a capture at mid-day, in bright sunlight, and without the ability to do any posing of my subject—not ideal conditions at all. In addition, this little duckling was in a wooden box, surrounded by several siblings. I decided to try to isolate the duckling, removing distractions, and to find out, by experimenting a bit, if there was a quality photograph in here by softening the background as well as darkening it.

On a Sea of Green

Built upon the same basic principle of emphasizing the subject by eliminating distraction, the initial capture for *On a Sea of Green* contained a good deal more detail in the leaves surrounding the dragonfly. Using selective focus, I left enough of the background to give a sense of place and a feeling of movement.

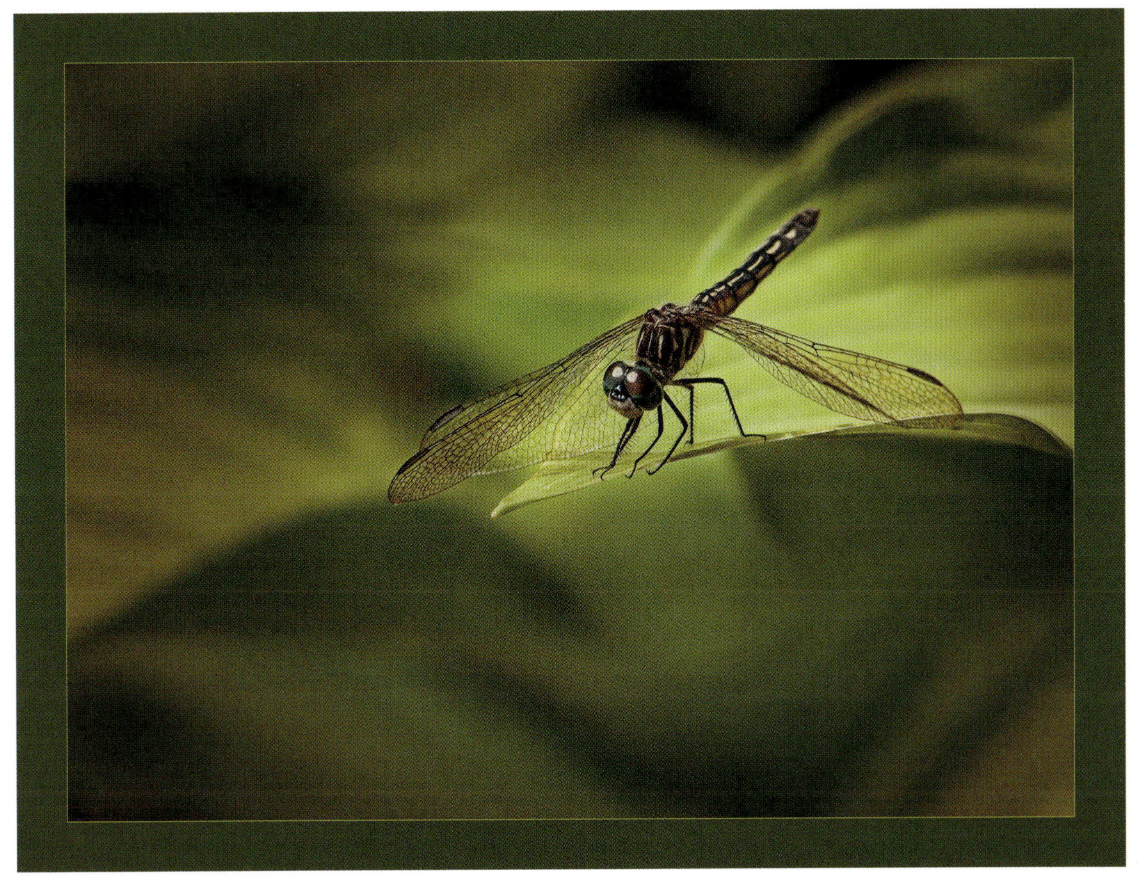

Raspberry

Raspberry began with a mid-afternoon shot of an old, somewhat bedraggled horse. I took the horse off the background by selecting and copying him onto a field of solid black. Since the lighting was far less then optimal, I decided to play up all the contrast I had in the image to create an almost line-drawing-like effect. Some sharpening was applied. More shape was added to the horse's head by using a standard technique of creating a layer in Soft Light mode and then painting it with black or white to burn and dodge. A quick flick of the brush added a few wisps of hair.

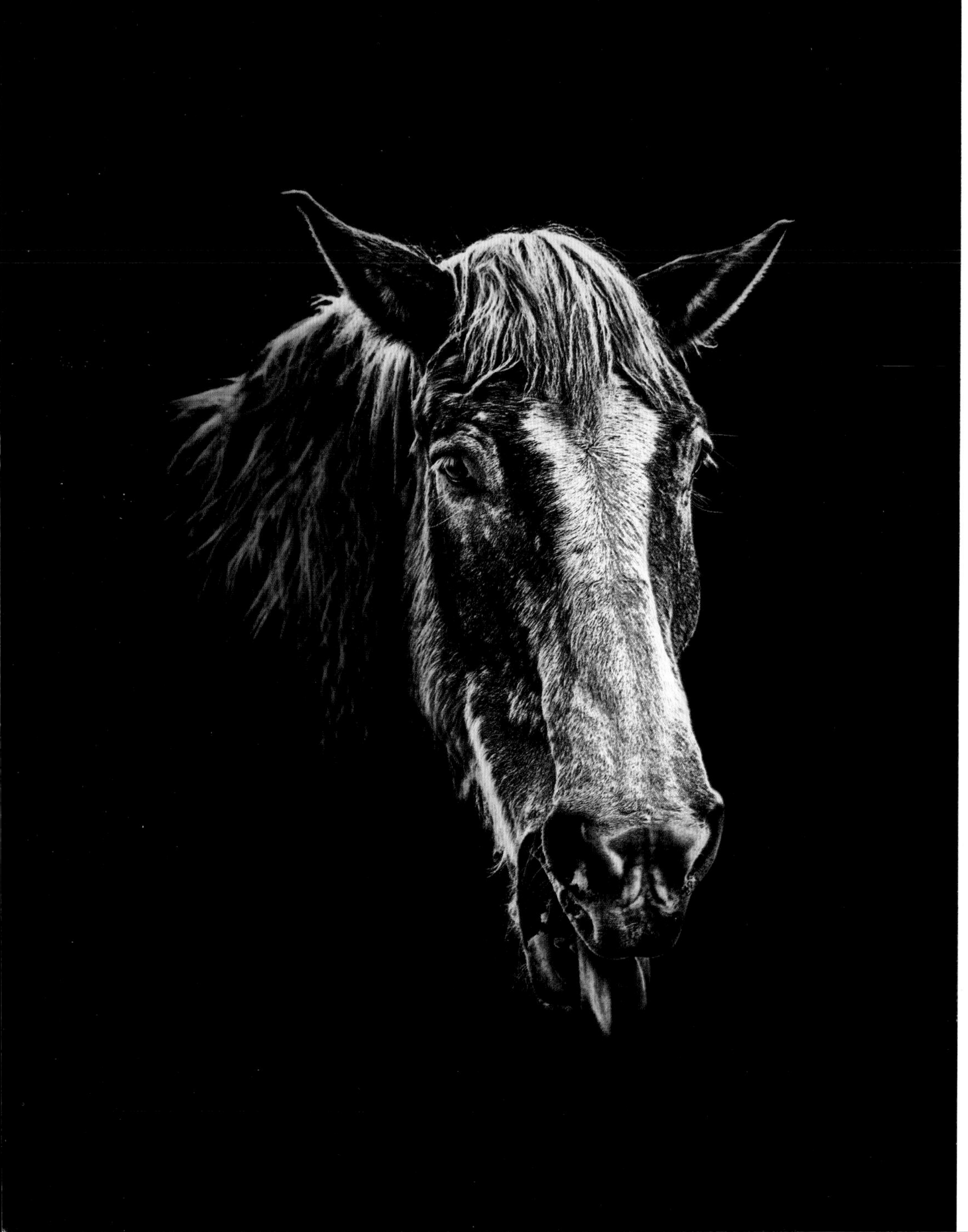

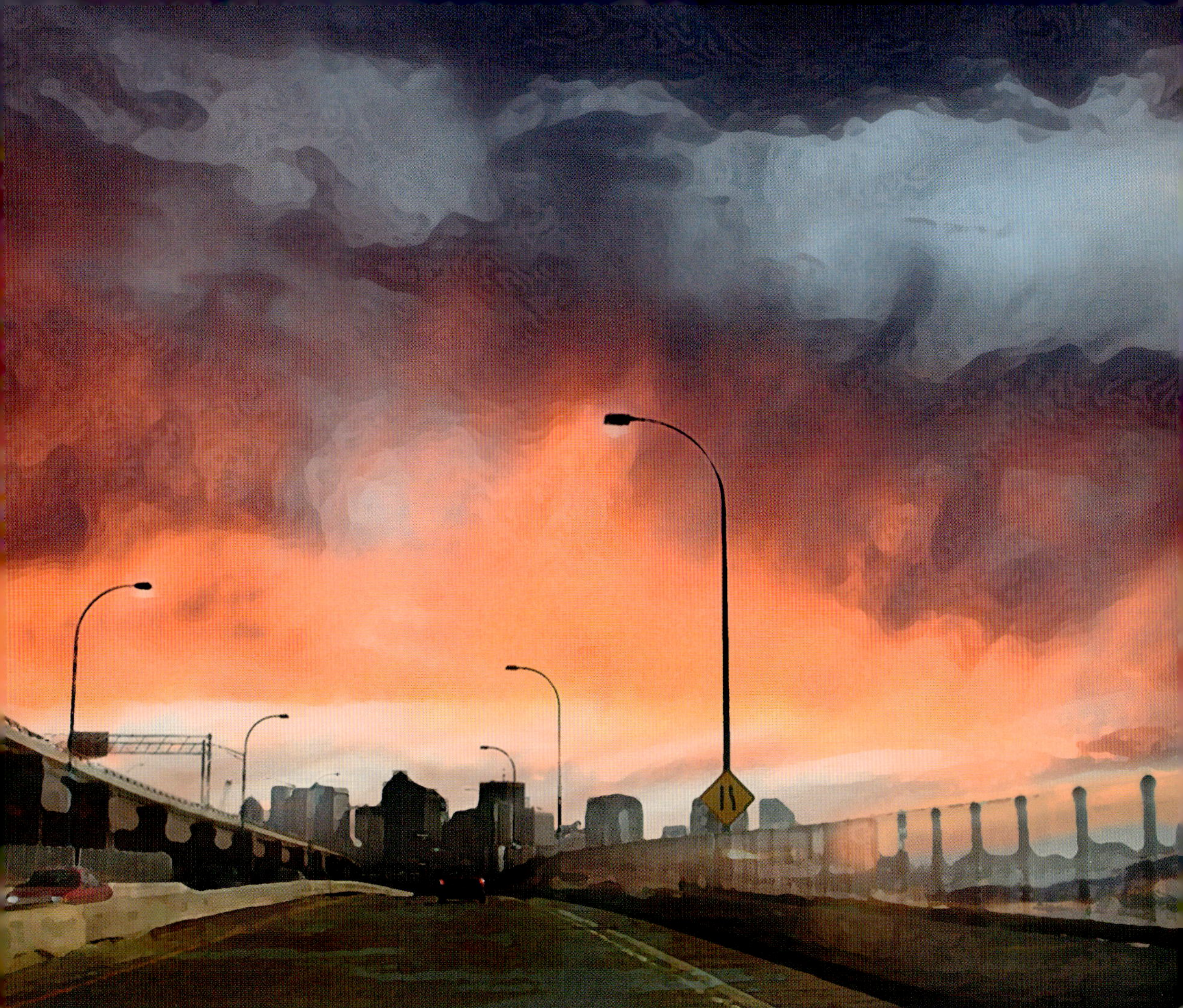

Blend Modes

I often use a sky from a different shot when the sky that existed in my base image is dull or without detail. This is one case where I used a New Mexican sunset on a Boston skyline. Blend modes, which allow you to choose the darker pixels of the active layer or the base layer, are very helpful in a situation like this. There was a good deal of experimentation with filters and painted effects and the result is this completed image.

Blend modes, which allow you to choose the darker pixels of the active layer or the base layer, are very helpful in a situation like this.

DANCING SERIES

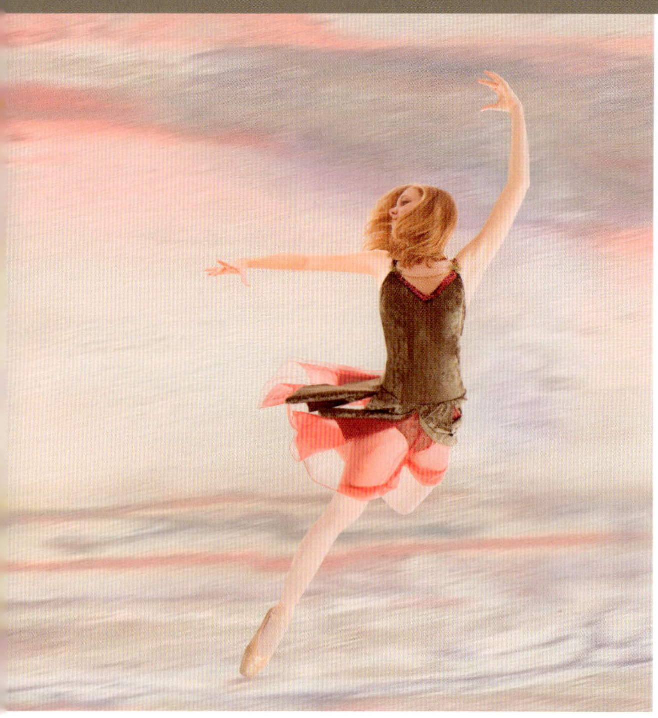

Series Work Encourages Artistic Development

This was the first image in a series of images centered around dancers. I've been working in series for about eight years now, even while I continue to work on other pieces. There are many reasons to do this. When you work in a series, you tend to exhaust the standard or cliched versions of whatever your subject might be rather quickly. After that initial easy period, you then have to start really searching for different and more creative ways to approach your subject. Finally you need to wring out every ounce of your own imagination to keep coming up with something more intriguing and interesting.

Dancing on the Wind ◄

In this piece, I worked in the studio and I had the dancer lean back with her feet and one hand on the floor. Then I rotated the image ninety degrees. While the dancer was in my studio, I also photographed her hands and feet and I replaced the original, supporting hand and awkward feet with these more graceful versions. I took her off the background and placed her over a layer of clouds. I then used the image adjustment Hue & Saturation to change the color of the clouds to harmonize with her outfit.

This is the initial photograph from which the image *Dancing on the Wind* was made. It's important to keep the direction of light consistent when reassembling a whole human from parts shot at different times. I had not planned out the final image when I did the photo session, so I had some tedious burning and dodging to do to create the effect of consistent lighting in this case.

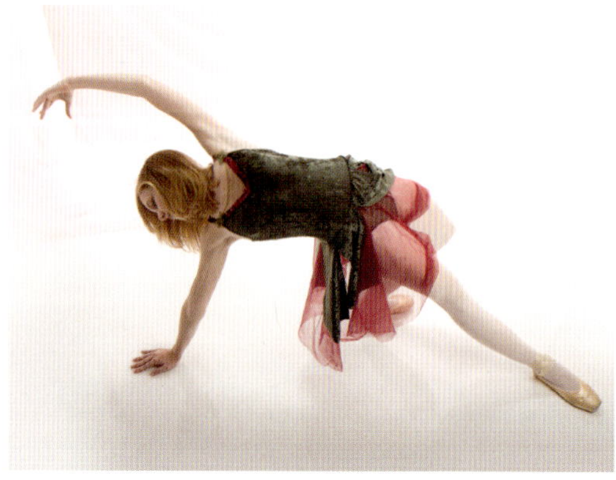

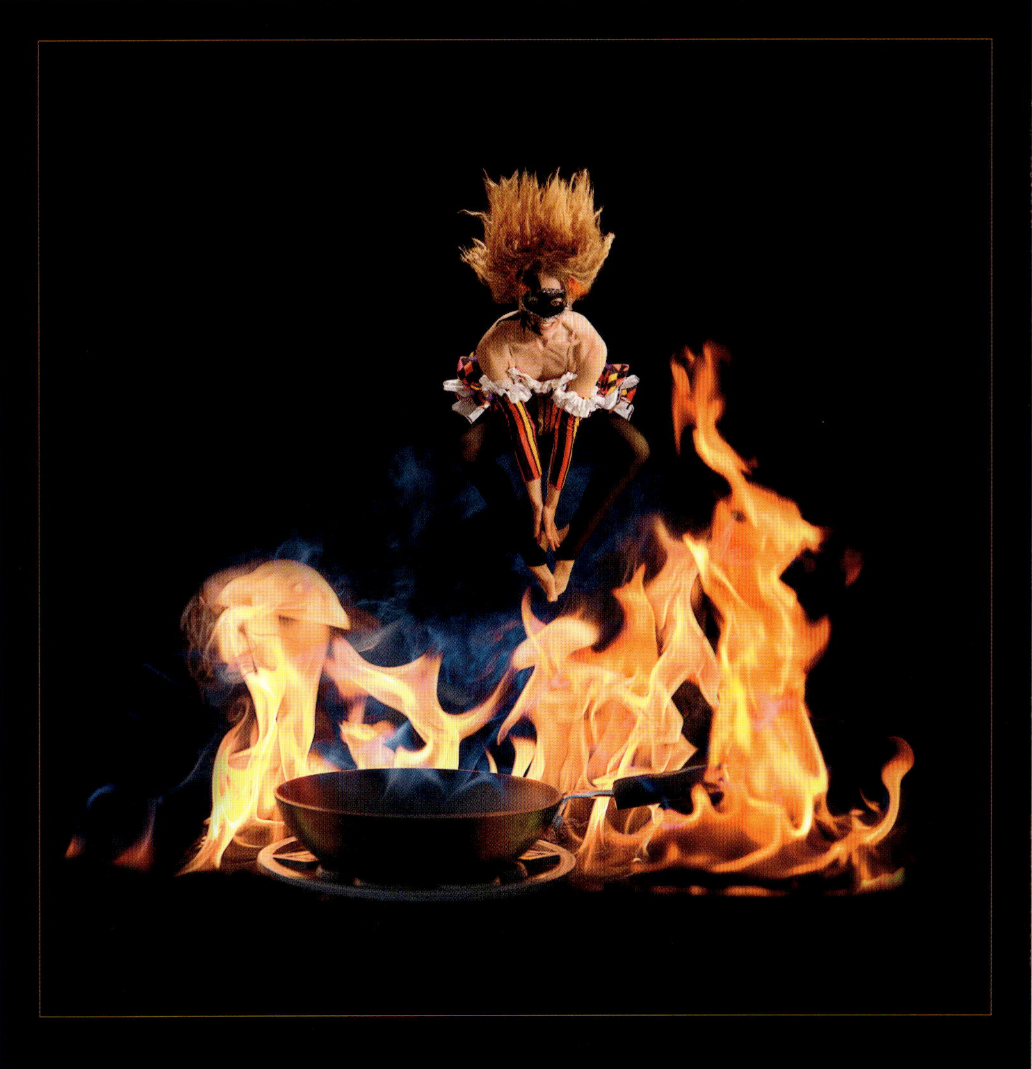

Into the Fire

The image *Into the Fire* is one case where the concept preceded the photography. I knew I wanted to have a frying pan on fire and a dancer jumping away from it. This dancer arrived with the perfect dance outfit to tie dancer and scene together.

Setting a frying pan on fire sufficiently so that the flames would show up well in a photograph was far more challenging than I'd supposed it would be. I set up a metal table outdoors with a black background behind it and tried charcoal lighter fluid and even gasoline, before finally settling on the fuel from a tiki torch and giving the fire some material to burn. Then I placed layers of flames over each other in Photoshop to give the flames sufficient visibility.

By the way, surprisingly, the burning experiment didn't even ruin this inexpensive frying pan.

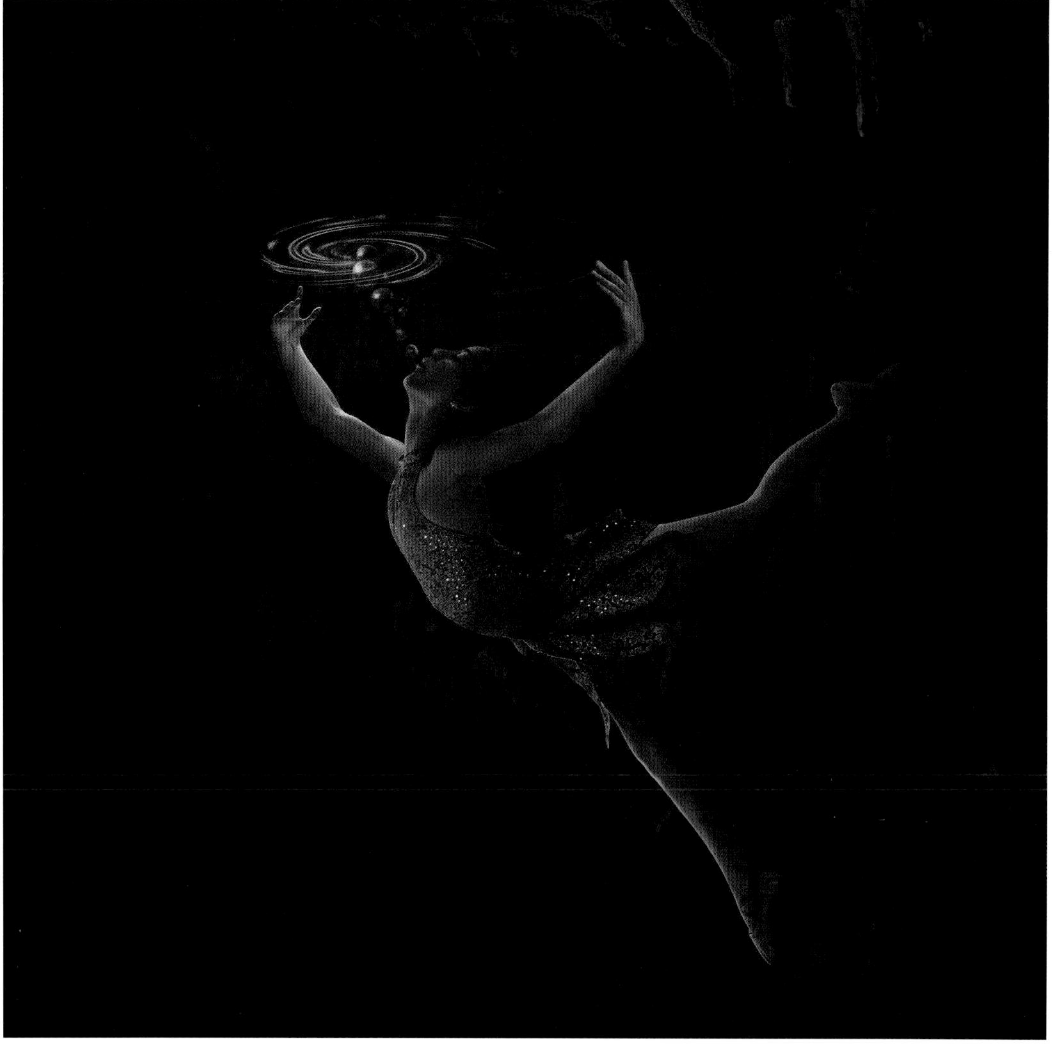

Underwater Dream

I had traveled with my husband to the Luray Caverns in Virginia and loved the stalactites and stalagmites. Unlike the larger caverns, the Luray Caverns are small enough that the lighting does a reasonably good job of showing off the terrain. I wanted to take the idea I started with in *Dancing on the Wind* and bring it a few steps further, but creating even more stretch and bend in the body with body replacement parts. This dancer is made up of parts from five separate photographs blended together. The background is the caverns, but unlike the warm tones of the original cavern shots, I've changed the color to purple.

I've added some water in post production for the dancer by adding bubbles, created from scratch in Photoshop and by using the Plastic Wrap artistic filter to give the newly synthesized water some watery highlights.

I stretched and painted her hair so that it looks like it's flowing on liquid currents and was careful to play up highlights on the edges of her face, arms, and legs so that the lighting is consistent with what one might see underwater when lit from above.

Combining Images for Free Falling

The image *Free Falling* was a very time-consuming piece to create mainly because of the large bird cage. I found the seven-foot tall birdcage at a secondhand shop and decided it would be a great prop for one of my dancer pieces. I painted it with shiny gold paint, which was a problem when trying to make a selection of the cage. The shiny surface reflected everything around it, making any kind of simple extraction impossible regardless of the background used. I eventually resorted to redrawing the bars of the cage for the final piece.

Here again, I used images of feet that were photographed separately to make the dancer appear as though falling through thin air. The bird is also a composite with wings of a hawk added to the body of an owl. The background is an Alaskan glacier. Leaves were placed to give added interest to the piece.

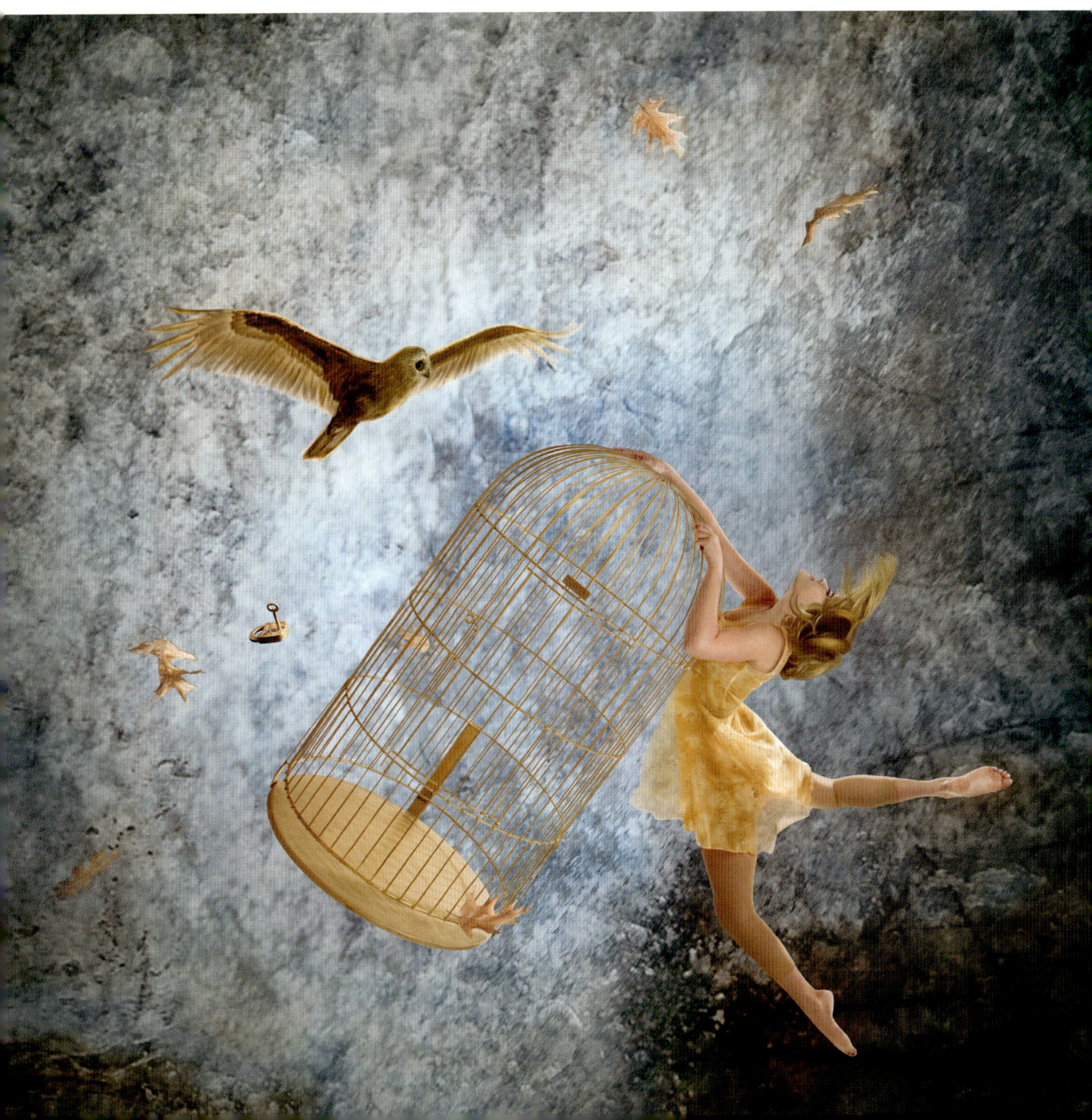

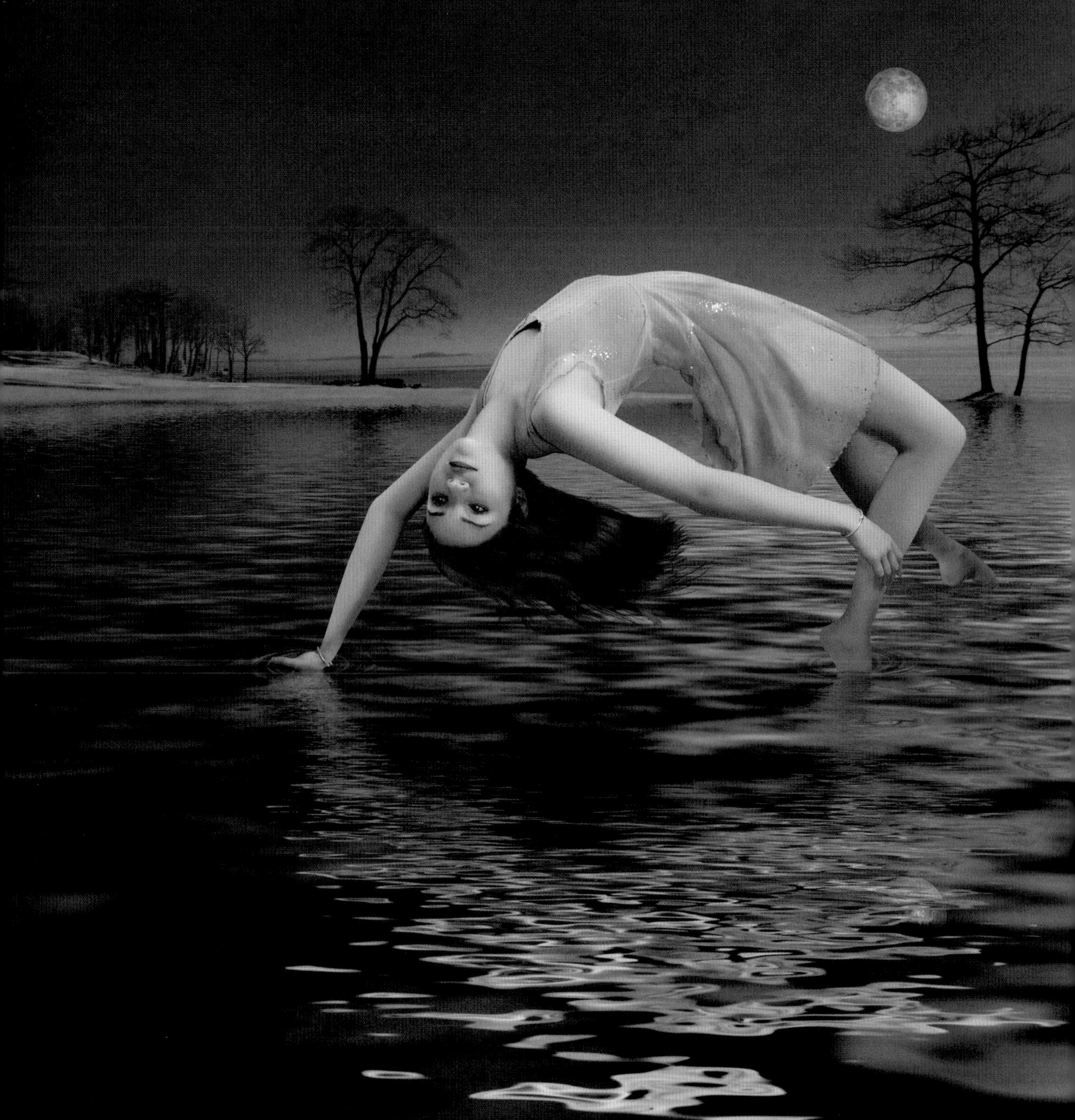

Floating on Air

Floating on Air, while in black & white, incorporates many elements from the previous color dancer images. A background shot on location in Maine was used, a moon photographed with a lens attached to a telescope was added, and the dancer appears to be suspended over the water by using body parts from different poses.

Reflections of the dancer were added into the water by using the layer blend modes and then adjusting the opacity of the layer until the reflections looked appropriate.

Holding Fast

Holding Fast is one of my most successful images, placing in the top ten in the world Grand Imaging Awards the year it was entered into competition. This image began in the studio with the dancer holding a sheer piece of fabric attached to a hook in the ceiling.

For the background, I used an image of a solitary tree taken in Virginia, and added a texture using the Overlay Blend Mode on the texture layer. The balloon was photographed in Albuquerque, New Mexico, during the annual balloon fiesta and taken off the background using the Pen Tool. The Pen Tool is probably the most ignored tool available to users, but the most precise for many selection situations. Lastly, I created clear, flexible straws-like lines, which were used as a transition element between the sheer fabric and the bottom of the balloon.

Cloning some of the grass so that it covers part of the dancer's feet creates the illusion that she was standing in the grass. Again, I enhanced some of the highlights at her edges to create depth and drama.

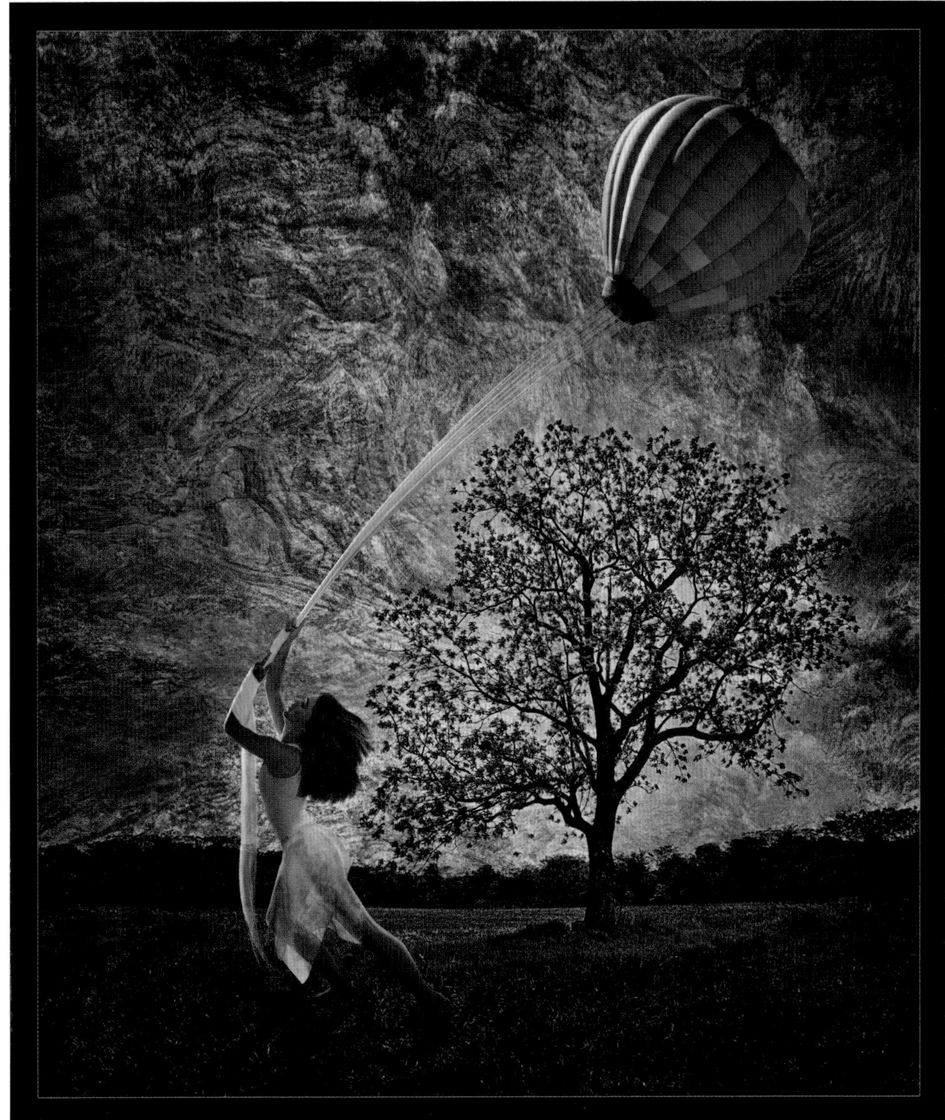

Lost Soul

The image *Lost Soul* is an example of taking the pieces of a living person and hollowing them out in Photoshop to make a living mannequin. To do this, one needs to visually dissect what happens when you have something hollowed out. Often it's a reversal of the lighting. Envision your light source and then build up the pieces you are working with from there. For instance, once you have selected your figure, cut out an oval shape just below the knee. You will exchange the darker areas with the lighter areas and vice versa. In this case, I could paint the piece that looks like the back section because I want the skin to look plastic-like. Using a soft-edged brush, I sampled the lighter color and then the darker color, using softer and less opaque brushes as I continued in order to blend smoothly. For the other limbs, you simply round the edges and then burn down the remaining piece to give it a rounded appearance.

In order to simulate the look of a wig for the inside of the hair (since I didn't have a wig on hand to photograph), I made a pattern of crisscrossing lines on a layer and then used the Liquify filter to shape it appropriately. Once the contours are right, change that layer's blend mode to Multiply. Then make a new layer above this and clone some of the hair over this layer to fill in the hair around the face. For even more dimension, you can add a subtle drop shadow.

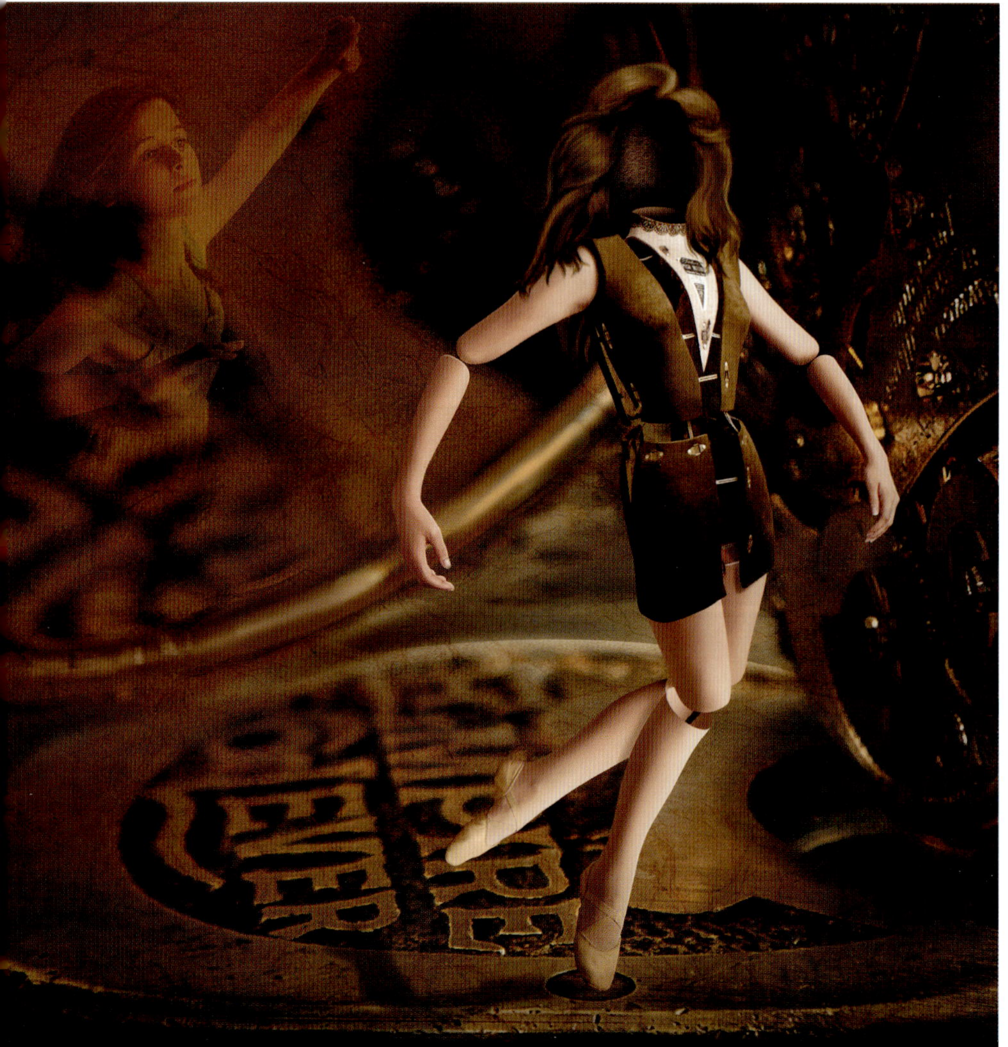

Helluva Angel ➤

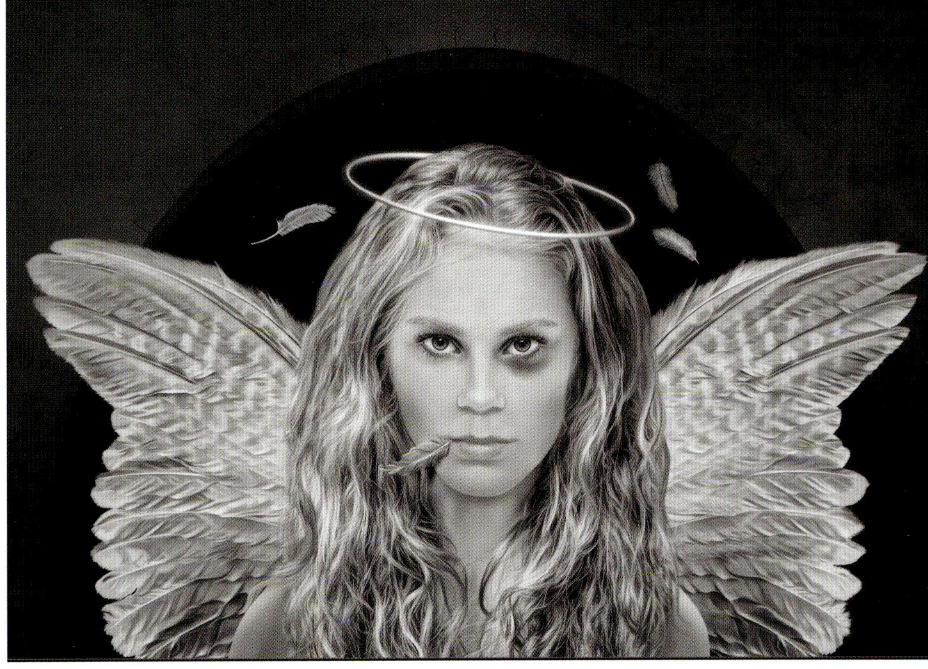

Helluva Angel was an experiment in flipping an image, or taking one side of the face and mirroring it so that the face is perfectly symmetrical. The dancer was selected and put on her own layer. Wings were added to the layer behind her. I happened to find a stuffed pheasant in a second-hand shop, and I used those wings. Likewise, I've also found preserved duck wings in a fishing/hunting supply shop—wonderfully authentic materials for imaging.

Of course, the hair needs to be filled in unless the subject has their hair styled with a center part. I enjoy using the Oil Paint filter, especially to give hair a softened, painted appearance. Take the Shine setting down to zero and then adjust to taste. Click on the Preview button to see what you can expect.

Her halo began as a simple elliptical selection. The next step: Select > Modify > Border. This always gives you fuzzy edges; then choose a substantial number to give your circle sufficient width. With your selection still active, press the keyboard Q key to go into Quick Mask mode. Then go to Image > Adjustment > Threshold. Leave the level at the default of 128. This will make the edges of your selection crisp. Click the Q key again to leave Quick Mask. Make a new layer and fill with the color of your choice. Use Bevel and Emboss in the Layer Styles window to add dimension.

Beginning Image ⌄

Her lips were closed by selecting the bottom lip plus feathering the selection into the chin area and copying that section to a new layer. The Warp tool was then used to close the mouth and the clone tool was used to blend the result together seamlessly.

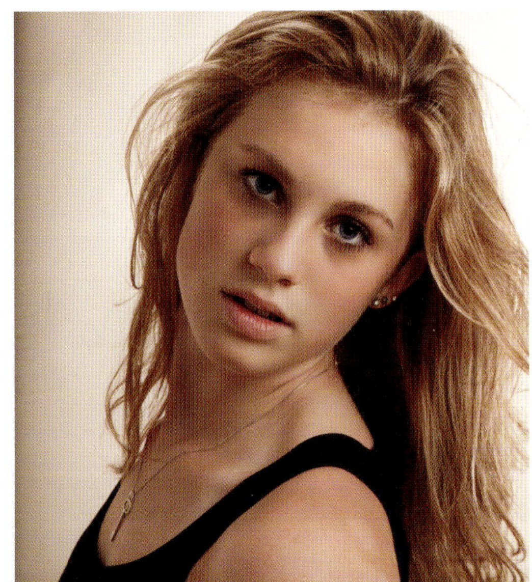

Caught Up in the Moment

Caught Up in the Moment was especially enjoyable to create. The dancer was photographed mid-leap with her hands out straight to the side. I took her off the background and used puppet-warp to bend her wrists because I wanted her to look as though she were being suspended air by chains or wires.

The lengthened and distorted hands of the clock were made using the Pen Tool. I made the lines with the Pen Tool and then, on a new layer, stroked them with a small, hard-edged Brush Tool in dark gray. I made the tips by Pen Tool as well, and used Fill rather than Stroke to fill in the triangular shape. Then I added a Bevel and Emboss layer style with a pattern overlay in Overlay mode to give the new distorted clock hands some texture and add interest. I repeated this procedure to add several layers of distorted hands and curled them around her wrists by erasing the parts of the lines that would, in real life, be behind her wrists and arm. Shadows were added, in this case by drawing them in, freehand, with a soft-edged, black brush, on a new layer with the layer blend mode of Soft Light. This will create a very editable shadow without distorting colors, although the Burn and Dodge Tools in the newest versions of Photoshop are not the awkward devices that they used to be. It's advantageous to work on a new layer for ease of editing.

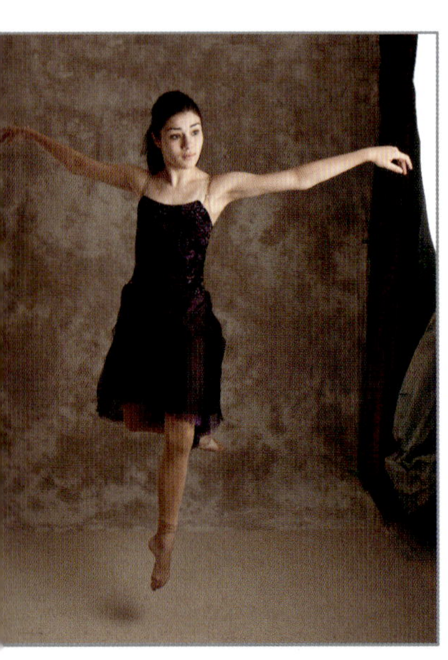

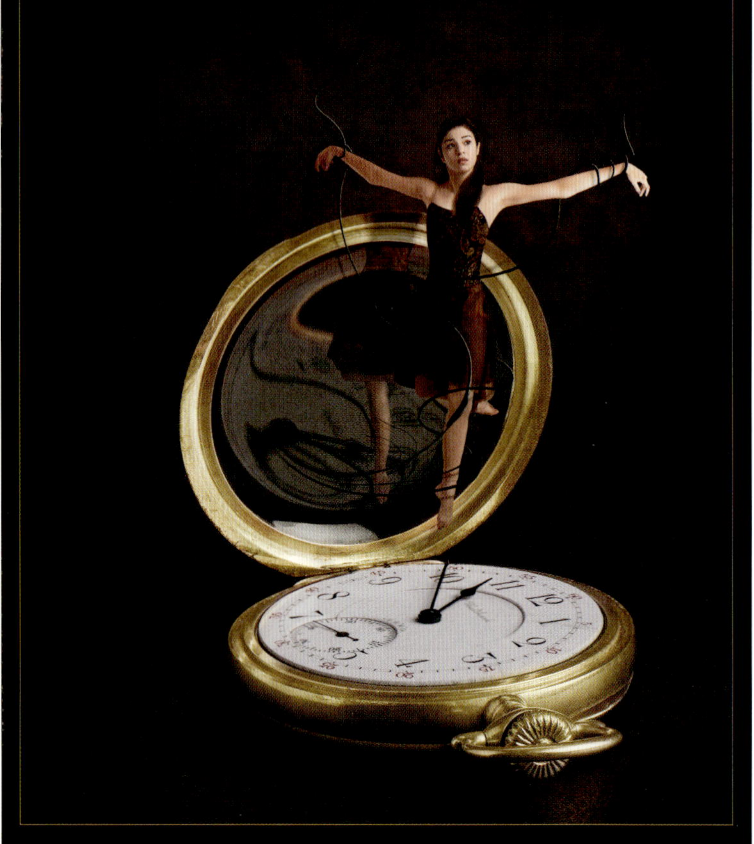

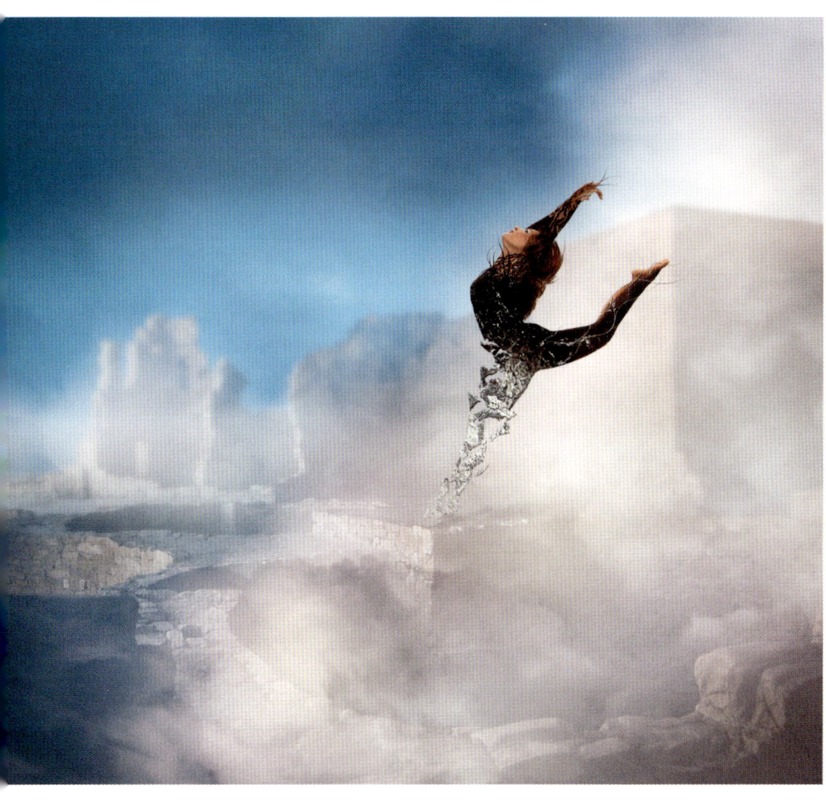

For this piece, I wanted her to appear to be breaking apart as she landed. To do this, I used the simple freehand Lasso tool to select segments of her legs and Cut and Paste those pieces to a new layer. A Bevel and Emboss layer style was then applied, along with a rocky-looking Pattern Overlay in Multiply layer style this time. This gives dimension to the pieces. Next, the layer Transform command was used to rotate them slightly and move them away from the body to give the desired effect of breaking apart.

Metamorphosis ▲

Metamorphosis was another piece I particularly enjoyed creating. I used the same technique as in *Caught Up in the Moment* to create the vines coming from her body.

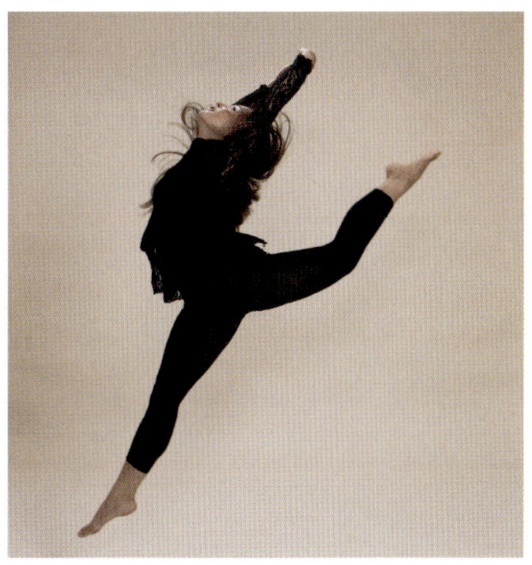

Make Your Own Patterns

Having patterns at your disposal in the Layer Styles is often a huge time saver. To add your own textures or patterns, open a file with the desired pattern and use the Rectangular Marquee tool to select the part of the pattern you want to use. Select the whole canvas if desired. Once selected, then go to Edit > Define Pattern. This places it into both the Layer Style window for use in any of the options using textures and in the Fill menu, found under patterns. Your newly saved pattern will appear as the last choice.

PHOTOGRAPHIC CAPTURE SERIES

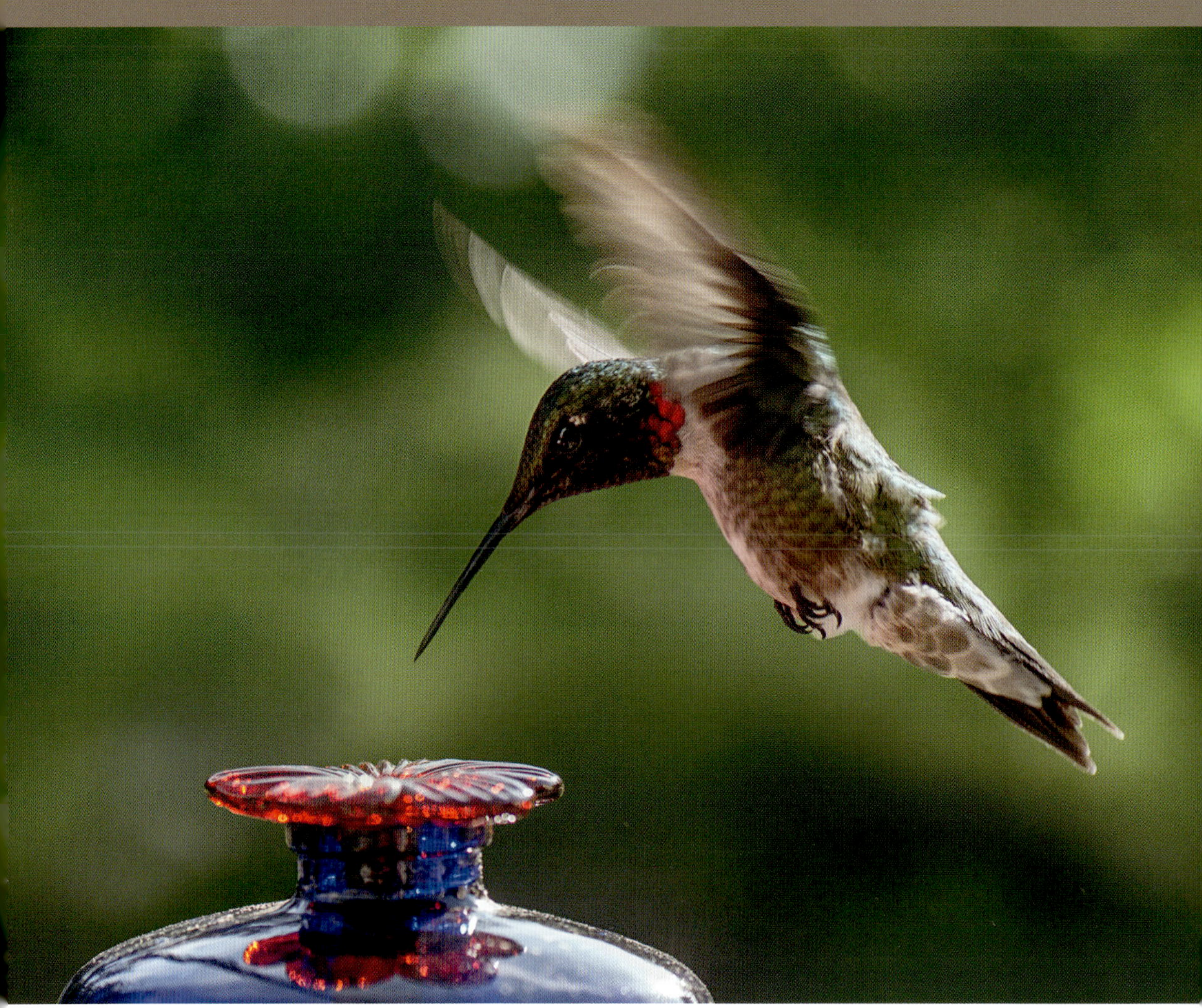

Hummingbird ▲

As I said earlier, I have been working in series for a while now. The next series was very much unlike my earlier work in that it was not manipulated. Instead, I went back to my photographic roots and focused on the capture.

I had just gotten my new Nikon D800E camera and it was January in New England, which tends to be gray and cold and can be just a bit depressing. I set up my new camera on a sturdy tripod and began taking photos of the birds that visited our bird feeders.

Backgrounds

Once the snow starts to fly, backgrounds can become lovely and crystalline, or just softly muted like this one. It's especially pleasing when you have the wonderful contrast of the red bird against all that white. Adjustments have to be made in exposure during the initial shot in order not to underexpose the bird.

It's especially pleasing when you have the wonderful contrast of the red bird against all that white.

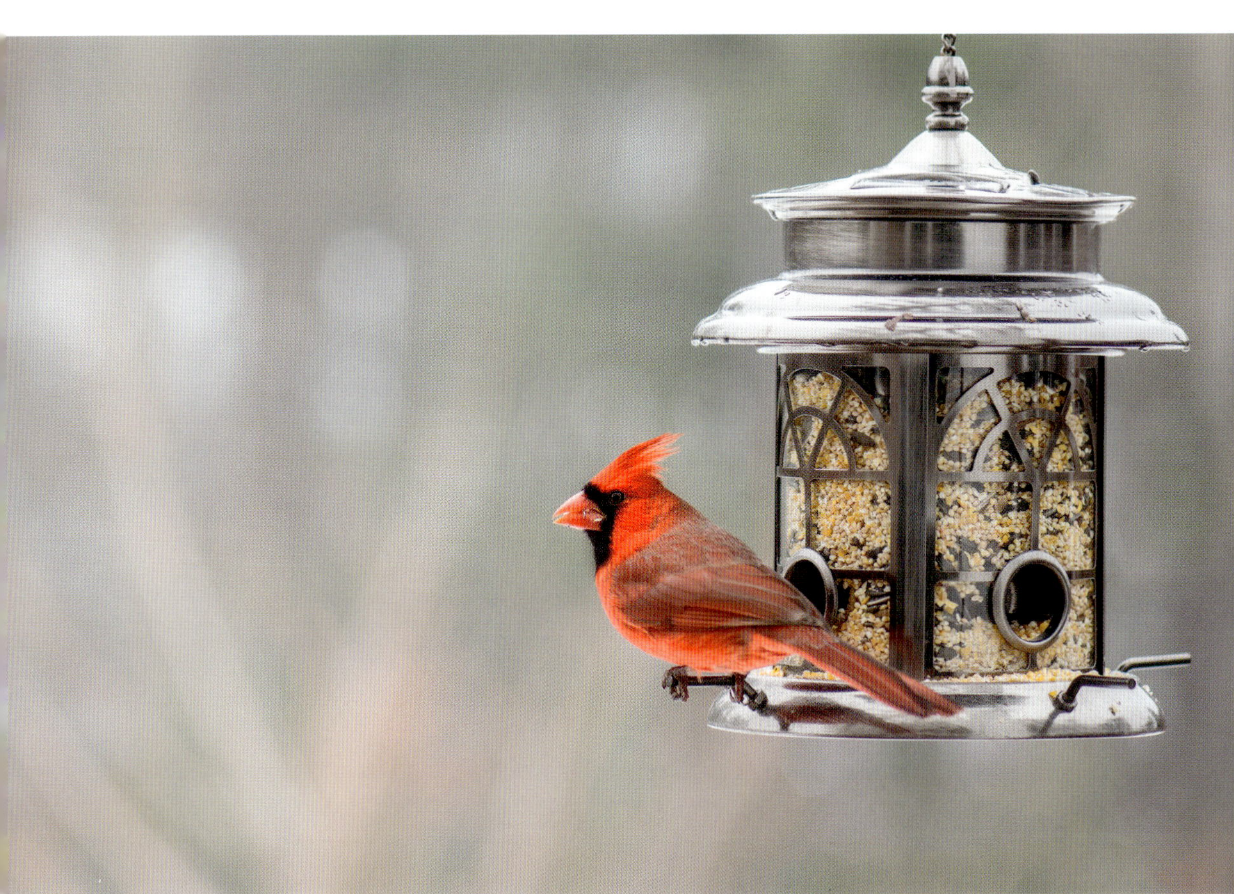

Free Range Chicken

I couldn't resist getting back to manipulating my images eventually. This rooster for *Free Range Chicken* was photographed on a street in Key West, and seemed like a great subject to experiment with using the relatively new Photoshop painting tools.

With the CC software versions, Adobe added the Mixer Brush, which allows the pixels to behave like wet paint. It's a fantastic option. There is an unlimited supply of brush tips, since you're able to create you own brushes, if you can't find a brush tip you like. You can also go to the Brushes window and edit any existing brushes in myriad ways.

Painting feathers is much like painting hair. It can seem tedious, but again, your patience will be rewarded. The bristle brushes are often a great place to start.

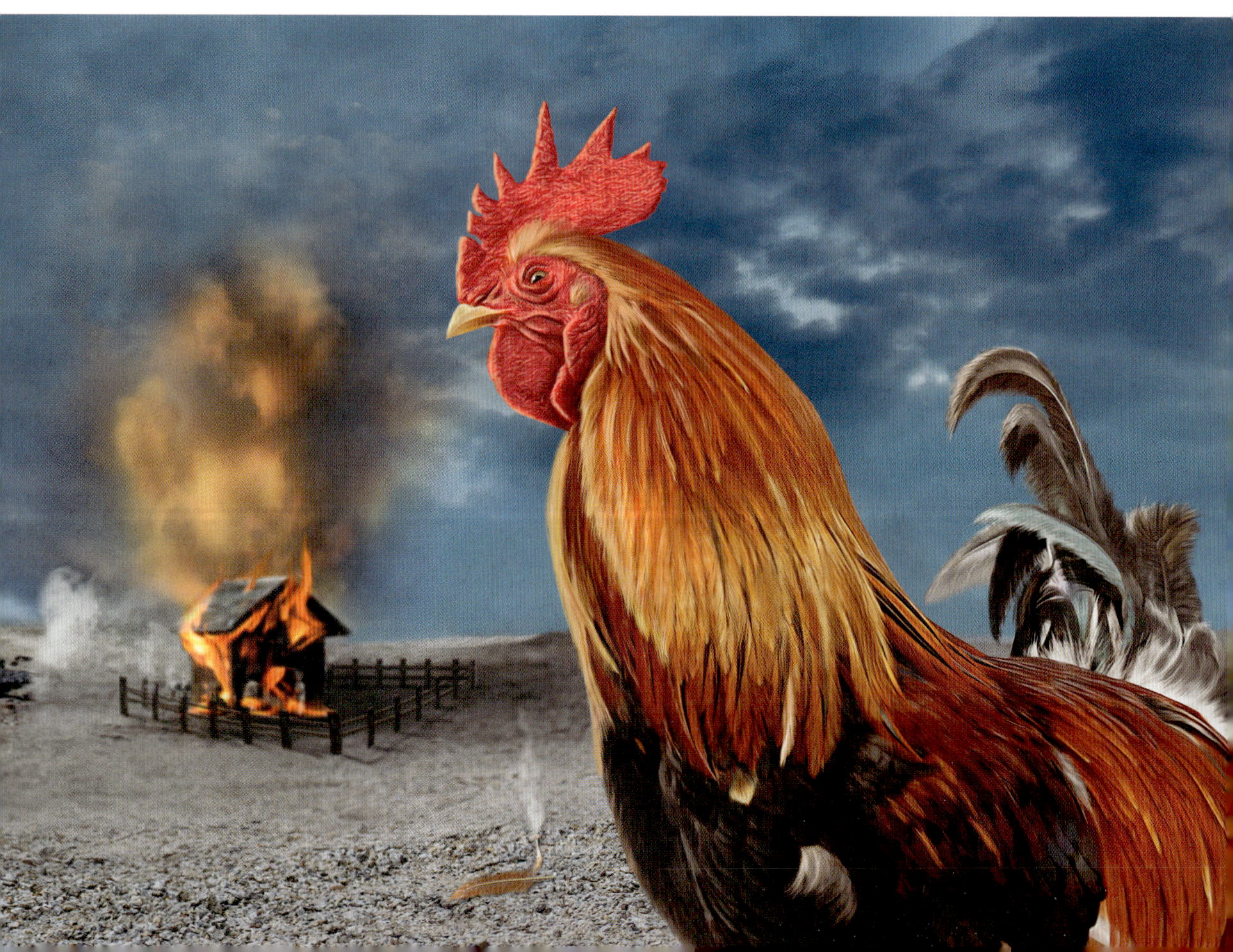

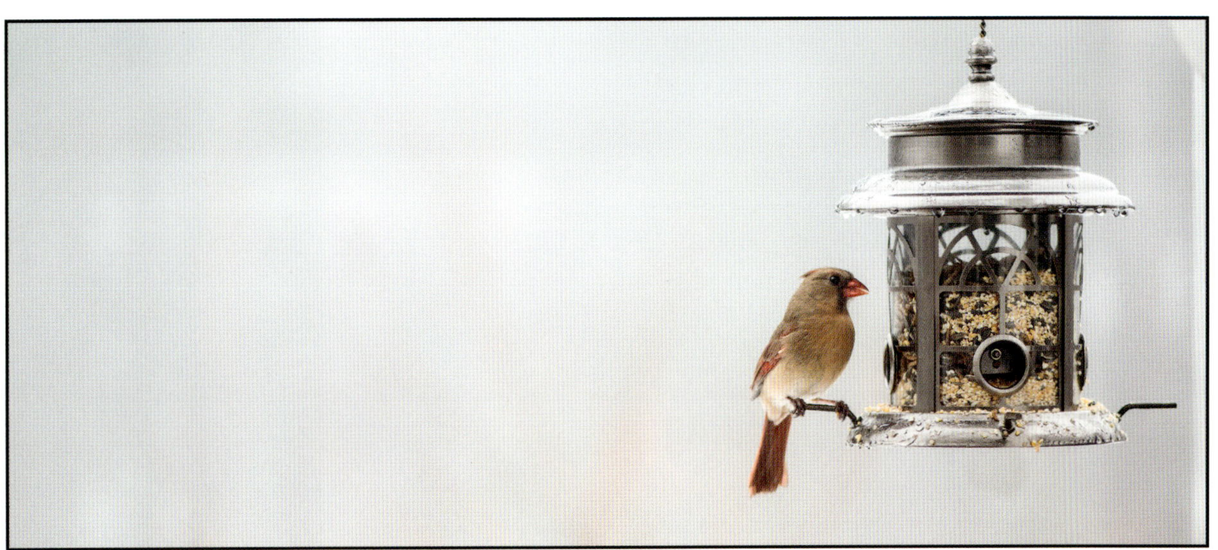

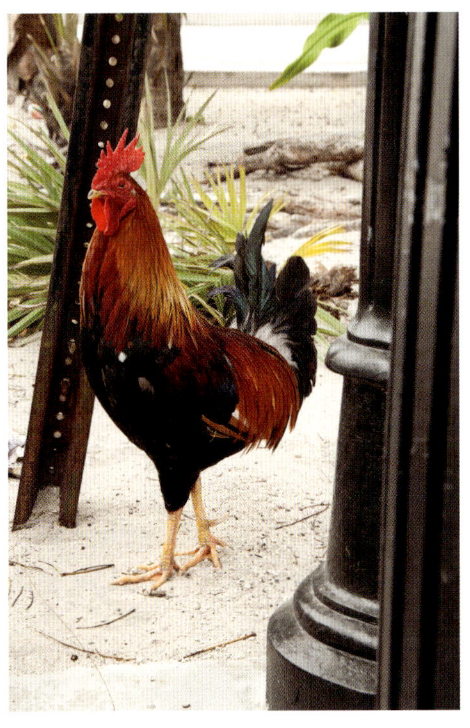

View from a Window ▲

With the large number of bird images I had, taken over the course of about three months, I was able to put a small book of the images together and title it *View from a Window*. Patience rewards the maker since, during this time, I was able to photograph an interesting array of interactions, as well as a wide variety of birds, ranging from woodpeckers to cardinals to tiny chickadees.

Cooper's Hawk

Painting this cooper's hawk was similar to that done on *Free Range Chicken*. I put the hawk on his own layer and simplified the background, since he was initially surrounded by a chaotic mess of limbs. When you are going to paint your subject, you don't have to be very careful about selection edges since you will be painting them.

High Pass Sharpening

I will sometimes paint a subject that can't be rescued by any sharpening method. My favorite method of sharpening is to make a copy of the layer, then go to Filter > Other > High Pass and use a setting of 6–10, lower for people and higher for landscapes.

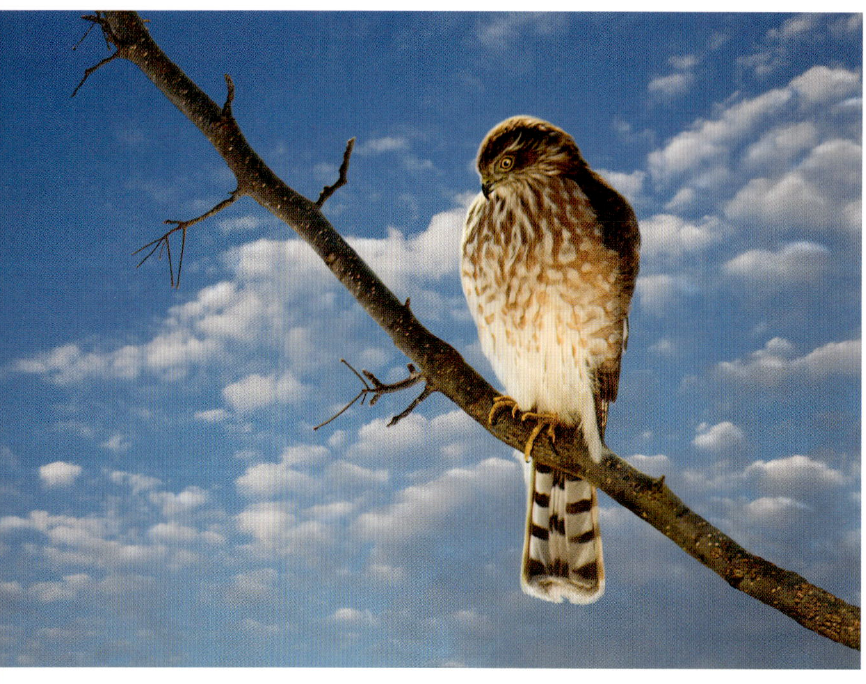

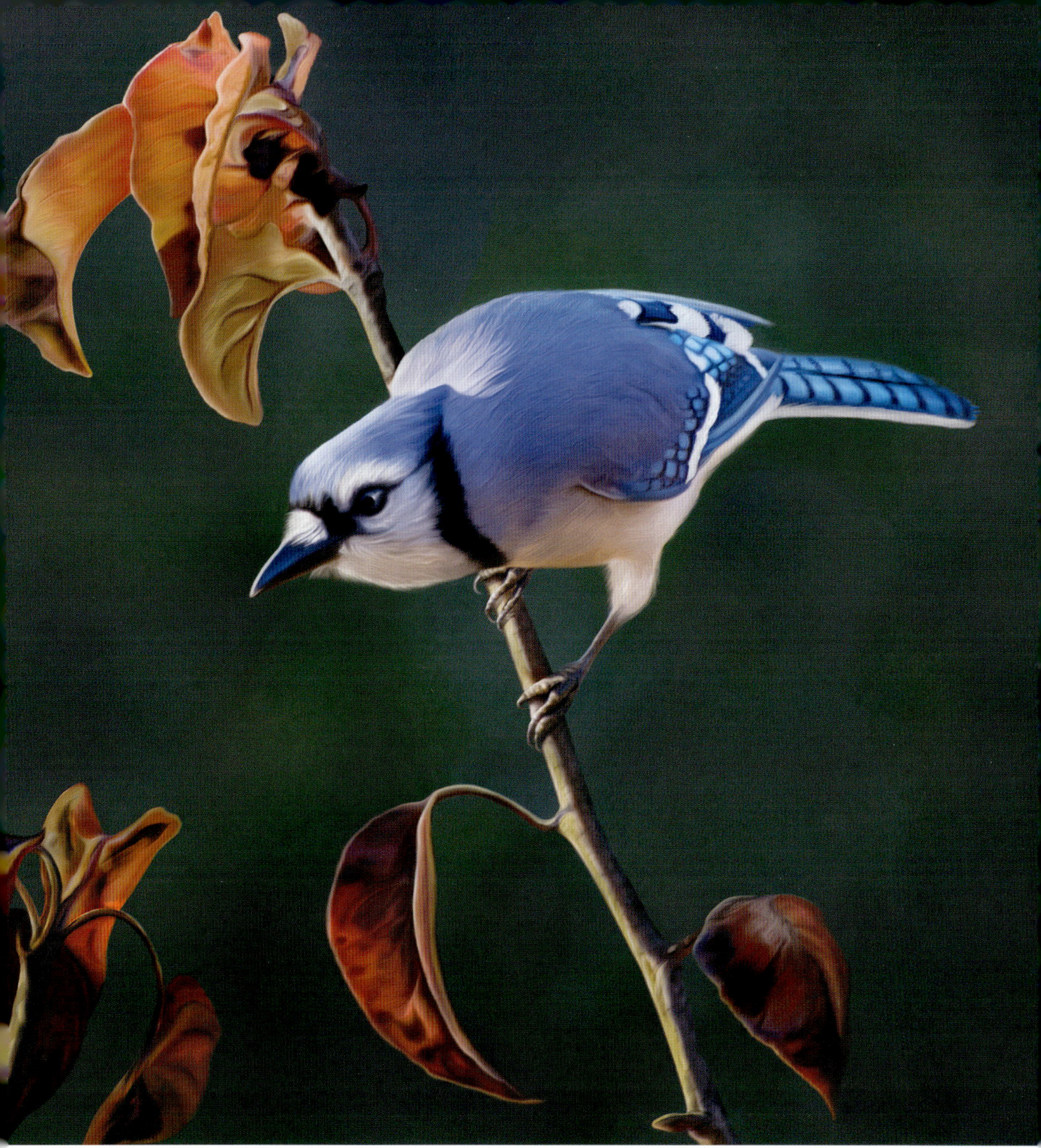

Then change that layer's blend mode to Soft Light or Overlay.

While the sharpening tools in Photoshop have improved greatly over time, this method has a great deal of flexibility as you can change the opacity of your sharpening layer, or even add a second sharpening layer to your file to get the desired result. This method tends to create fewer halos at the edges where lights and darks meet.

Flowers: A Self Challenge Series

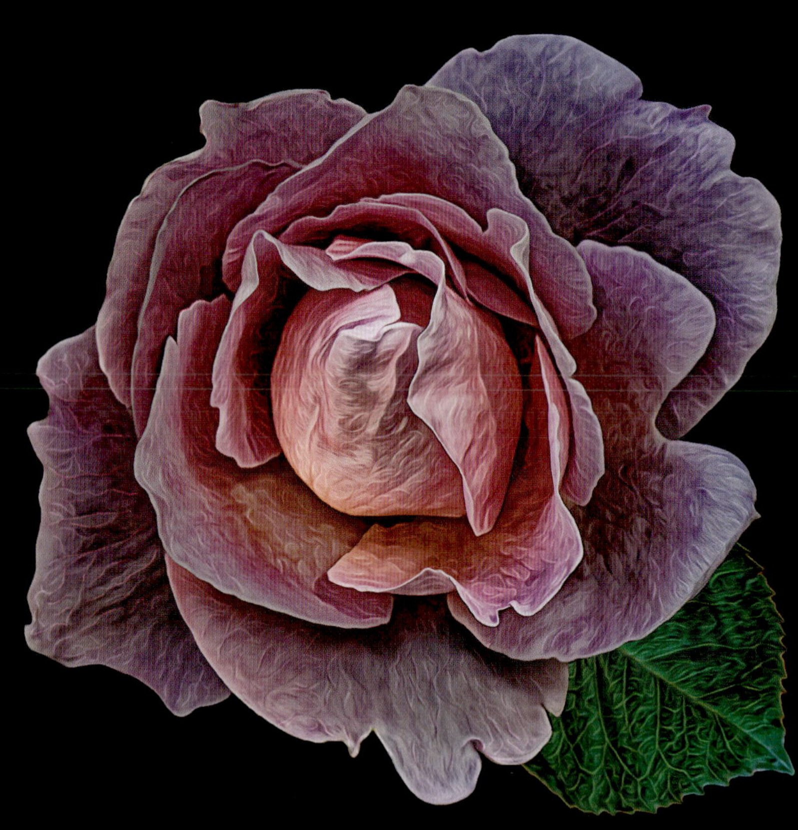

I began by experimenting with taking the rose apart in Photoshop, petal by petal . . .

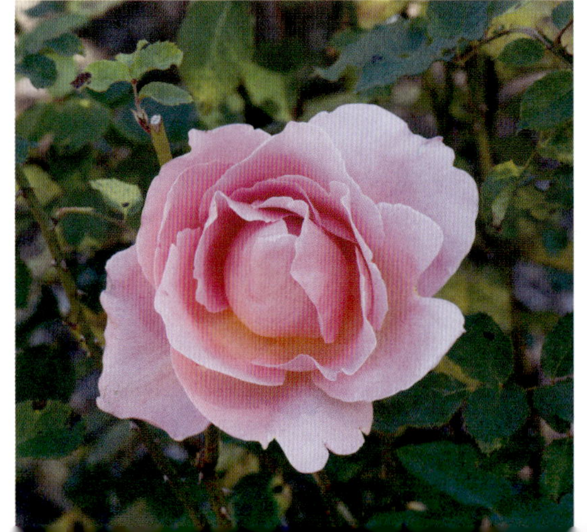

One of the Most Photographed Subjects

There are so many instances where you can't dictate the time of day you are able to take a photograph. I photographed this rose in the garden at mid-day as I traveled from one spot to another. I decided to see if I could create a far more pleasing image from it, in spite of the harsh afternoon lighting conditions.

This self-challenge began another series of images; this time a long series of flower images. How do I take one of the most photographed subjects in the world and make something more surprising?

Changing the Lighting After Capture

I began by experimenting with taking the rose apart in Photoshop, petal by petal and putting each petal on a different layer. I wanted to change the lighting from the initial capture. I put a solid black layer beneath all the layers of petals, and then proceeded to change the opacity of each petal layer with the less opaque layers at the edges and the more opaque layers toward the center of the flower.

This resulted in an almost glowing effect and, for me, it was far more interesting than the original lighting.

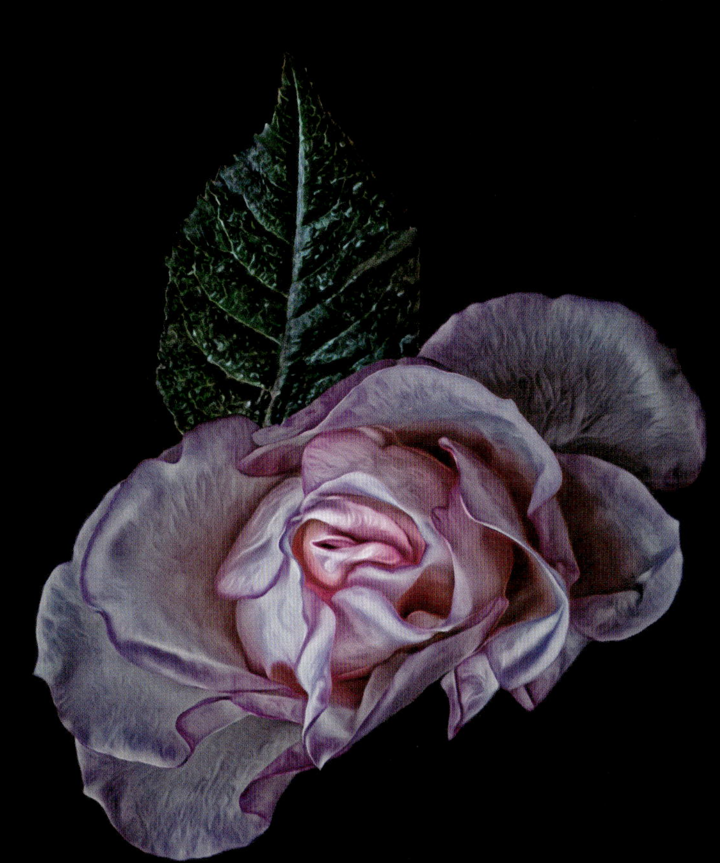

Burn and Dodge

I inspected the flowers veins and lines by zooming in, and by using the Burn and Dodge tools, I lightened the lighter parts and darkened the areas right next to those highlights. This added a great deal of dimension to the previously subtle lines in the rose petals. And yes, it takes a while. This isn't production work; it's an attempt to create art.

I inspected the flowers veins and lines by zooming in

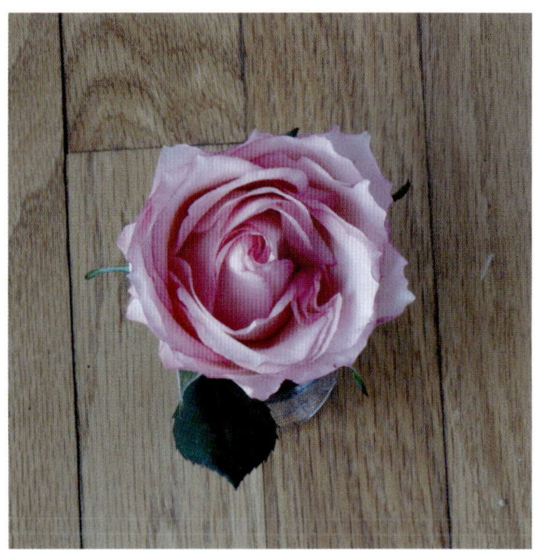

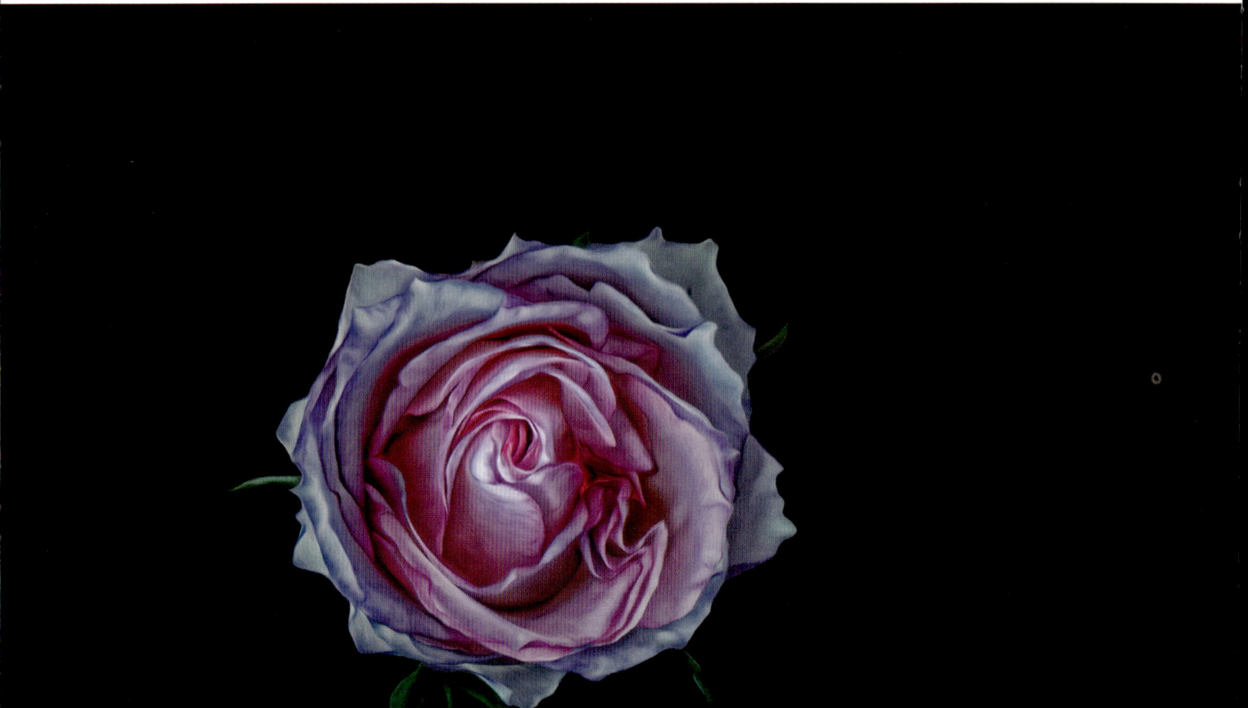

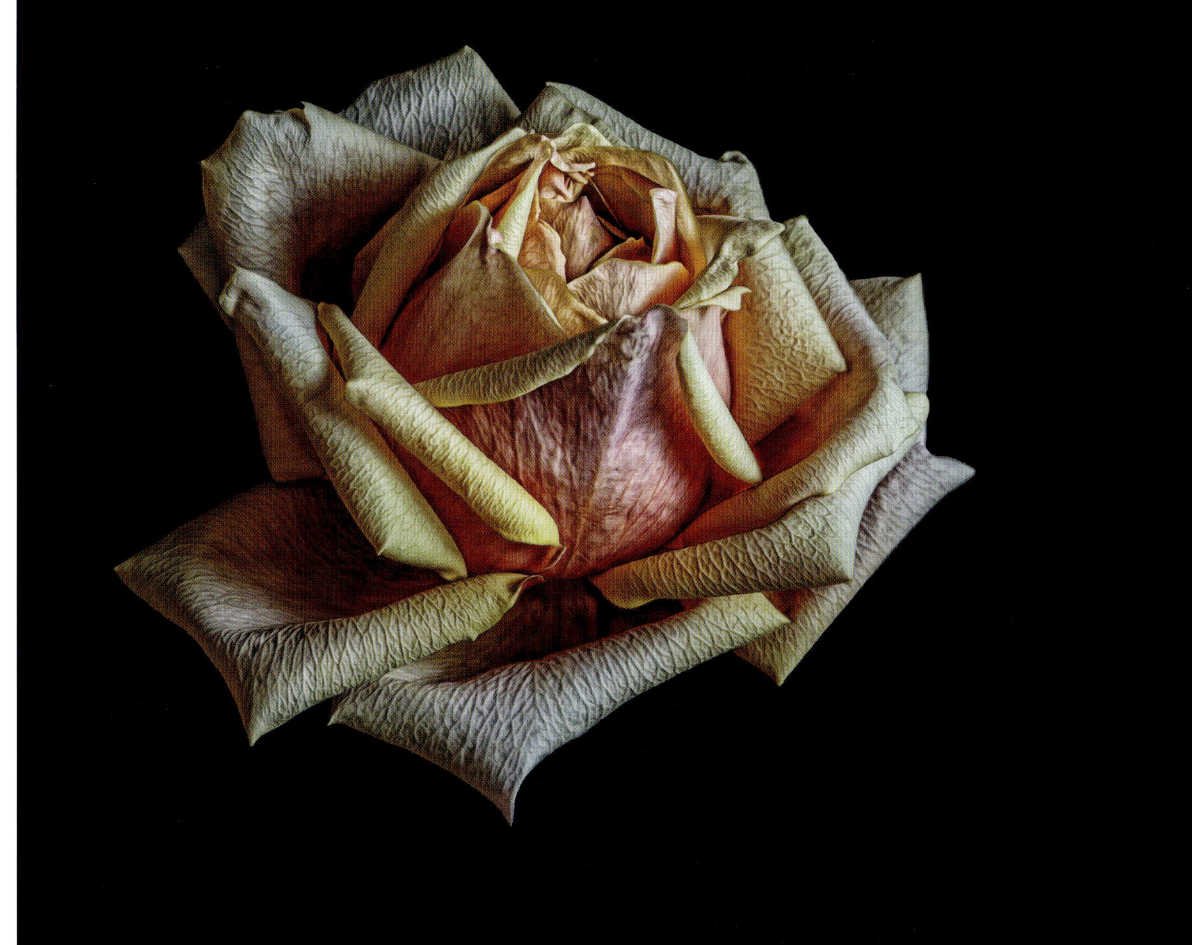

Oil Paint Filter ▲

After highlighting and adding shadows to accentuate the lines in the flower petals, I then applied the Oil Paint filter to each petal. I used a pretty subtle setting: Stylization: 4, Cleanliness: 6, Scale: 4, Bristle Detail: 4, and the lighting angle adjusted to match the original light source. Remember to set the Shine to zero. I don't want the filter's effect to be immediately apparent. This gives the petals a lovely, softly painted feel. The amounts will vary depending on the resolution of your image, as with many of the filters in Photoshop.

I don't want the filter's effect to be immediately apparent.

Enhancing Shadows and Highlights

This flower required a different approach. Separating the petals into different layers would have a very different result, since these petals are only a single layer deep for each flower. However, enhancing the shadows and highlights works well to add pop and dimension, and the Oil Paint filter, applied with subtlety, gives the flowers a nice finish.

. . . enhancing the shadows and highlights works well to add pop and dimension . . .

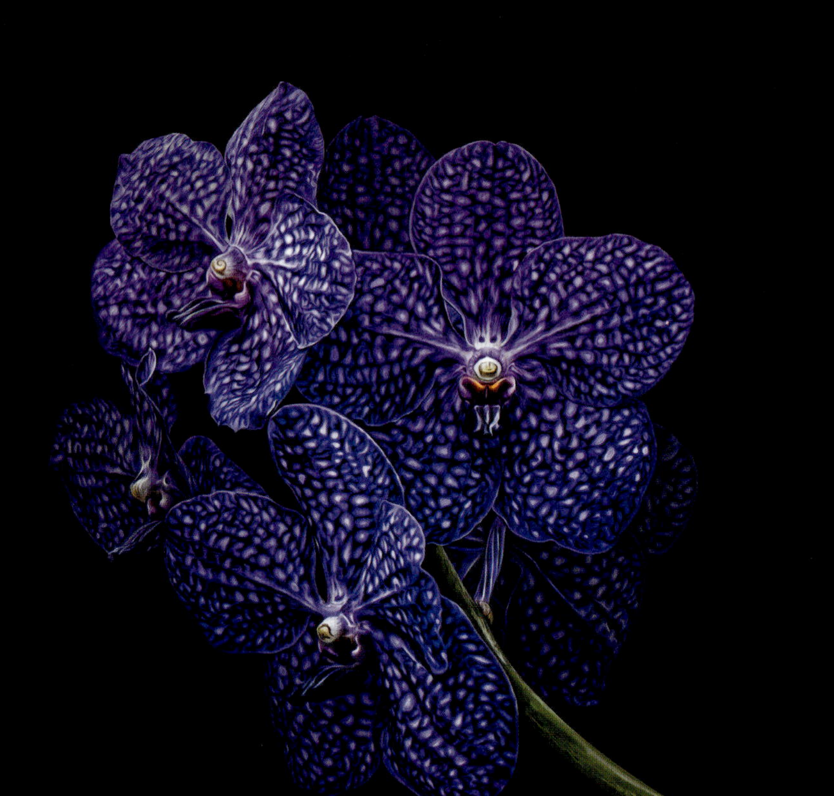

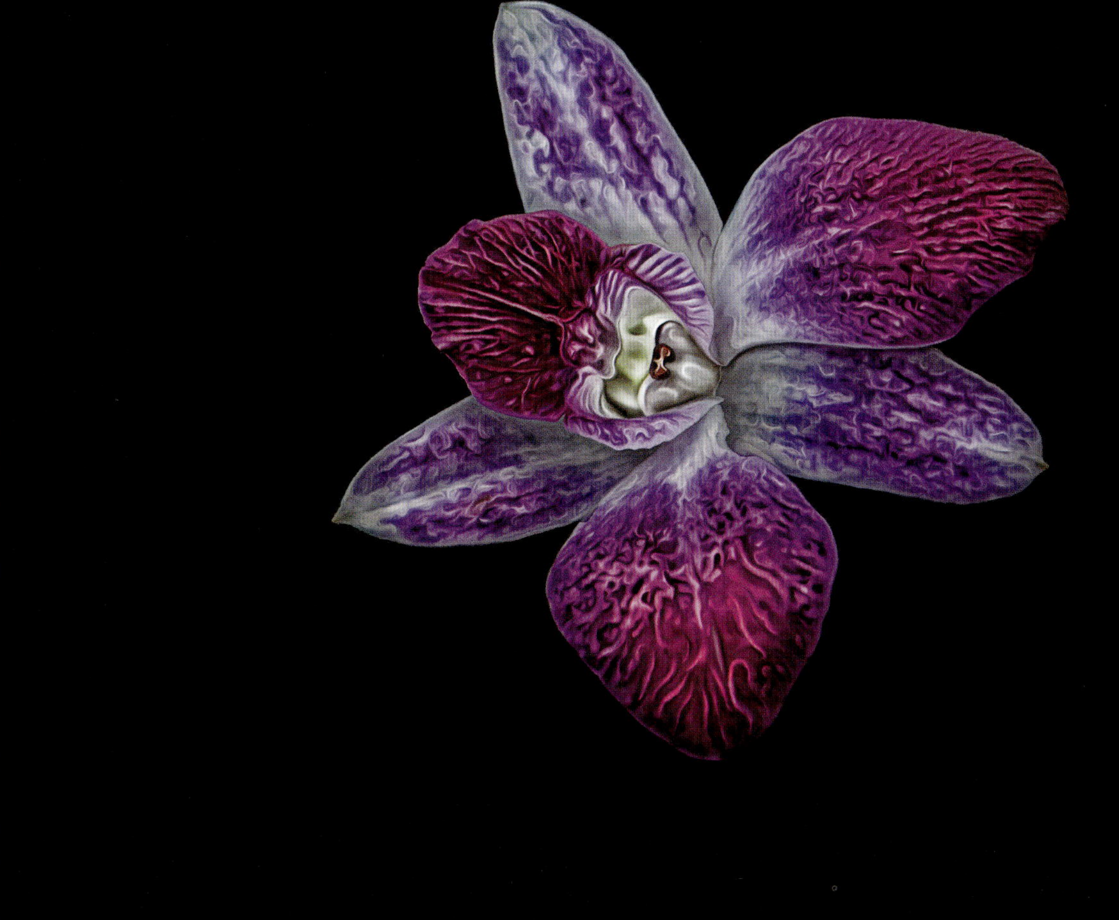

Quick Selection ▲

This is a prime example of using the Burn and Dodge tools to create extra dimension with the flower. With all of these flowers, I used the Quick Selection tool to make the selections of petals and to take the flowers off of their original backgrounds. This one tool, for me, is worth the price of upgrading from the old CS versions of Photoshop. The Quick Selection tool works very well for many selections, including hair.

This one tool, for me, is worth the price of upgrading from the old CS versions of Photoshop.

Quick Selection Tool

To use the Quick Selection tool, you just activate the tool which is clustered in the tools panel with the old, faithful Magic Wand tool. The Quick Selection tool is the only selection tool that doesn't require using the Shift key or the *Add to selection* option in the options bar to keep adding pixels to your selection. Just keep clicking.

The sensitivity of your Quick Selection tool is based on the tolerance setting for the Magic Wand tool, and on the size of the brush tip you select. If you want more sensitivity, then lower the tolerance setting for the Magic Wand tool, make your brush size smaller, or both.

Petals on Individual Layers

I used the technique of selecting petals and putting them on their own layers with differing opacity settings for this tulip. In addition, I used the Oil Paint filter. To make the rain drops appear more distinct, I copied the layer over itself and applied a layer mask to the copy layer. (Hold down the Opt or Alt key when making a new layer mask. This will create a black layer mask.) That copied layer's blend mode was then changed to Color Dodge. Then, with the white brush, paint over the raindrops. If they are too light or too harsh looking, simply lower the opacity of that copy layer until you get the right amount of shine.

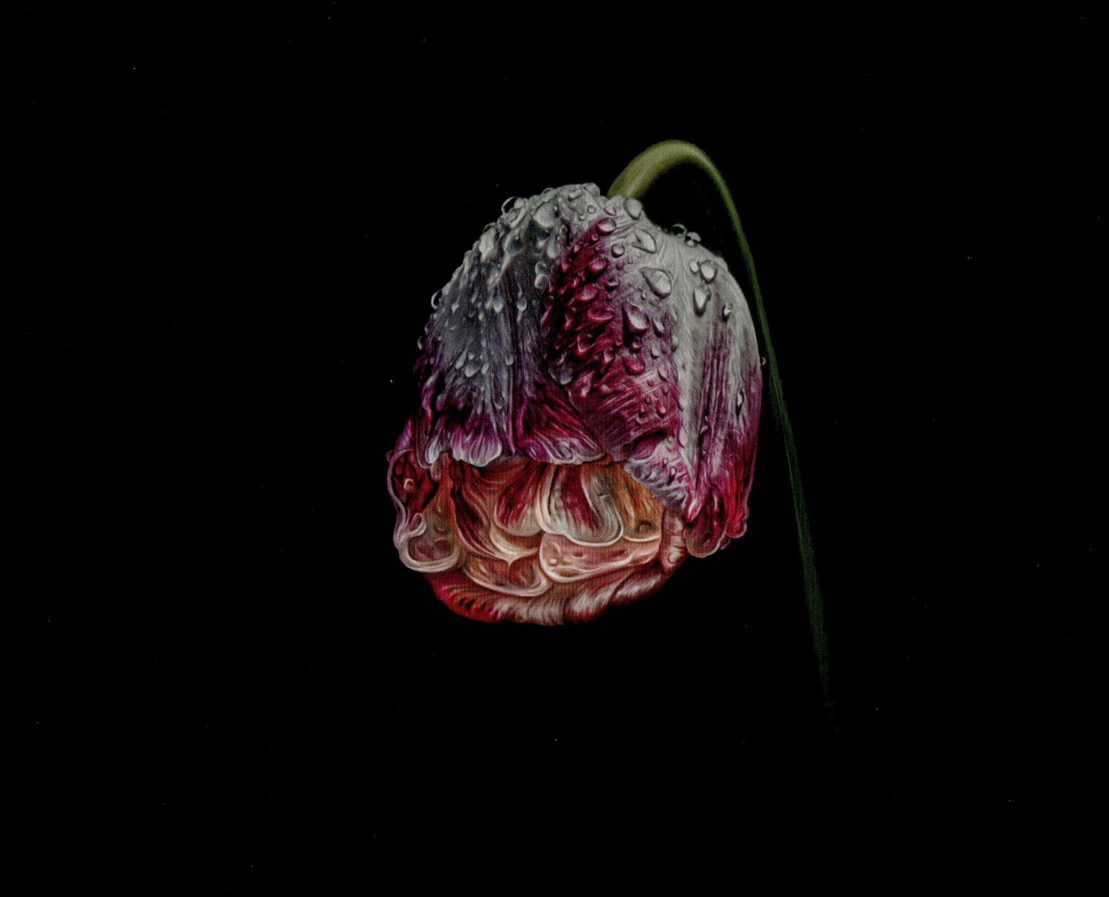

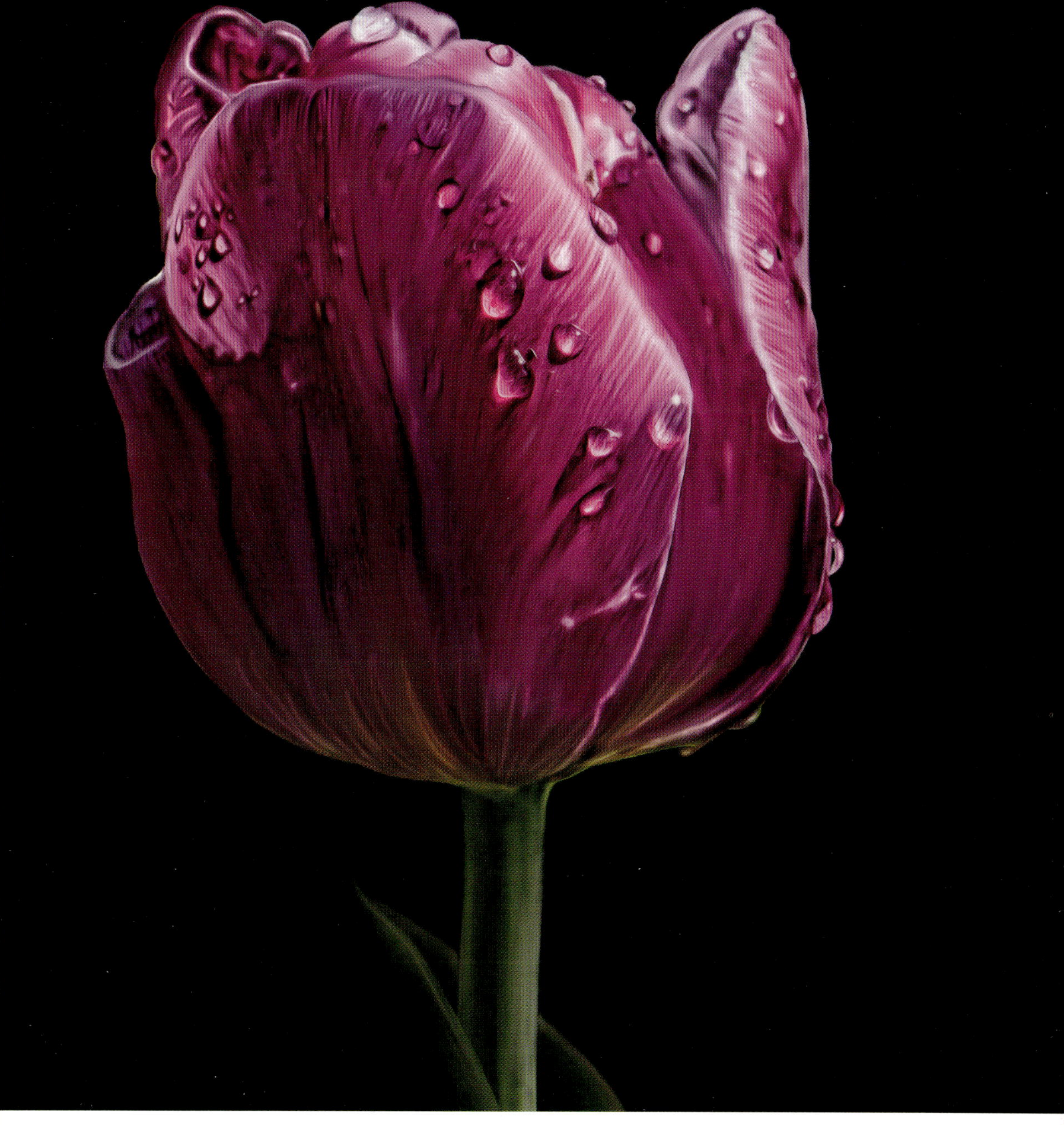

Then, with the white brush, paint over the raindrops.

Shy Rose

This is one of my favorite flower images. The off-centered flower and the glow that occurred is exactly what I wanted for this flower. In addition to the other techniques I've already described for the flower series, I dodged additional areas near the origin of each petal and burned down the edges to add more dimension and drama to the flower.

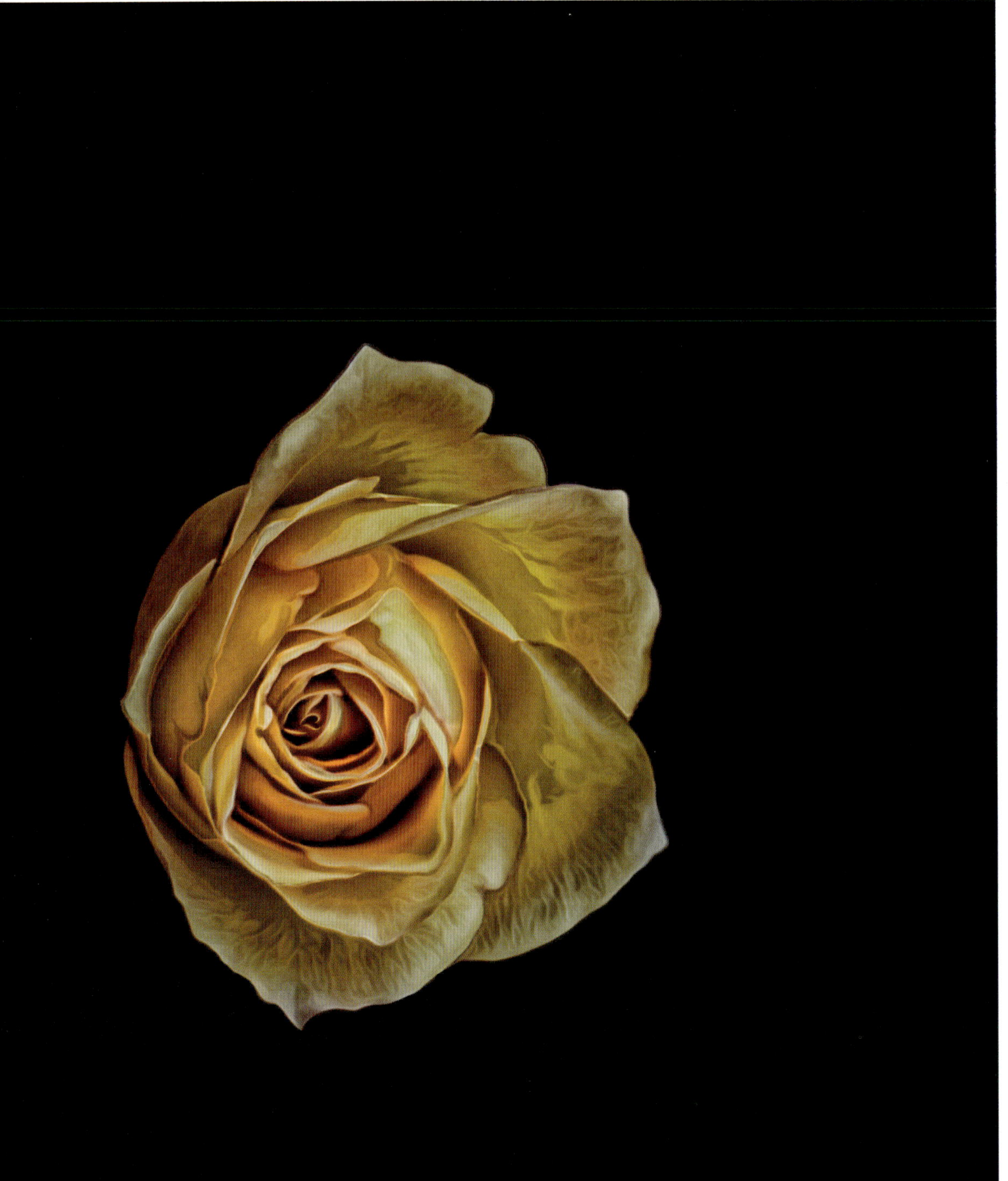

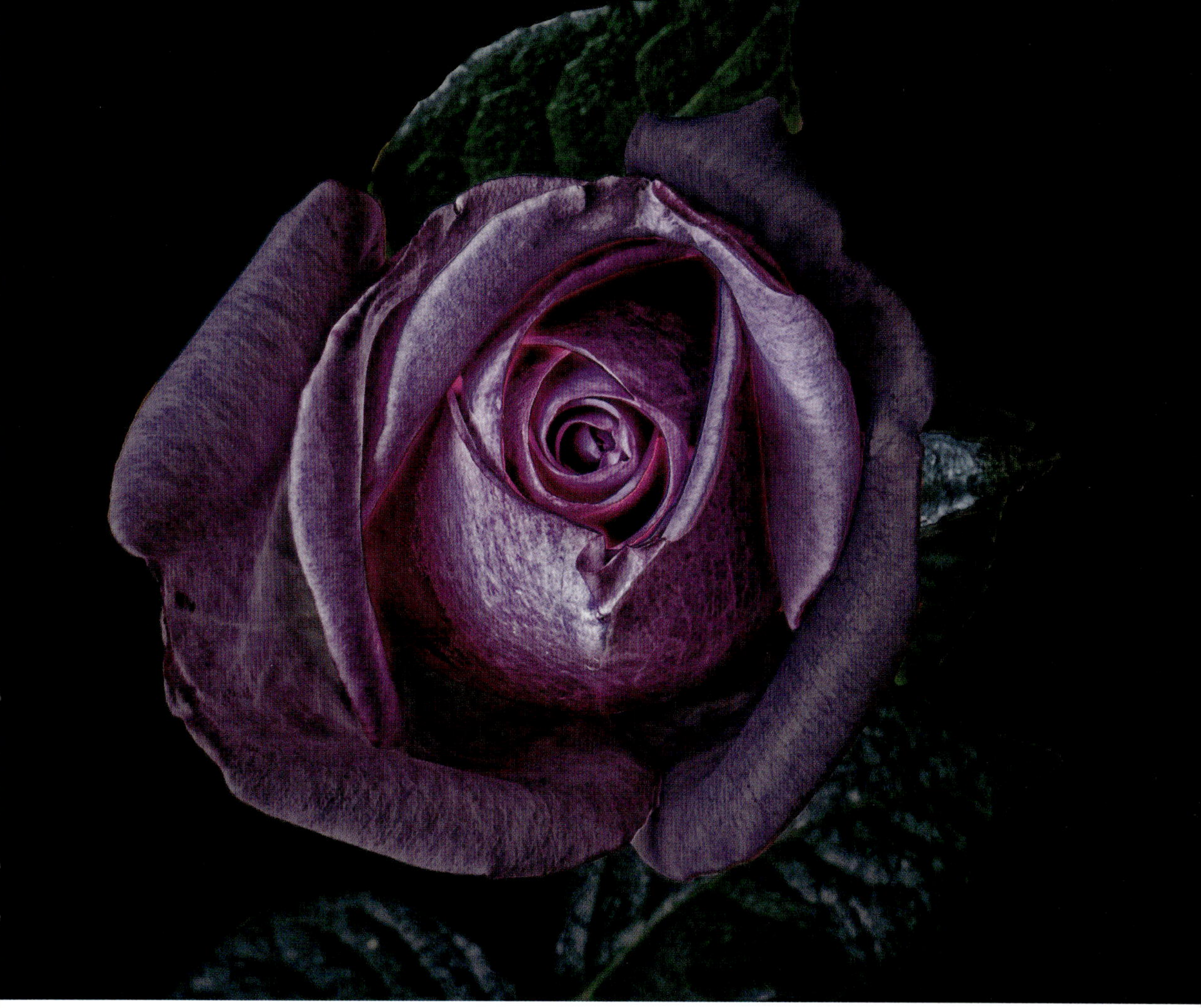

More with Layering Techniques ▲

This layering of techniques works on flowers of all colors. I continued the effect on the leaves in this one as well, adding dimension with the burn and dodge technique. Also, I softened with the Burn and Dodge tools, and I enlarged the brush to subtly add brightness and depth to certain areas of the flower, such as the top ridge of those inside petals.

I enlarged the brush to subtly add brightness and depth to certain areas . . .

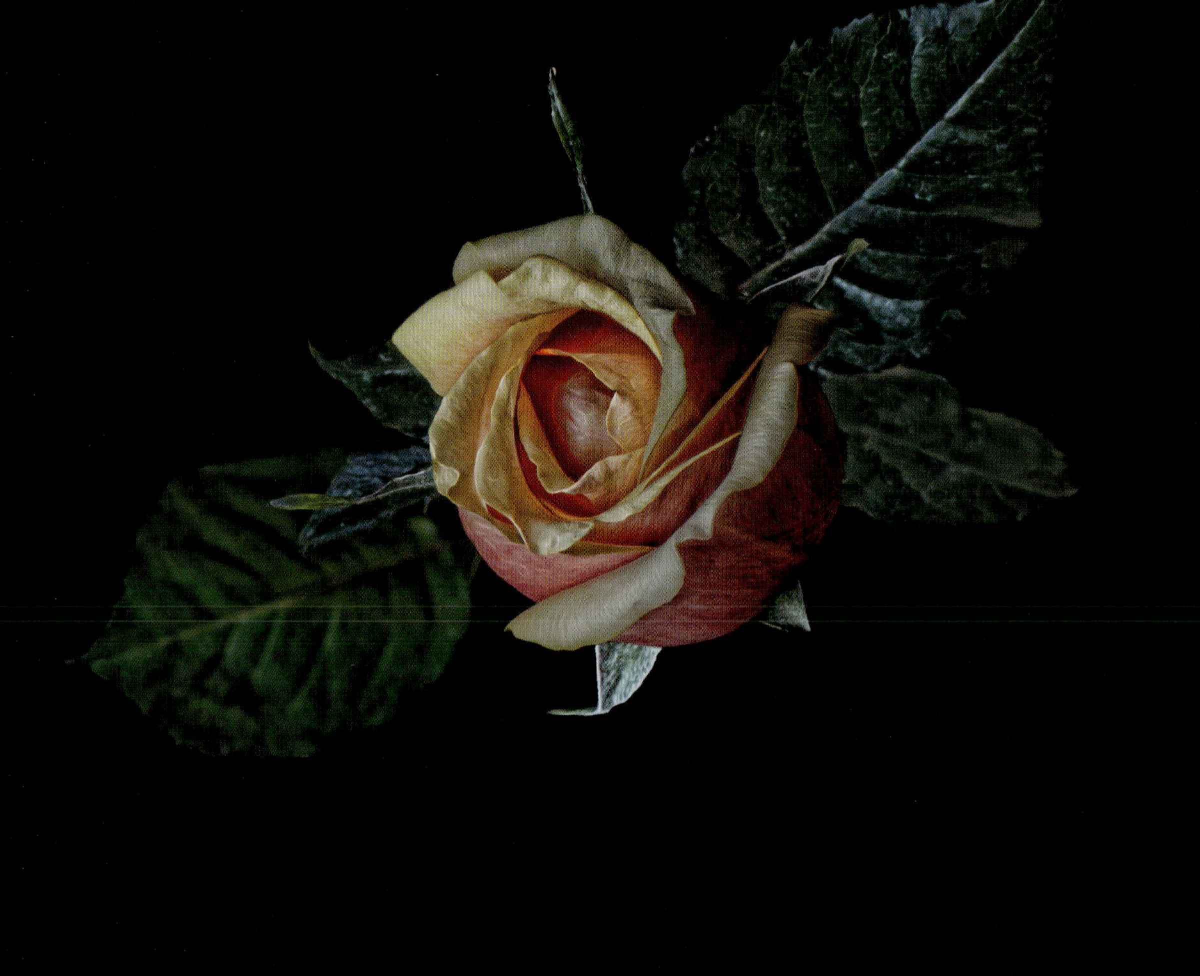

Closed Bud Flower ▲

It's more difficult and less obvious to use the petals-on-different-layers technique with a closed-bud flower or with a flower that is more in profile to the camera position. Judicious dodging and burning before painting techniques are applied will still be effective.

Modifying Selections ▶

It's tempting to let the selection edges become less precise as you make your selections of the petals, but it's important that they be accurate. You have a number of Modify options under the Select pull-down menu. Among those are: Feather, Expand, Contract, and Border. You can soften the edge of a selection to allow it to blend into a new scene more effectively. I generally subscribe to the theory that every selection of a living thing needs at least a .5 pixel feather on it. If you find your Quick Selection tool is a bit shy about hitting the edges of your petal, then go to the Expand command under the Modify menu. Generally, it only takes a setting of 2–3 pixels to catch the edges you might have missed, but a very accurate setting will take a bit of practice, since it will be different for different resolution images.

You can soften the edge of a selection to allow it to blend . . .

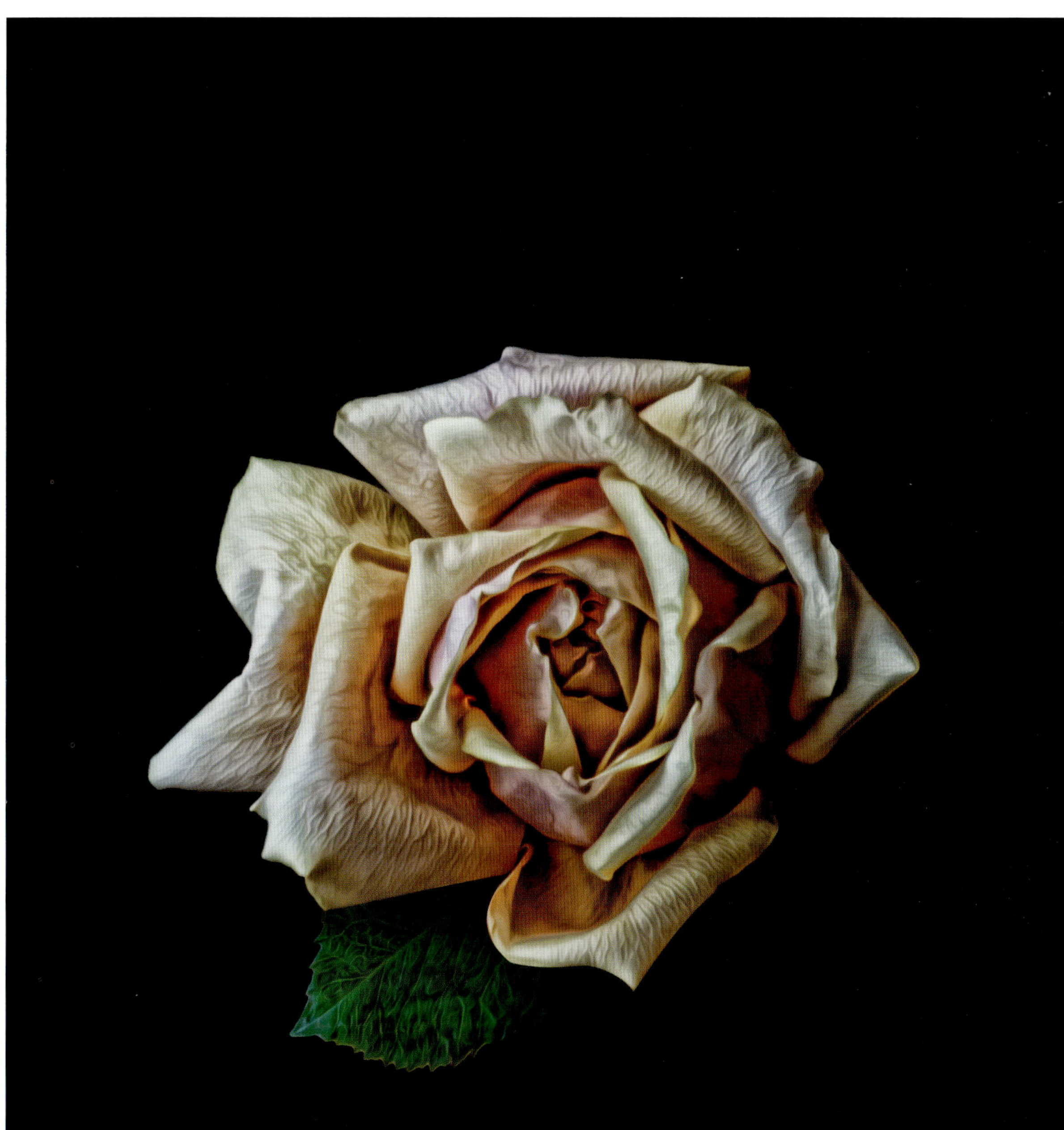

Dismantle, Enhance, and Reassemble

This is another example of the technique where the rose gets dismantled in Photoshop, enhanced, and then reassembled at different opacities. It gives the center of the flower prominence. In this case, I took a leaf from another rose and added it to the composition, using the same enhancement techniques for the leaf. Details were brought out by use of sharpening techniques, in addition to selectively burning and dodging.

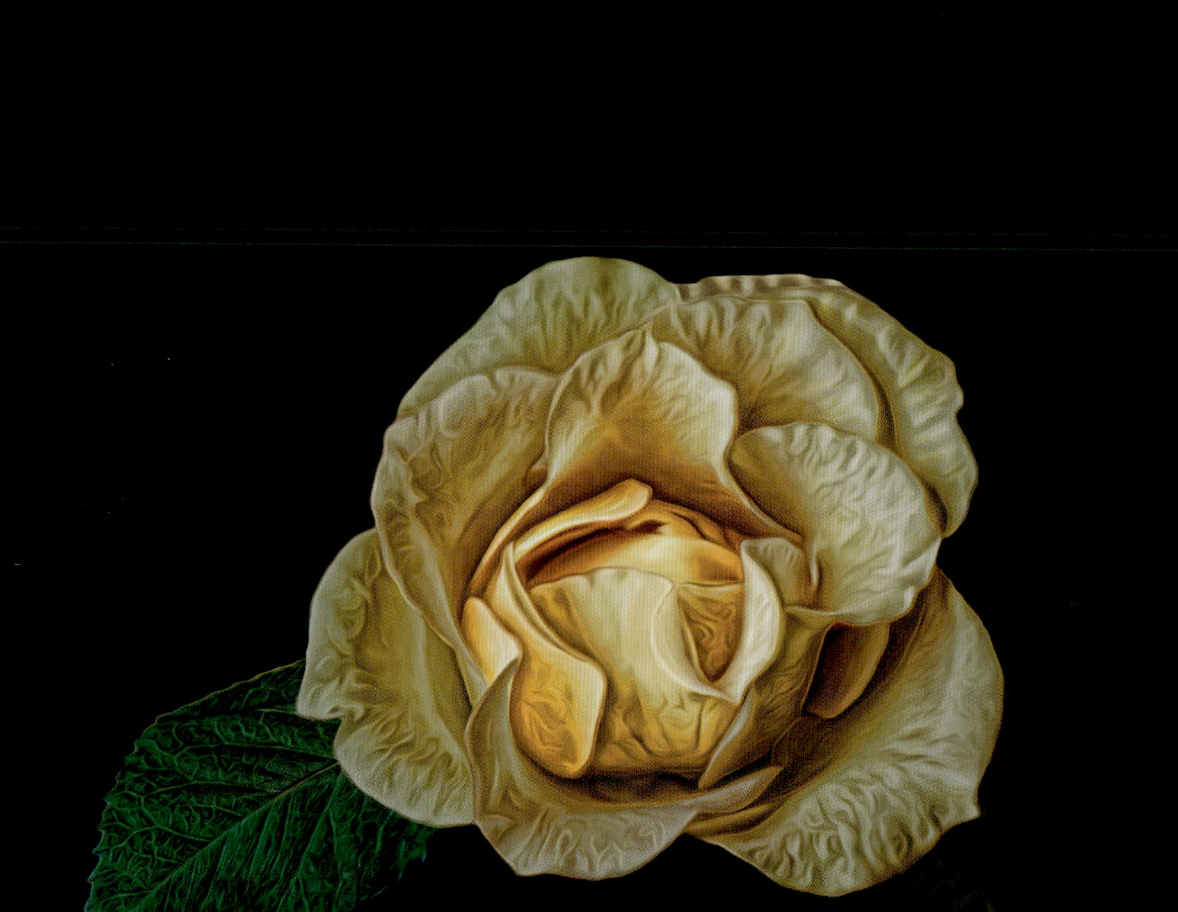

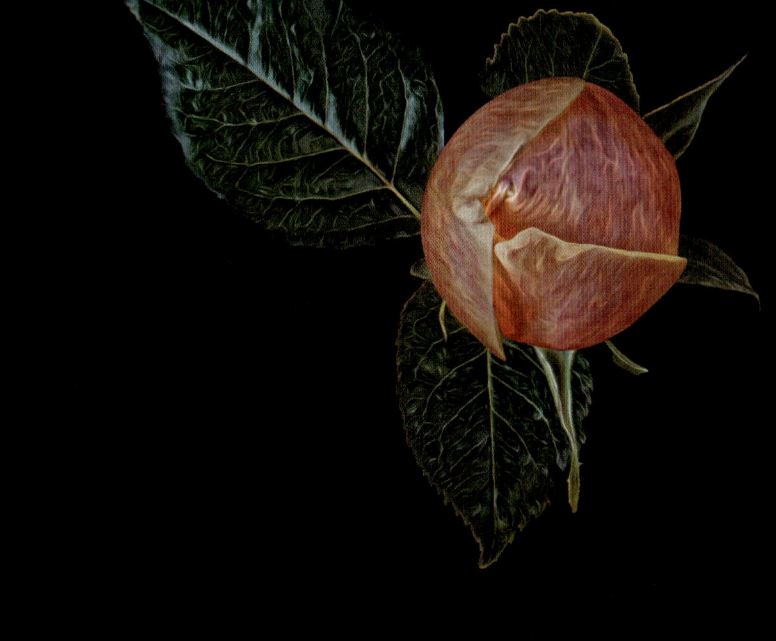

Using Layers to Control Opacity

With flowers whose buds are tightly closed, there are only a few petals visible. In this case, the technique was to use a layer mask to control the opacity in different parts of the petal rather than keeping the entire layer with each petal at the same opacity. In other words, the outer part of a petal is less opaque than the part near the center of the bud. Using a black, very soft-edged brush at a lowered opacity, for instance 20 percent, will allow you to paint away the opacity smoothly.

The technique was to use a layer mask to control the opacity in different parts of the petal . . .

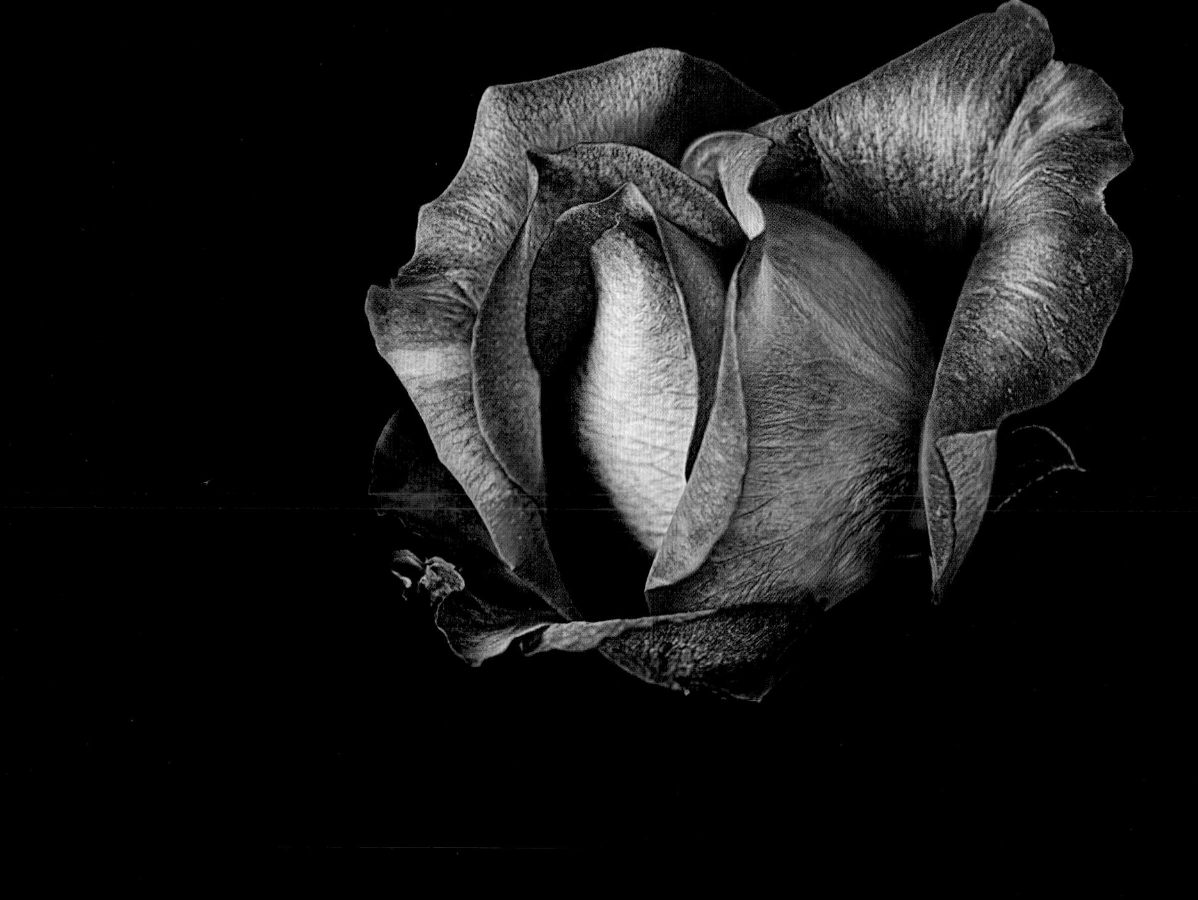

A More Dramatic Result

These results are more subtle, but still interesting.

After finishing several dozen flowers in color, I decided to try the technique as a black & white image. These results are more subtle, but still interesting. The change in saturation that happens with the opacity changes of the color images results in a more dramatic result in black & white images. Nonetheless, this is an evocative and different way to look at flower photography.

Pressure-Sensitive Tablets

This rosebud in a vase makes ample use of Photoshop's ability to burn and dodge, as well as the technique of separating petals and changing the opacity. Using a pressure-sensitive tablet allows the Photoshop user a great deal of control in using all of the painting capabilities inside the program.

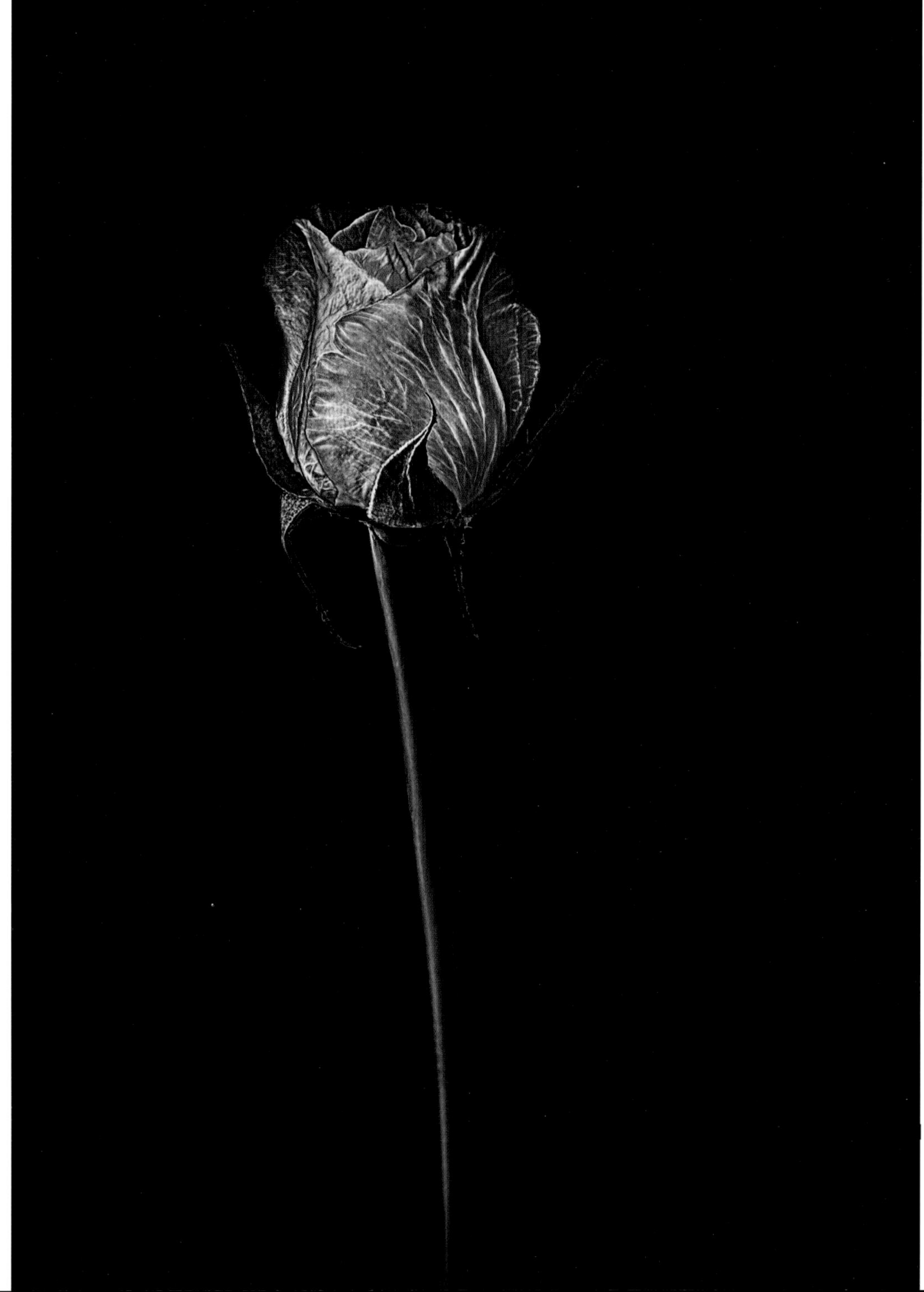

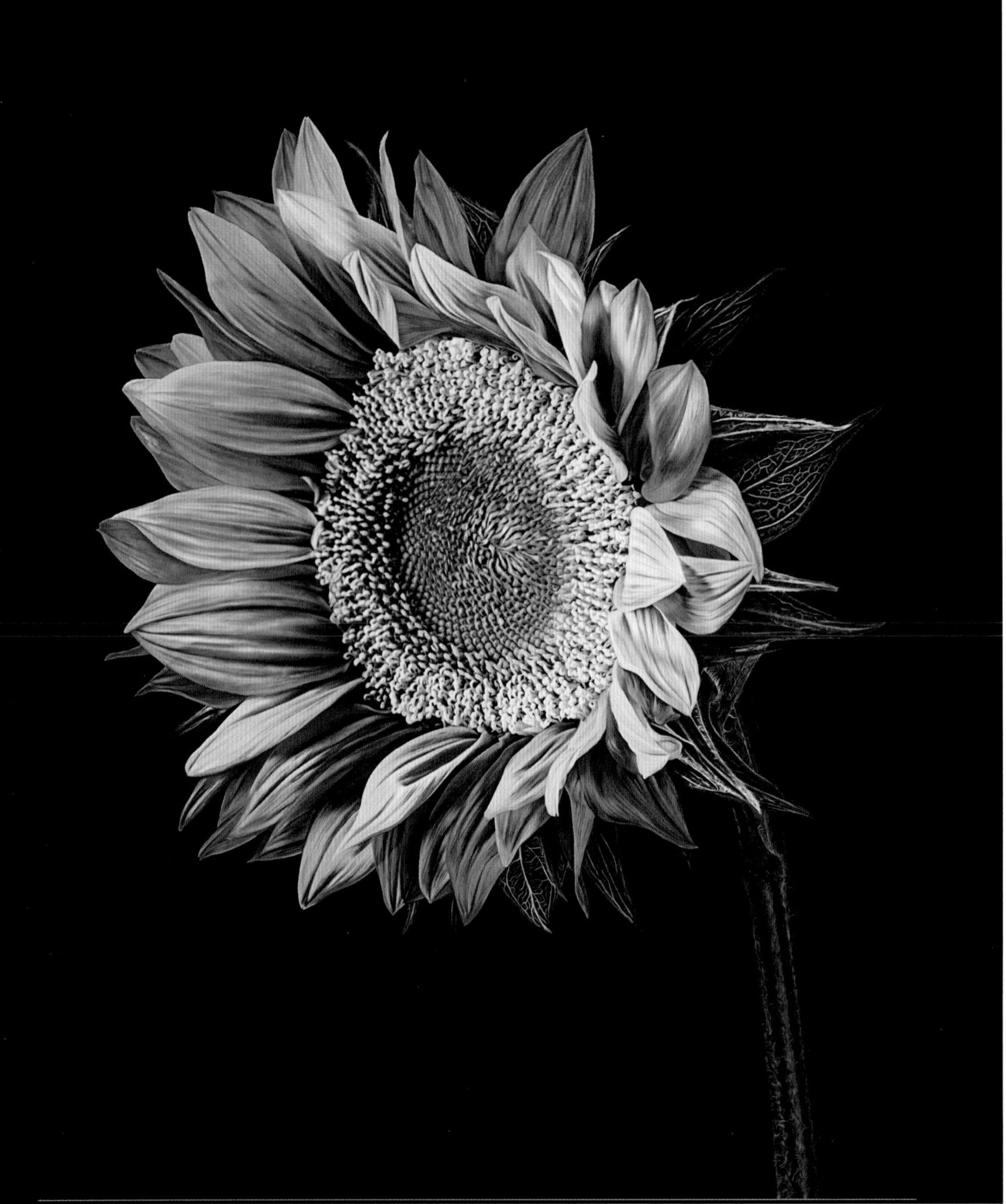

Sunshiny Day

The sunflower in this image, *Sunshiny Day*, uses the opacity changes from the center of the flower to the edges, as well as detail enhancement. In this case, the fact that the image is presented in black & white creates an even more translucent appearance for the outside petals.

Using a Pen Tool to Create More Detail

This image, *Tight Rope,* of a Queen Anne's lace flower was photographed in front of a dark background, using video lights. The thread was created using the Pen tool to make the line, and then the Brush tool to stoke the line. Water drops were photographed and added to the thread, and then the spider was added, from another image, in post-processing. Some of the leaves were stripped away to simplify the composition.

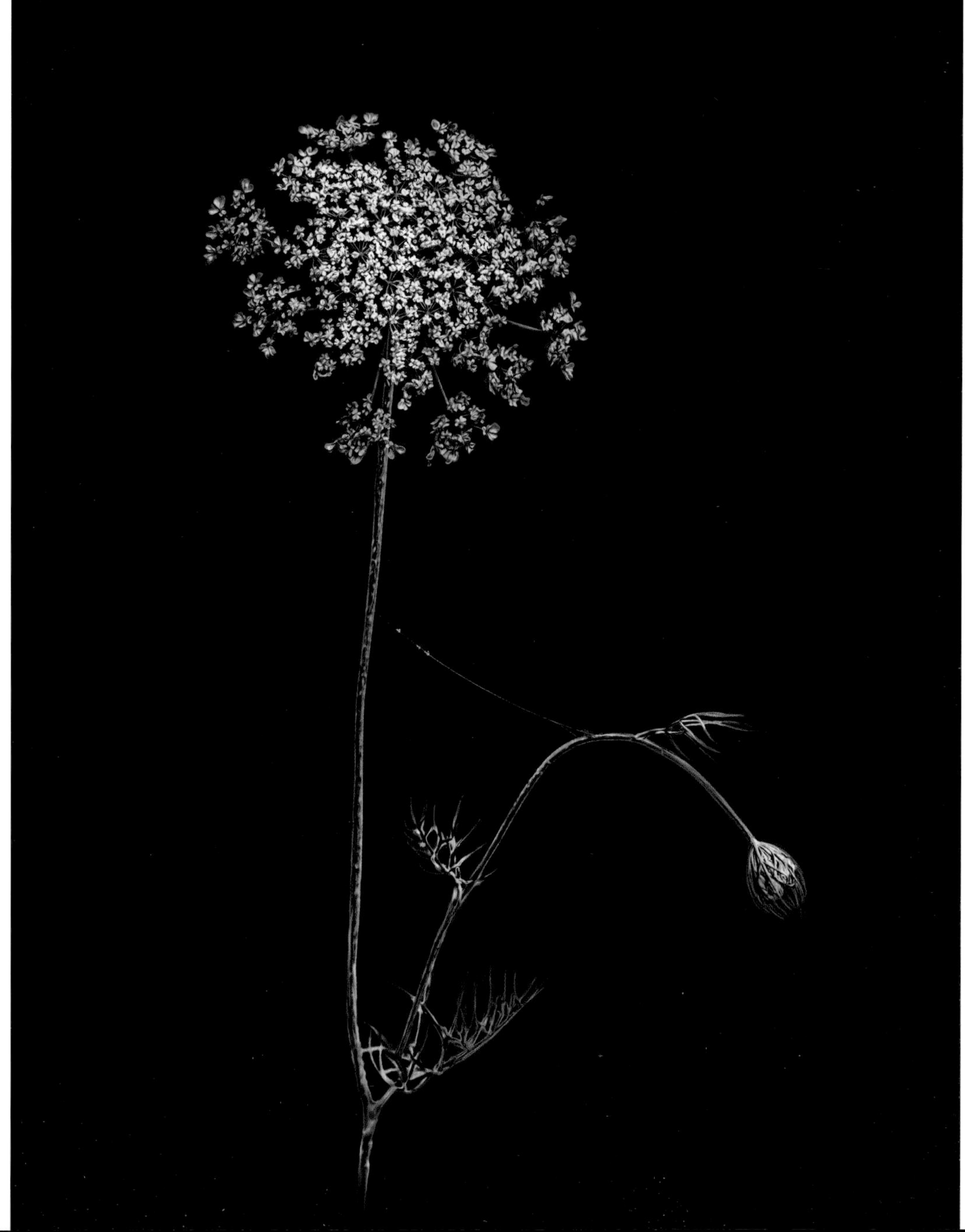

A Light Background

I love using a black background. It's clean, dramatic and gives the subject the spotlight in a big way. There are times, however, when the subject is more delicate—then a black background is just too heavy or overpowering. These wildflowers, the coneflower *(below)* and the flowering maple *(right)* are cases in point.

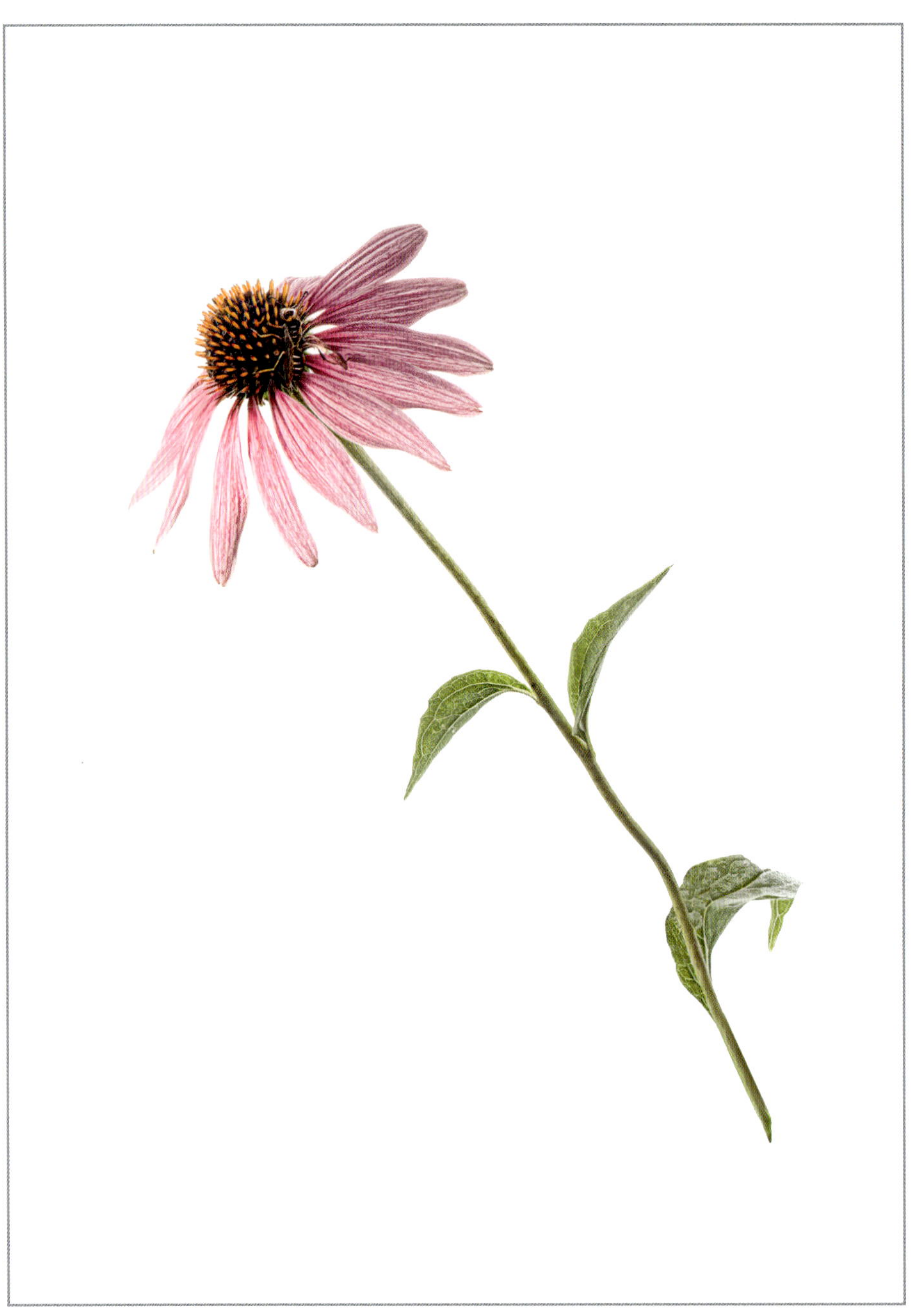

Establishing Place with Drop Shadow

The image *Flowering Maple* has quite a bit of white in its patterning. A black background could have overpowered it. In the case of this image, I've added a drop shadow to place the flower in the scene.

To do this, use Layer Styles > Drop Shadow to create a drop shadow. You can use the default settings because you are going to be able to edit this shadow as much as you like. Then go to the Layer pull-down menu, then choose Layer Style > Create Layer. This will put all of your layer styles on distinct layers. You'll have to highlight the drop shadow layer in the Layers panel. Now you can activate the Transform command, and with the Control/Command key pressed, drag on the center point at the top of the transformation box. You can pull the drop shadow over so that it looks like it's going across the floor. Since it's on its own layer, you could also add a layer mask and fade the drop shadow as it gets farther from the flower's base.

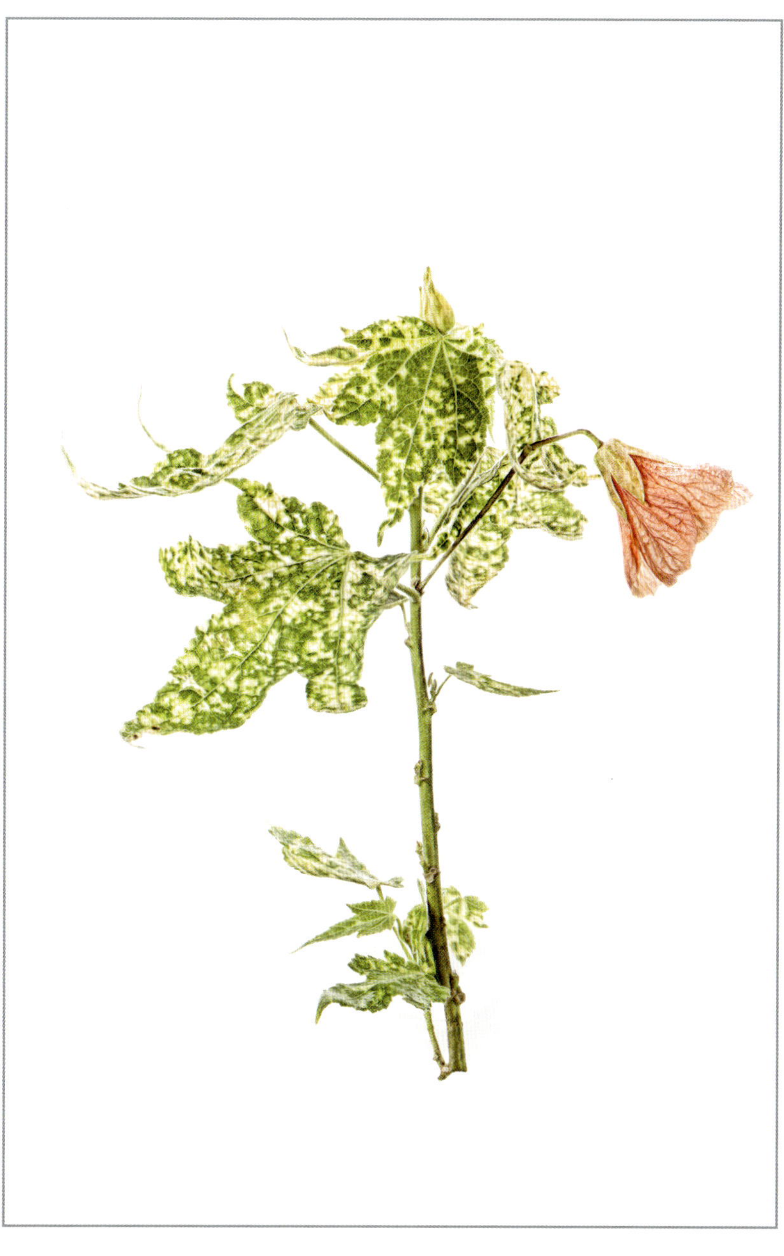

A Delicate Touch

This geranium cried out for a very delicate touch. When I selected this pale, purple flower and took it off its original background, it appeared to be too hard-edged. Opacity is a powerful tool with many uses. Lowering the opacity of the petals and the small seed bulbs on the side of the stalk gave this portrait of a flower a much softer and, for me, a much more pleasing result.

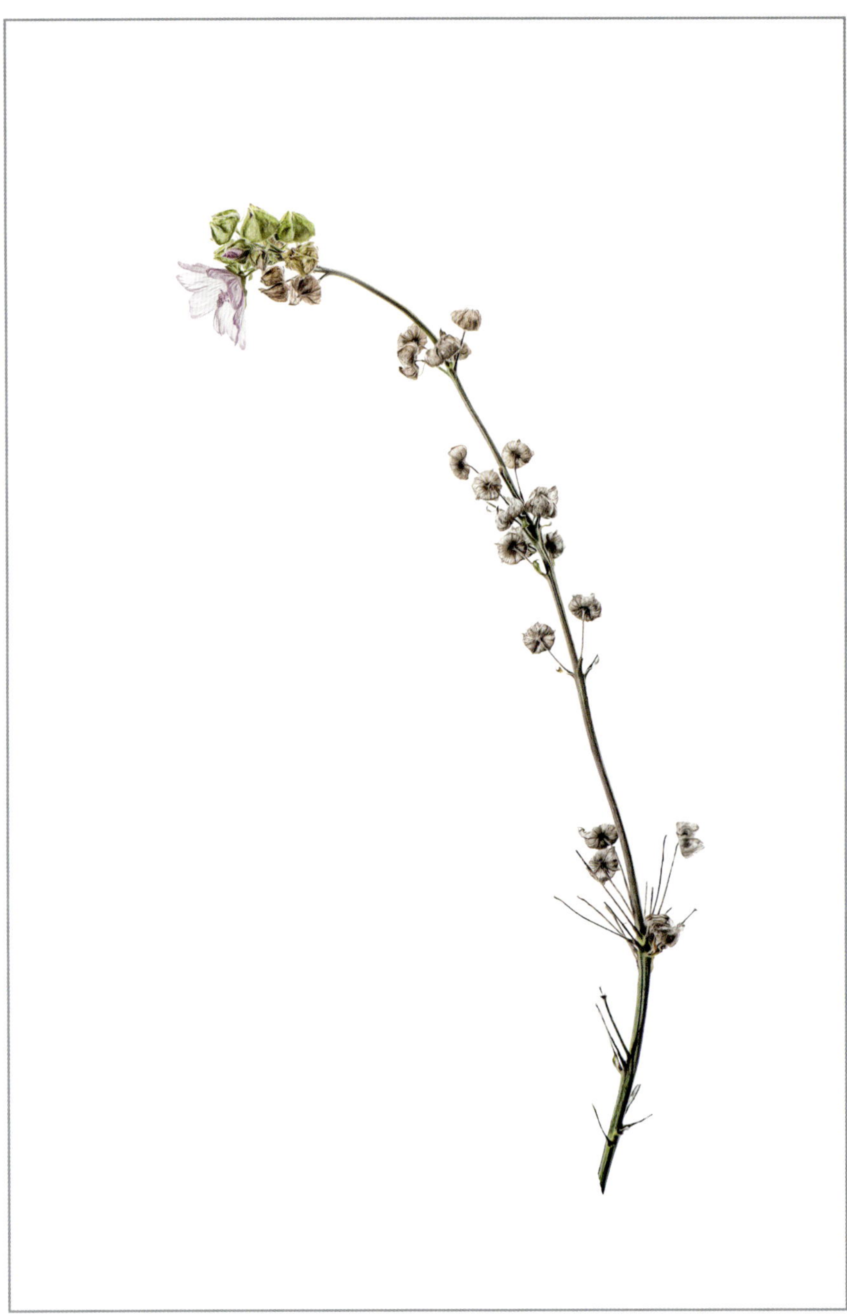

Painting from History >

This image *Rose of Sharon* uses nearly all the techniques described, including varied opacities, Oil Paint filter, burn, and dodging. I've also used selective painting from history as well. Using the History panel as a tool for artistic interpretation gives the image maker a huge range of possibilities from which to choose. It's a time machine for Photoshop. It's magic. Image makers can not just combine different images, but different points in time from each image.

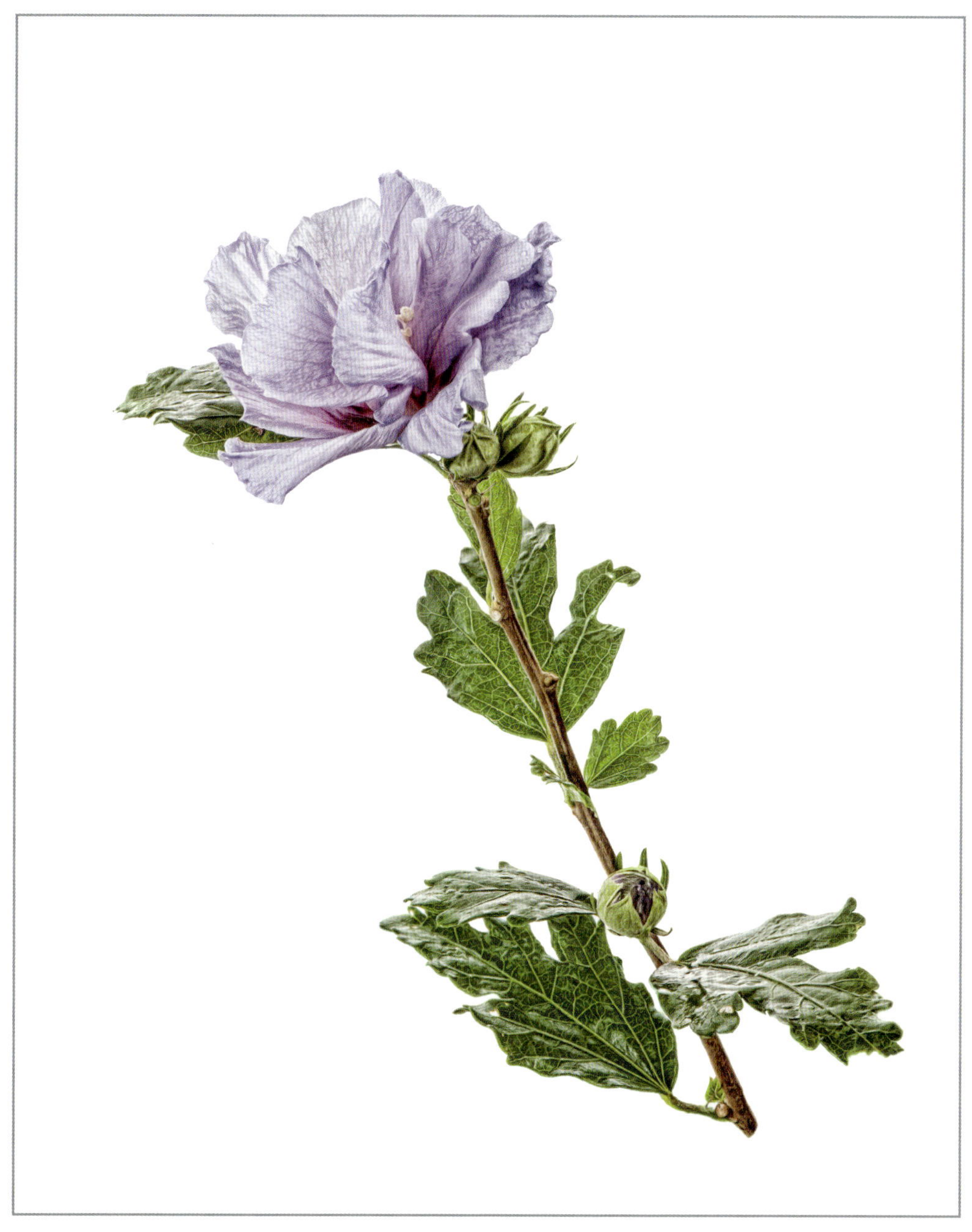

Damage Series

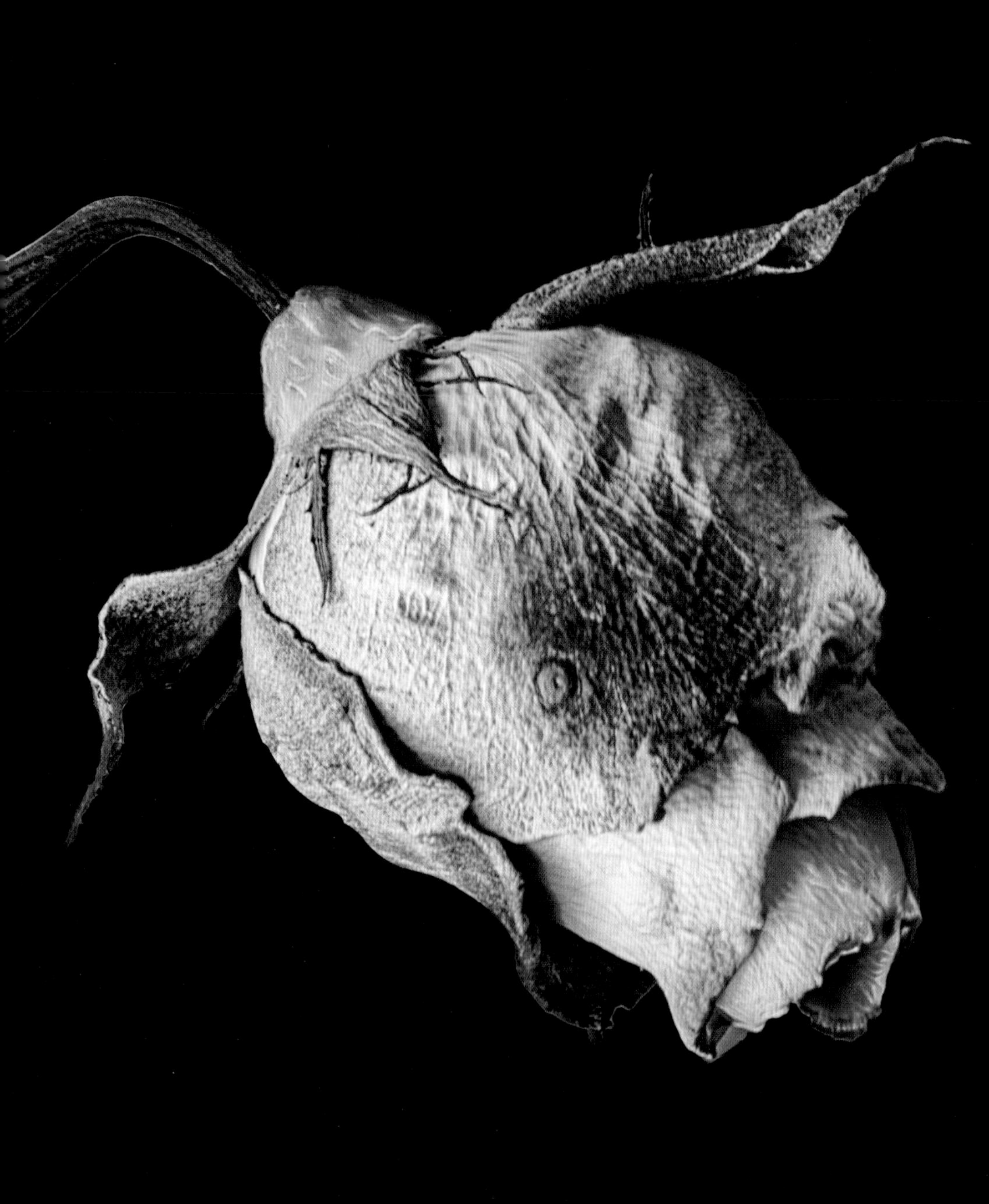

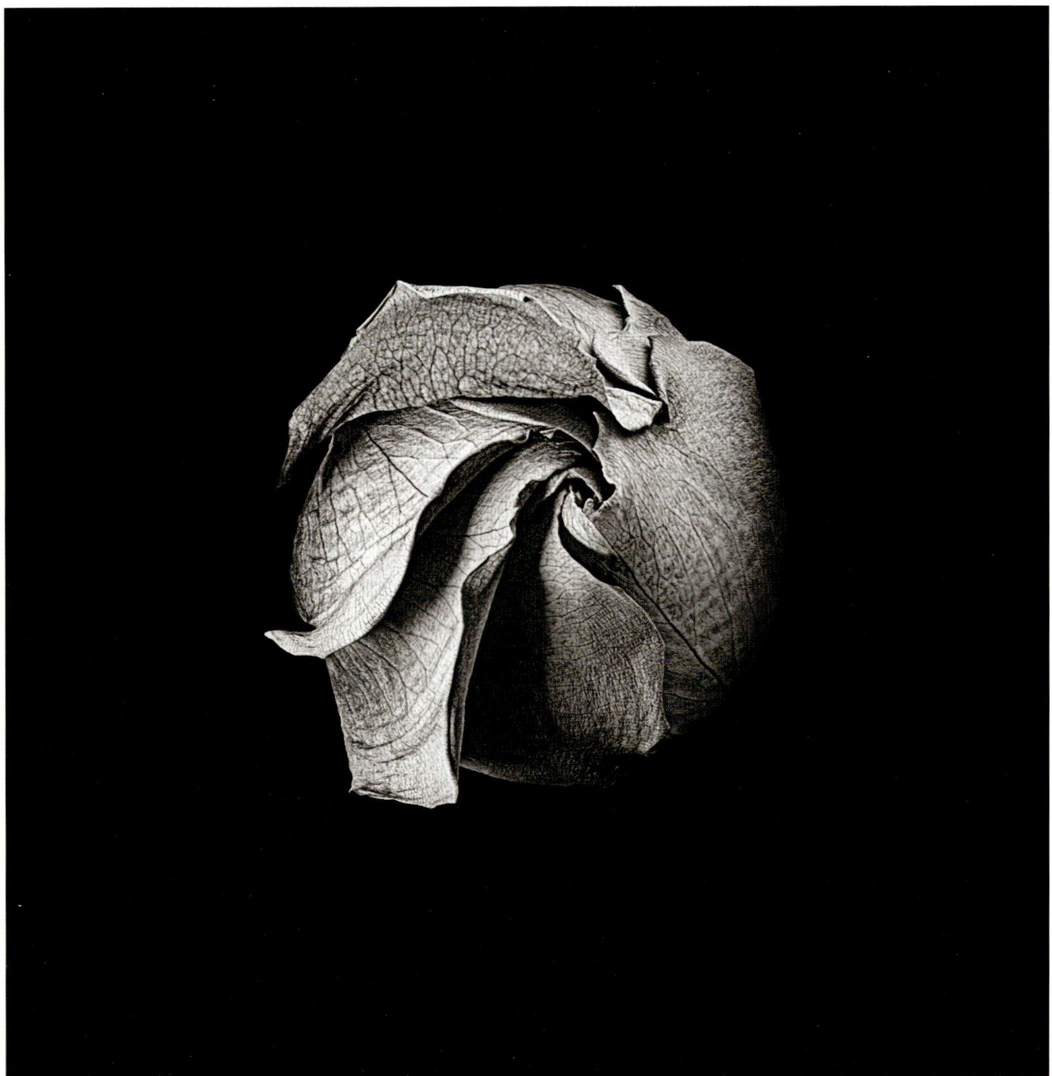

Other Ways to View Flowers ◀

After working through a series, including a few dozen flowers in a similar way, I felt the need to strike out in a different direction. Rather than focusing on how beautiful the flower could be, I wanted to investigate other ways to view flowers. What if the flowers weren't so beautiful?

Pulled, Dissected, and Cross Sectioned ▲

This is how the *Damage* series began. I dried flowers, let them die, baked them, and even fried them. I pulled them apart, dissected them, looked at them in cross section, and every other way I could imagine. I was trying to see the flower, not for its beauty, but for other attributes.

Not Seeking Beauty

In spite of the fact that I was not seeking out beauty in this series of flower images, this baked rose has a certain kind of appeal. The formerly soft, pastel blossom seems to have developed the grain of some exotic type of wood as it dried. The leaves appear to be so close to cracking apart, that they have become all the more delicate and ethereal.

Other Ways to See and Photograph

This dried lily seems suspended on the wind. In spite of being very dried out, it is held in the grip of endless motion. Had I not been experimenting with other ways to see and photograph flowers, I never would have stumbled across this.

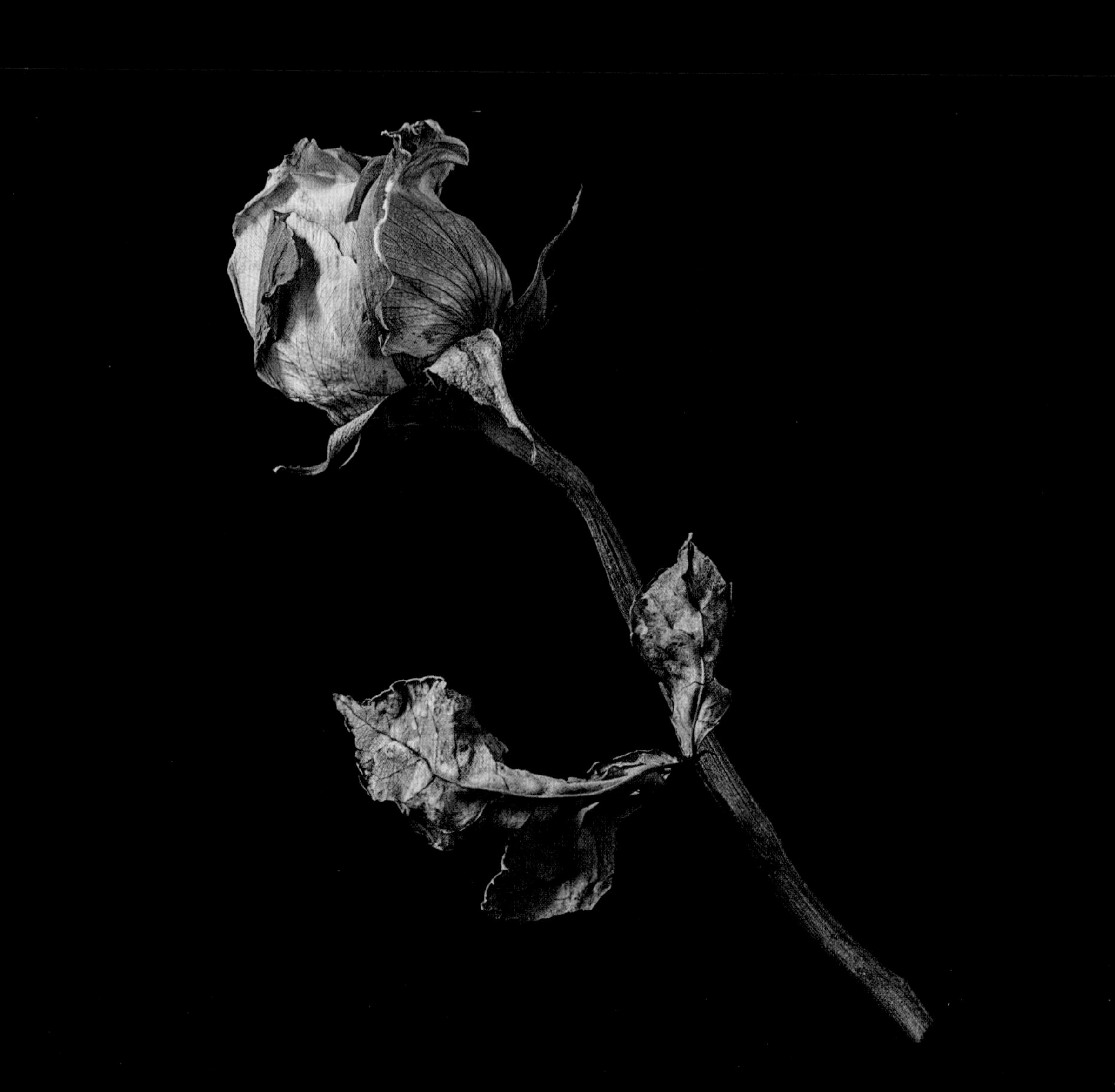

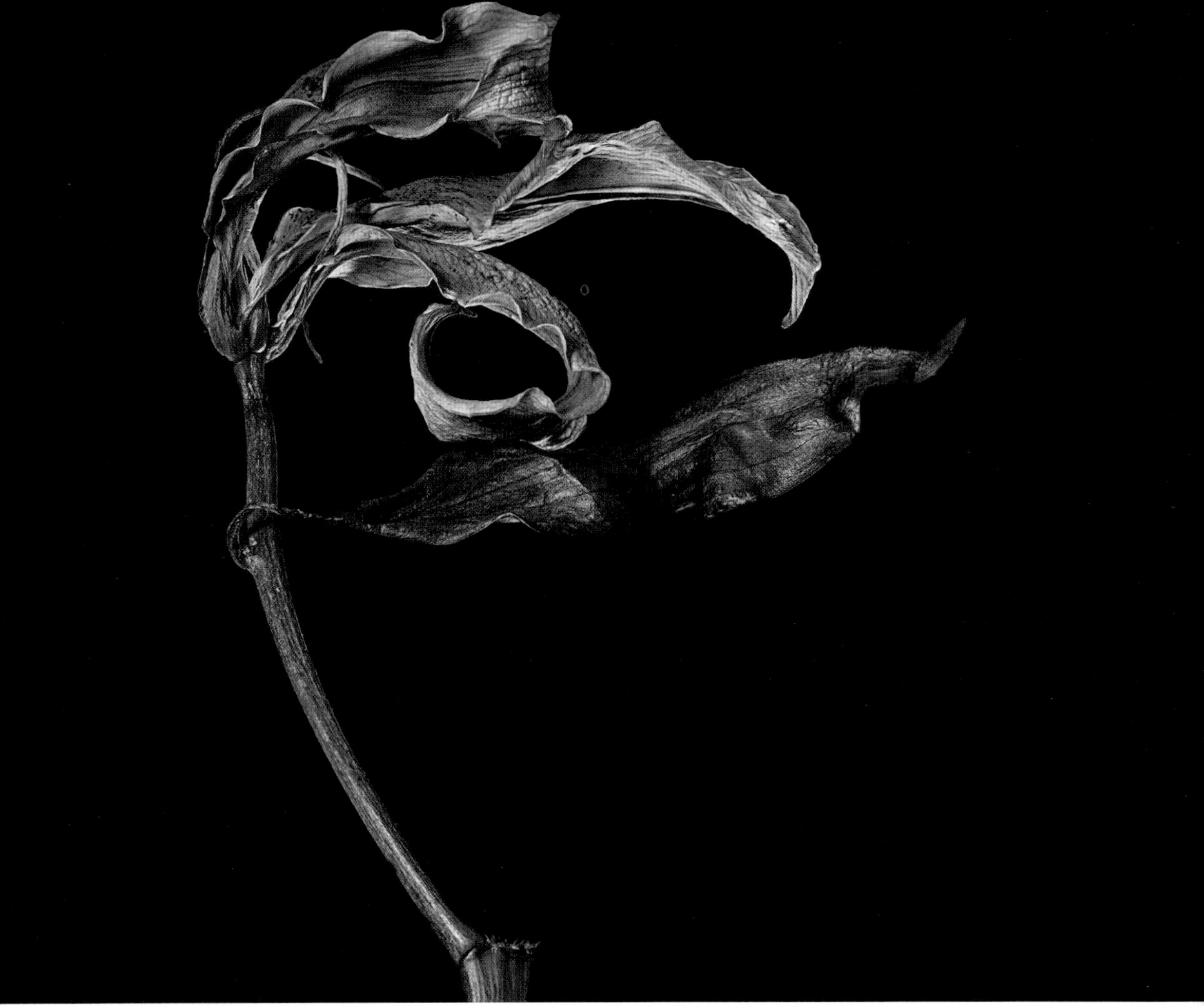

Had I not been experimenting . . . I never would have stumbled across this.

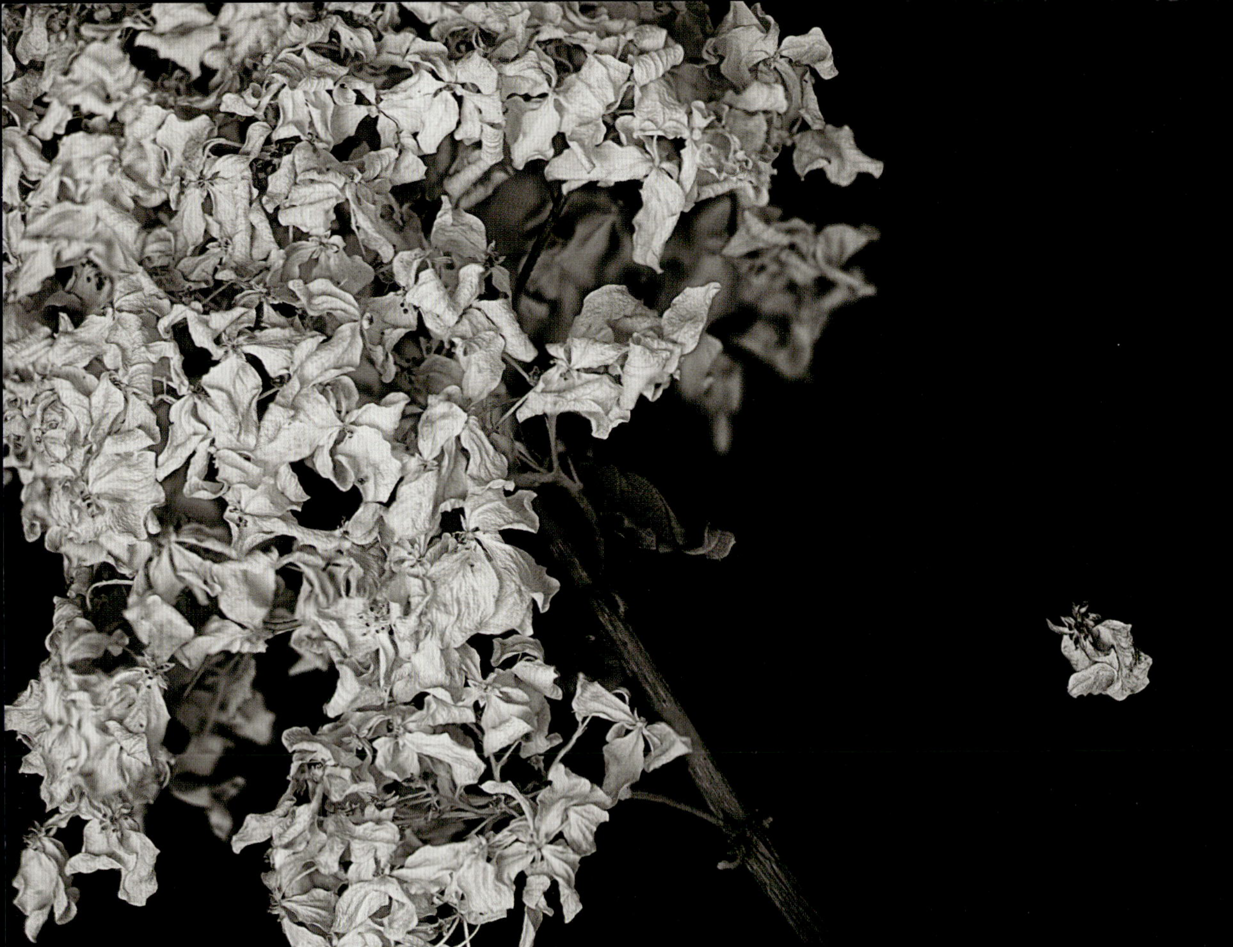

Focus Stacking

This flower was baked in an oven and then allowed to age slowly over the course of several weeks. I then photographed it using window light and a very simple, white card, approximately one foot by one foot, as a reflector. Taking four frames, focusing on different parts of the flower, I was then able to use focus stacking, by selecting all the layers, then choosing Edit > Align Layers, and Edit > Blend Layers in Photoshop to get maximum depth of field for this image.

. . . focusing on different parts of the flower, I was then able to use focus stacking . . .

Align and Blend Layers

Many of these images in the *Damage* series were the result of the subject being photographed multiple times with the camera on a tripod and changing the point of focus of multiple exposures. These were then imported as separate layers, which were then blended together in Photoshop using Edit > Auto Align Layers, then Auto Blend Layers.

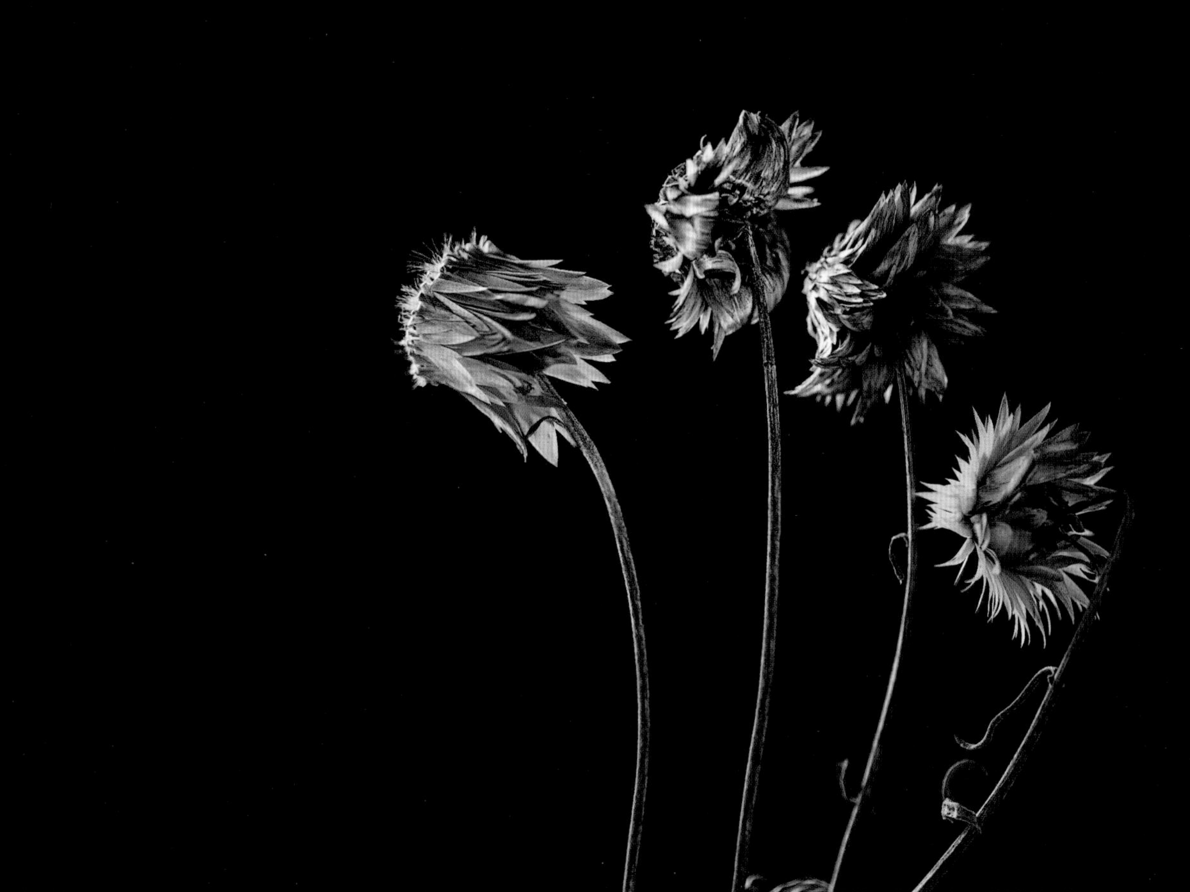

Pen and Brush

Again, I used focus stacking for maximum depth of field for this image, but with this image, I wanted to create an eerier feeling overall. Originally, the leaf on the top right simply ended just outside of the stem. I used the Clone tool to copy parts of the leaf and stretch it so that it wrapped around the stem. I then used the Pen tool and stroked the resultant paths with the Brush tool to create the tendrils that wrap around the stem. I added drop shadows for the tendrils to place

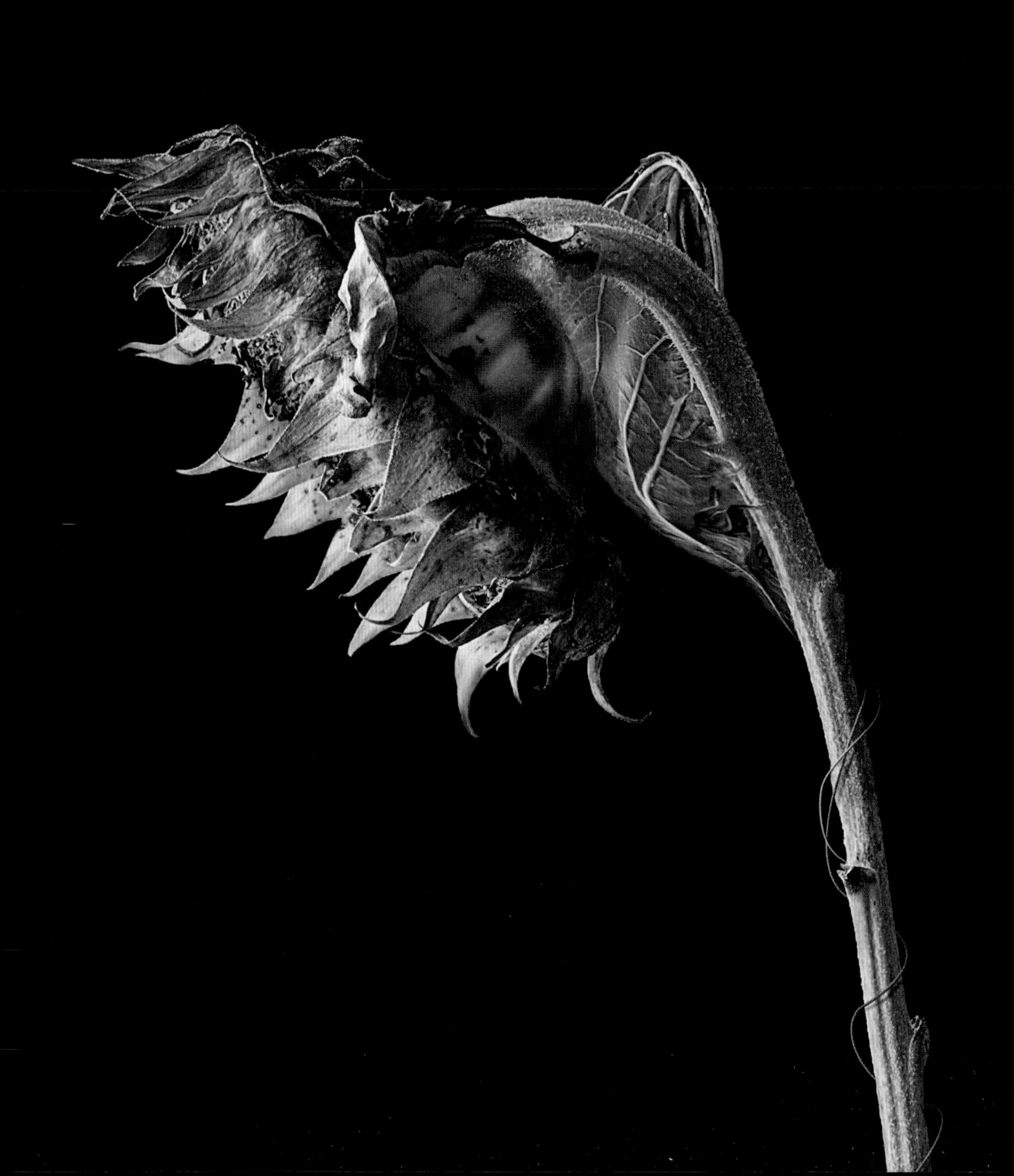

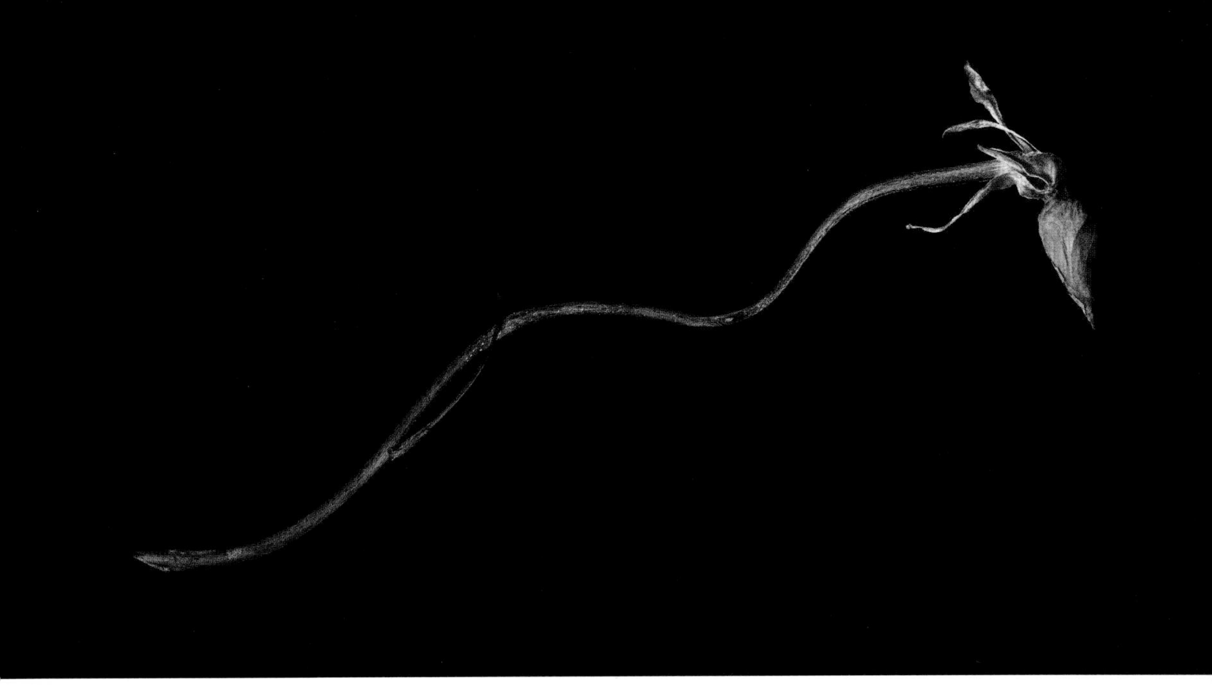

them in the scene. Rather then a simple dried sunflower, the subject becomes strangely clingy and surreal.

Warp and Liquify ▲

For this rose bud, I curved the stem using the Warp tool in Photoshop. This was done after selecting the rose and putting it on its own layer. The Warp tool is a relatively new tool in Photoshop and allows the user to bend pixels. The Liquify tool does this as well, but the two tools work somewhat differently. The Liquify tool has a number of different options, while the Warp tool creates a grid, which the user simply pulls around to distort and bend the subject.

I added drop shadows for the tendrils to place them in the scene.

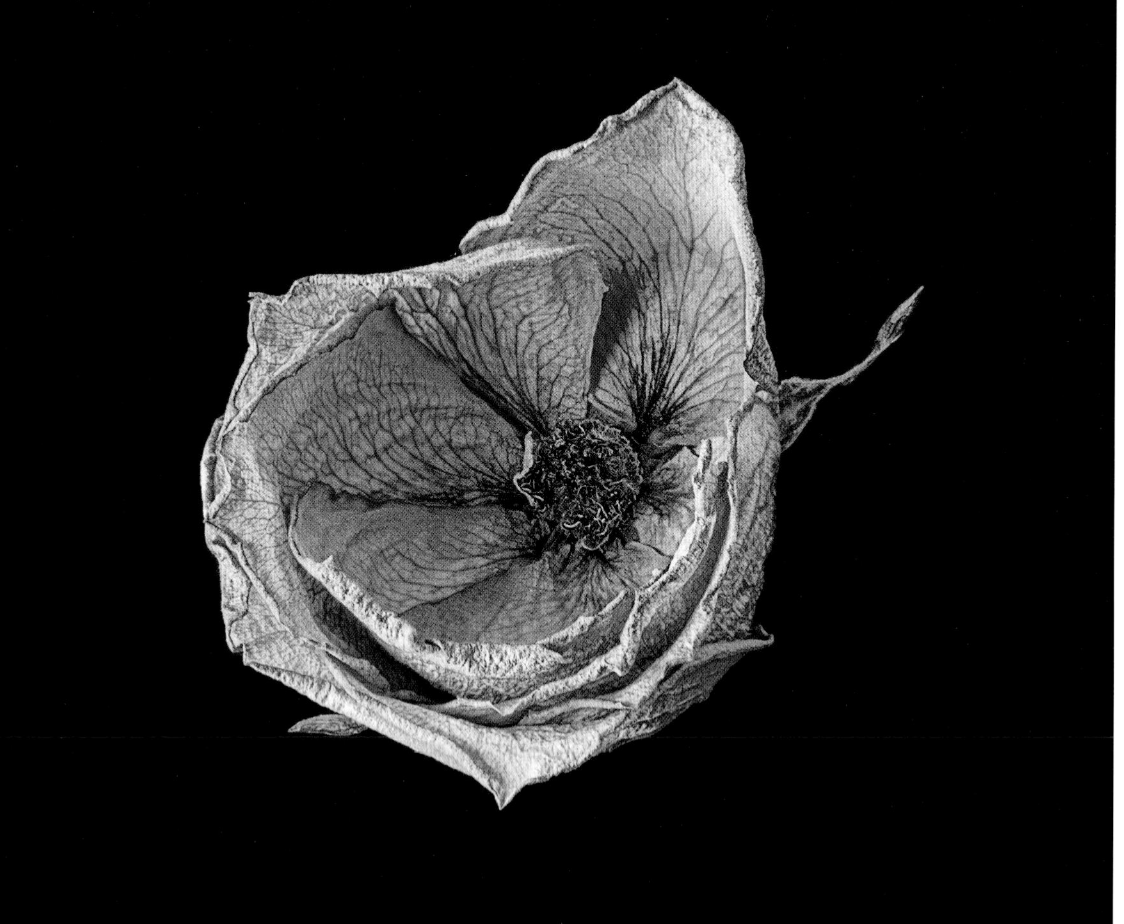

I heated up cooking oil and fried this rose.

The technique was used of enhancing the veins by using the Burn and Dodge tools.

Fried Rose

For this image *(below)* from the *Damage* series, I heated up cooking oil and fried this rose. Interestingly, frying turned the rose petals translucent and very shiny. The translucency was very appealing. To see this even more clearly, I plucked out the center petals and backlit the rose, again using a very simple, white reflector for fill light.

Enhancing Details

Another version of a hollowed out rose *(facing page)*, this time dried, shows virtually the same flower in a completely different way. This time the rose is papery in appearance. I enhanced the veins by using the Burn and Dodge tools

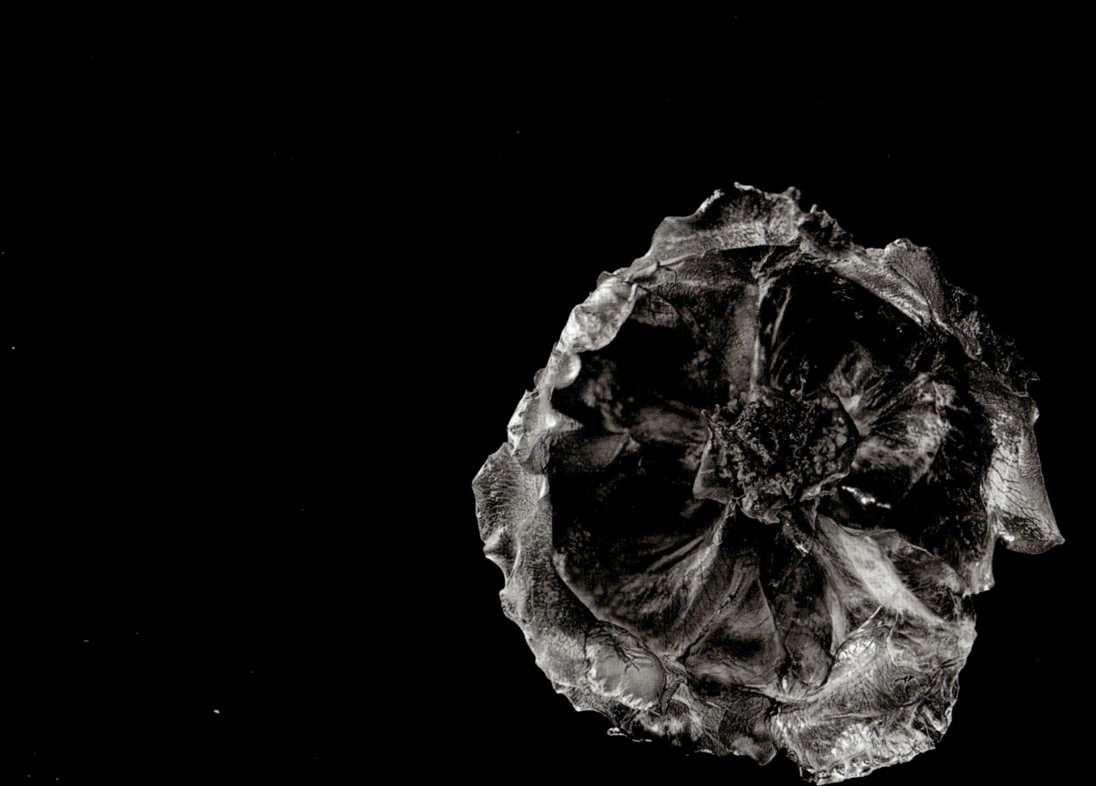

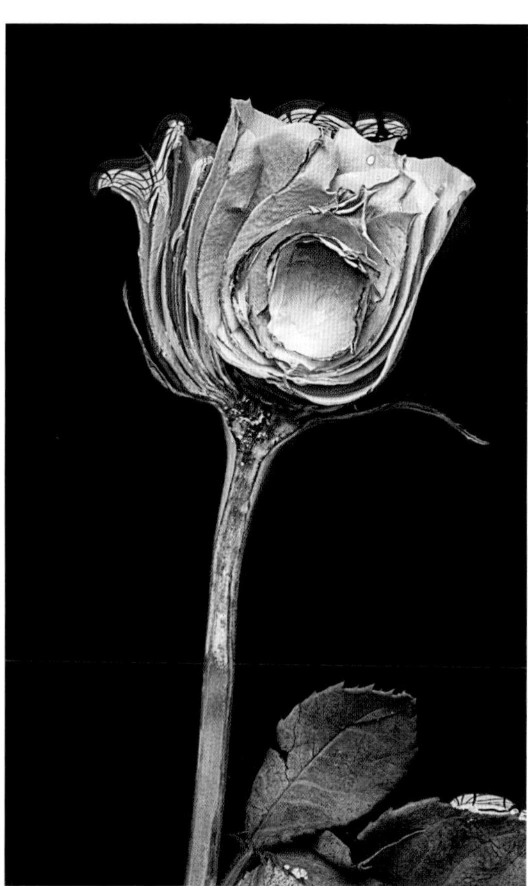

Graceful Repetition of Lines

This rose was dissected, including the stem, and in the center, a face seemed to appear. In this case, the flower is floating in a pool of dark water which virtually disappears, but there are water droplets visible on some of the petals' edges. The edges of the dissection create a graceful repetition of lines around the center.

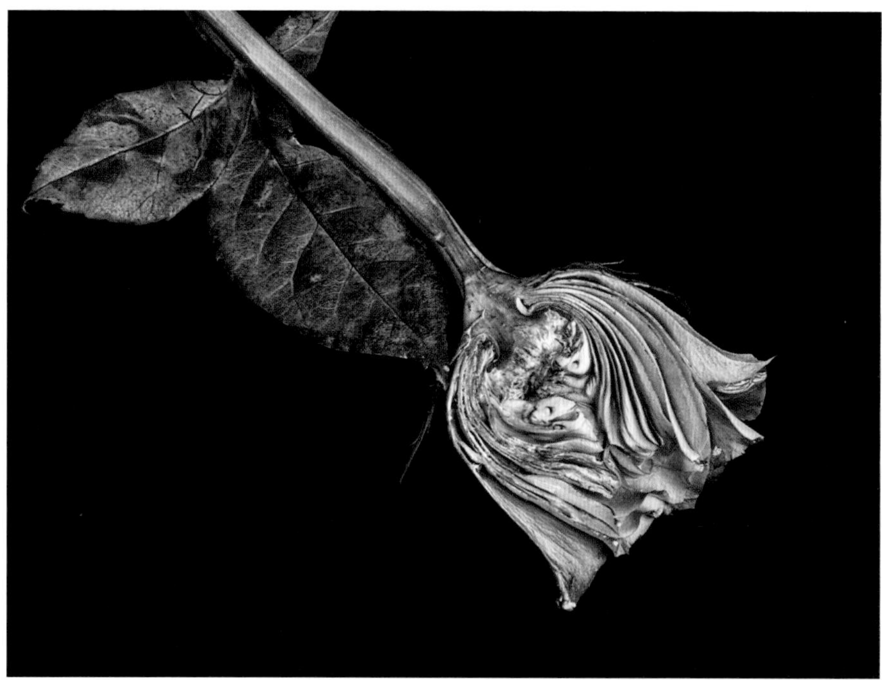

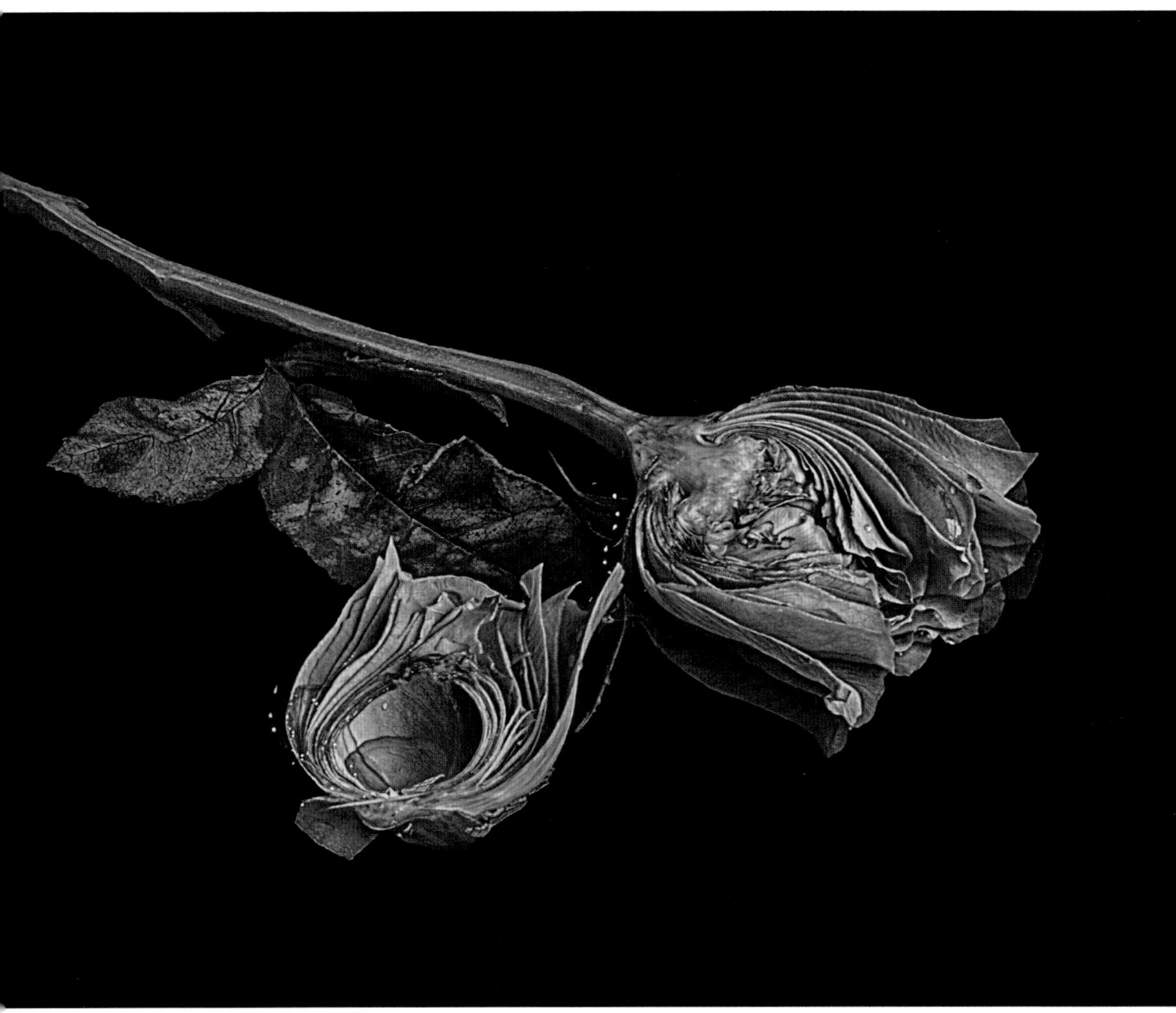

Flower Cutaway ▲

It is even more evident here that the flowers are floating in a water bath. The cutaway portion lies next to the other section of rose with a small pool of water inside. Water drops dance around the edges. Working with different textures, including water, can add a new feeling to the imagery.

Working with different textures, including water, can add a new feeling to the imagery.

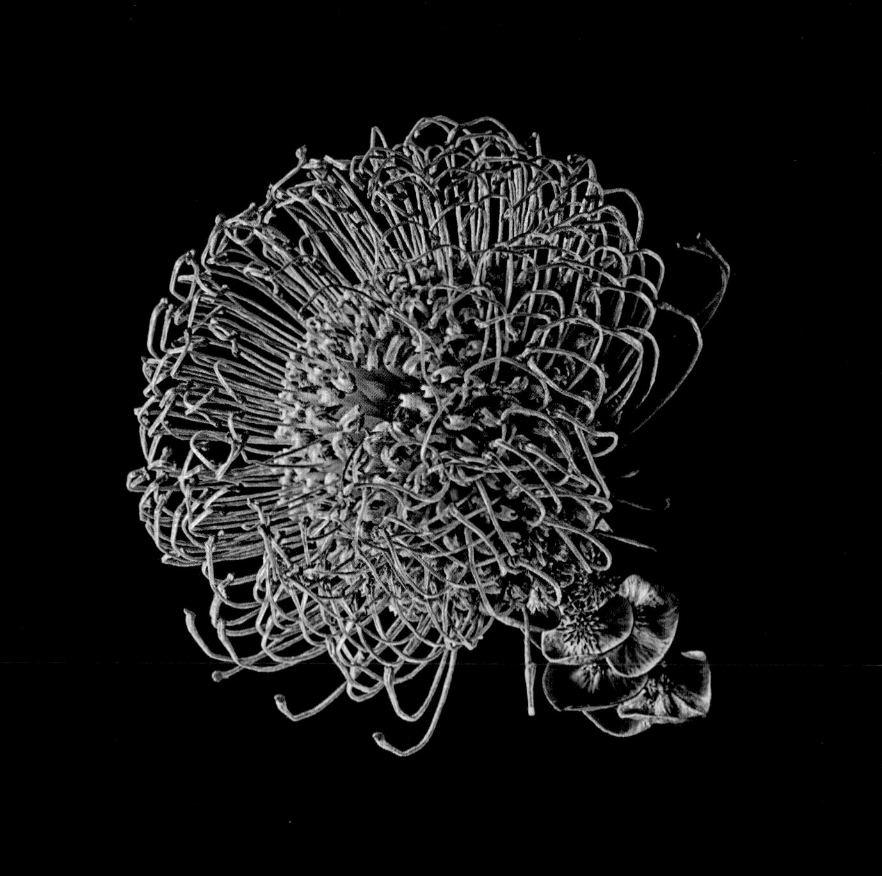

Man Eater ▲

I happened to find this strange flower in a local florist's shop. It was spiky and orange, and I photographed it as it dried over several weeks time. This was the final stage before it began to fall apart, and it seemed to be reaching out in an effort to grab anything—or anyone—that might come close. I called this one *Man Eater* for that reason.

Door into the Heart

Not as cleanly dissected, this rose functions like a door into the heart of the flower, showing its center surrounded by gently curving petals, which arch protectively over it. Using Photoshop's Oil Paint Filter on just the center gives it a very different texture from the rest of the flower. There are several methods for applying a filter to just part of a layer. The method I used in this image is to copy the layer and go to Layer > Smart Objects > Convert to Smart Object. Then add a layer mask, filled with black, and then use the Brush tool in white to paint in the filter effect wherever you want the filter effect. If you over paint or make a mistake, simply switch to black and paint away the effect. You can switch between black to make the filtered part disappear or white to make the filtered part visible.

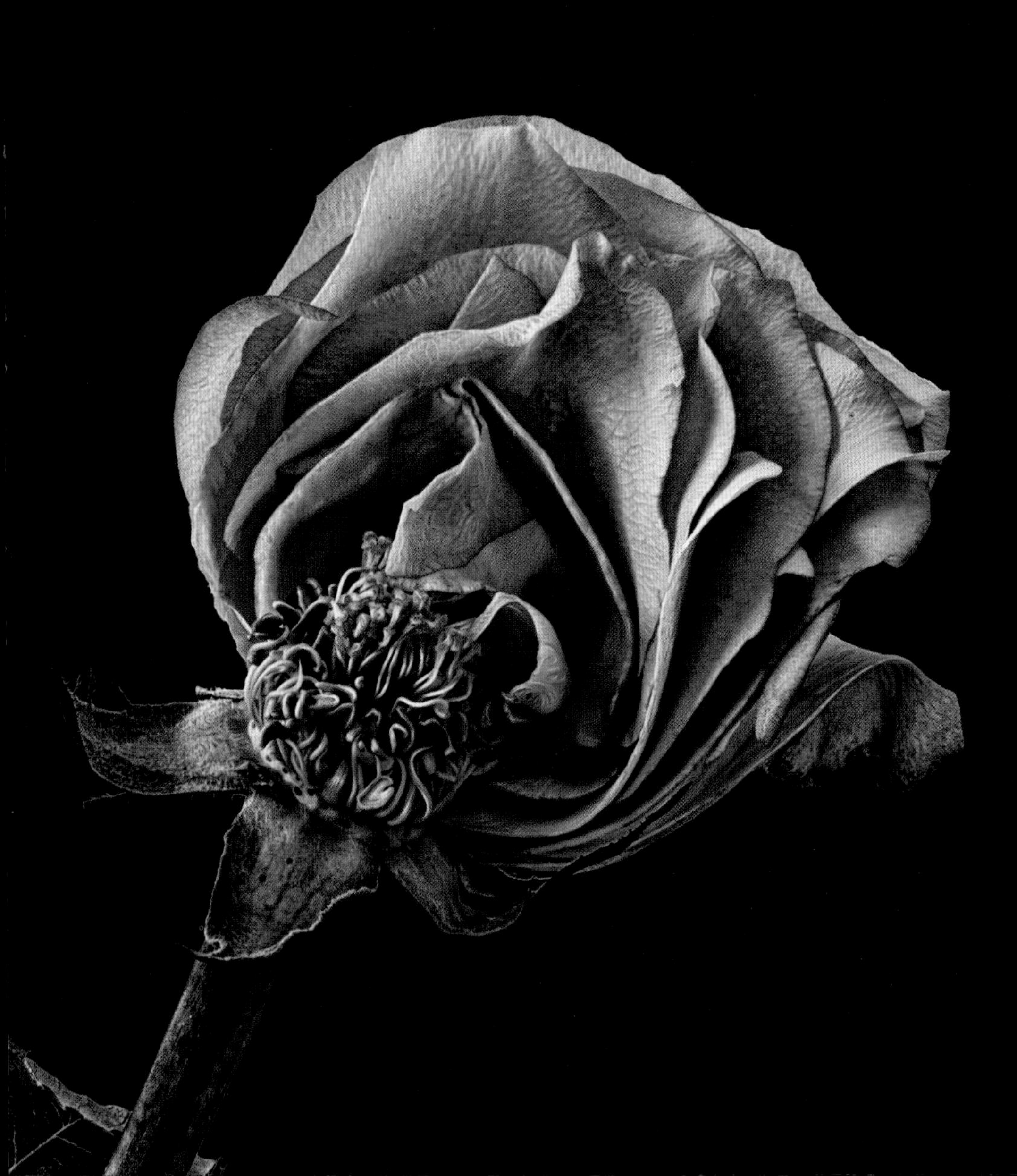

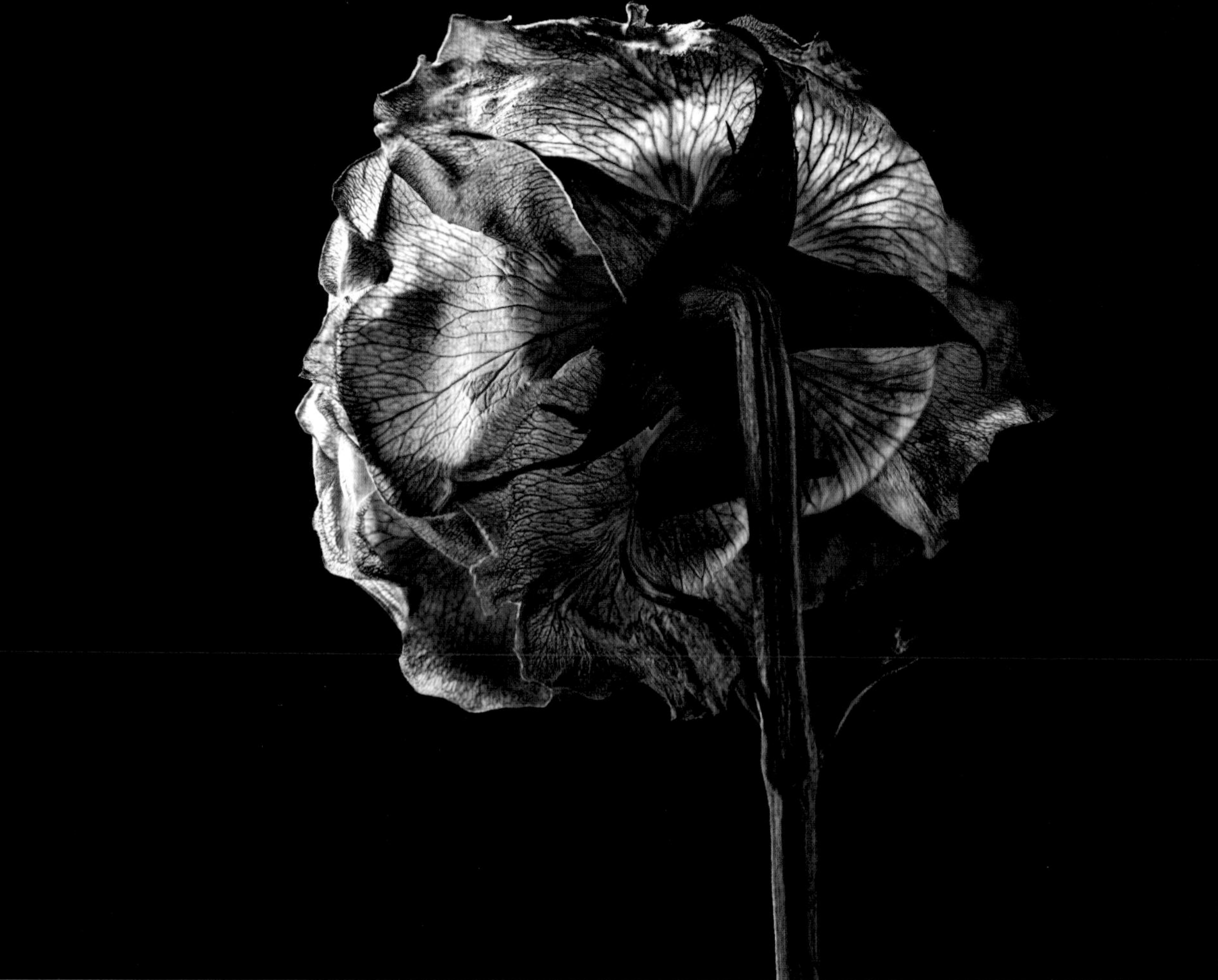

Carefully Enhanced Details

Delicate Beauty is another image of a rose that was fried, but the center was left partially intact. Also backlit and photographed several times for maximum depth of field, the photographs were compiled and blended and the details enhanced carefully.

The photographs were compiled and blended and the details enhanced carefully.

Entrapment: Eliminating Parts of the Subject

Adding a blank layer and changing the blend mode of that layer to Multiply allowed me to use a slightly soft-edge black brush in medium low opacity.

The image *Entrapment* began with a more standard photograph of a mum blossom. I plucked just a few of the petals for a better view into the flower's center. I used a video light placed to the side and a reflector to light the flower. I put the flower onto its own layer and then decided to surround the flower in a cage of metal vines.

I used the Pen tool to create the vines, erasing just the parts that seemed to visually go behind the flower and adding the Bevel and Emboss layer style to the metal vines to give them dimension. A Pattern Overlay was also added, using the Multiply Blend Mode to darken and add a texture to the metal vines. Adding a blank layer and changing the Blend Mode of that layer to Multiply allowed me to use a slightly softer-edged black brush in medium low opacity (25–35 percent). Stroke where the shadows would naturally appear.

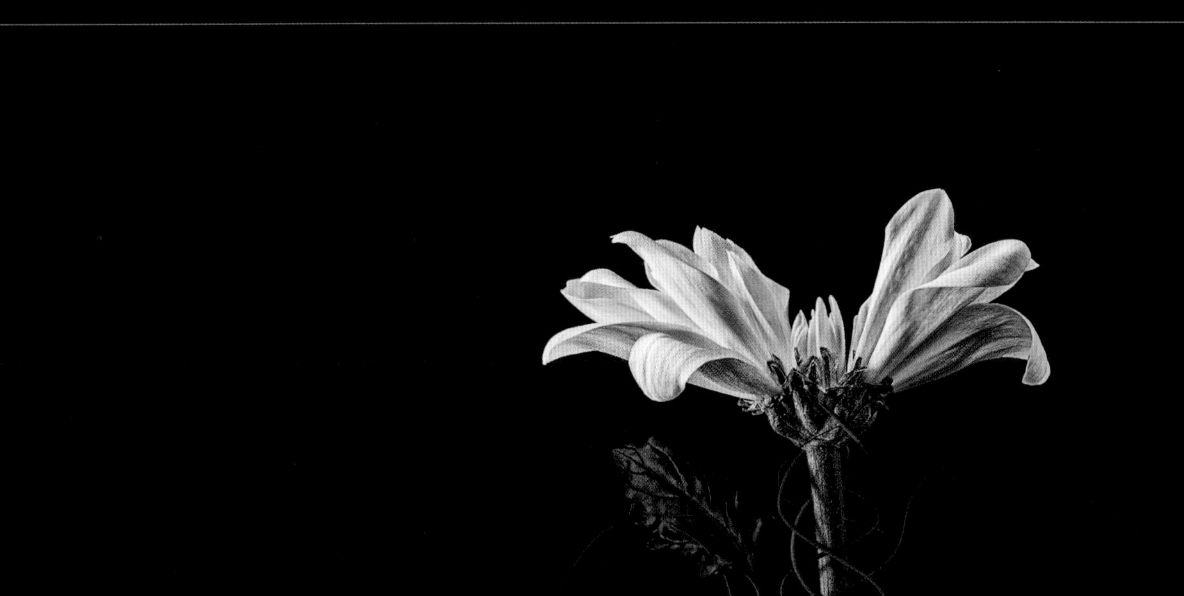

Experimenting with Hybrid Combinations

For an exploration of more ways to work with the *Damage* flower series, I experimented with hybrid combinations, adding small animal parts to the flower and blending carefully. This is a very dried-out sunflower, naturally dried, past its prime, in the garden. It had a great texture to it naturally. I found the mouse outside, also past its prime and photographed it.

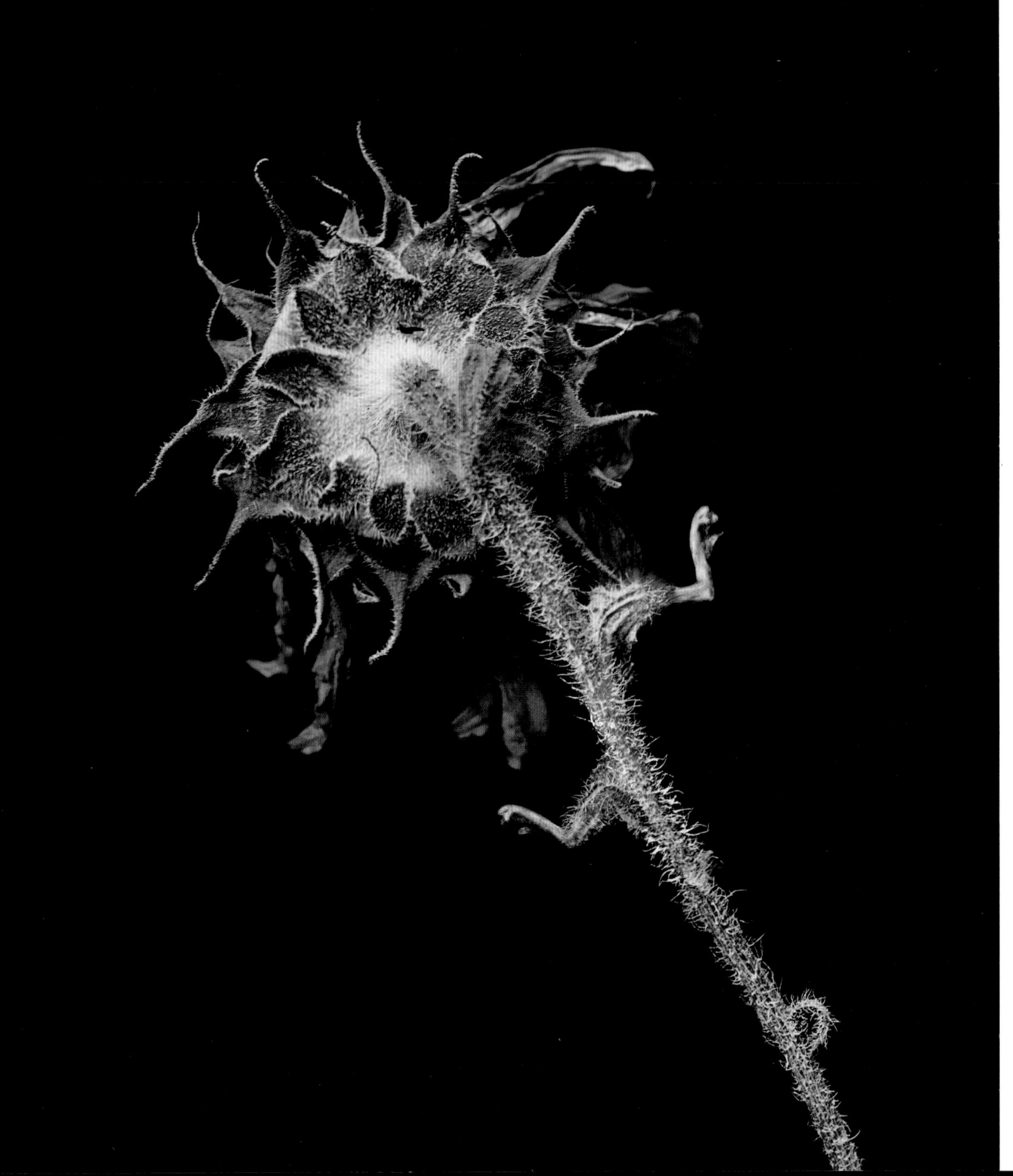

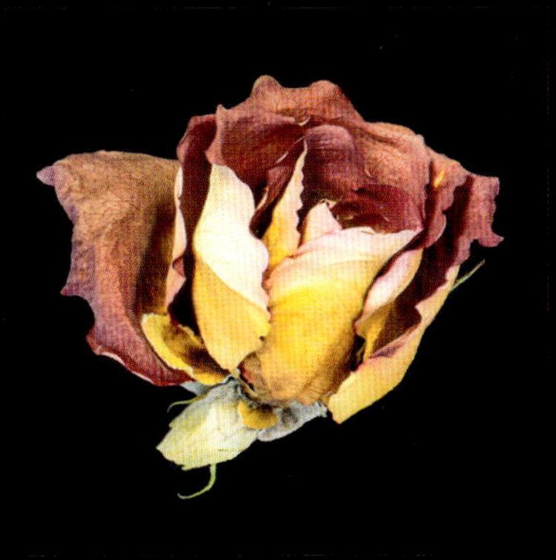

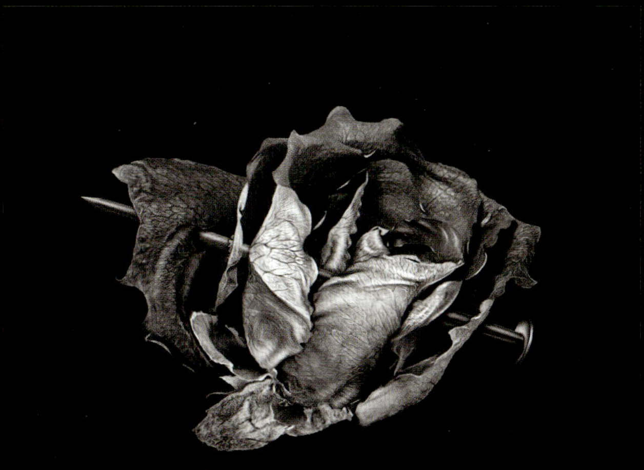

Building a Nail ▲

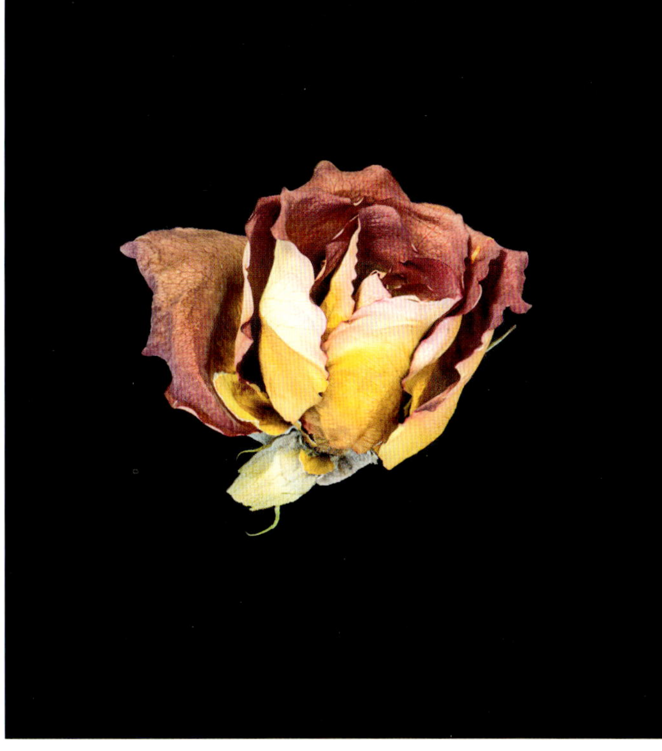

The nail in this image is built in Photoshop and stabbed through the flower only digitally. To do this, build the nail first. It's simply a rectangle, with a point added to one end, then a circle added to the other end. I used a Bevel and Emboss layer style on the circle giving it dimension, like on the nail head, and then filled in the shaft of the nail with a color, burning one side and dodging the other to give it form. Adding a texture creates a more realistic looking nail. The completed nail was placed on its own layer and then layer mask was added. A small, hard-edged black brush was used to paint a layer mask black where the petals needed to appear to be in front of the nail.

Happy Accidents

A deep frying process and backlighting resulted in some very vibrantly colored flowers, especially when combined with backlighting. This was one of the happy accidents that can delight photographers. With its broad range of color and saturations, the resulting image is very different from the initial flowers series.

Using the Familiar

Photographed from the back of the rose rather than the front, the same rose becomes gestural and evokes a very different feeling. In part, this is because the rose is now seen as a familiar shape. This version of the rose is lit from the side, similarly to the lighting one might see for a portrait—adding another familiar element to its construction.

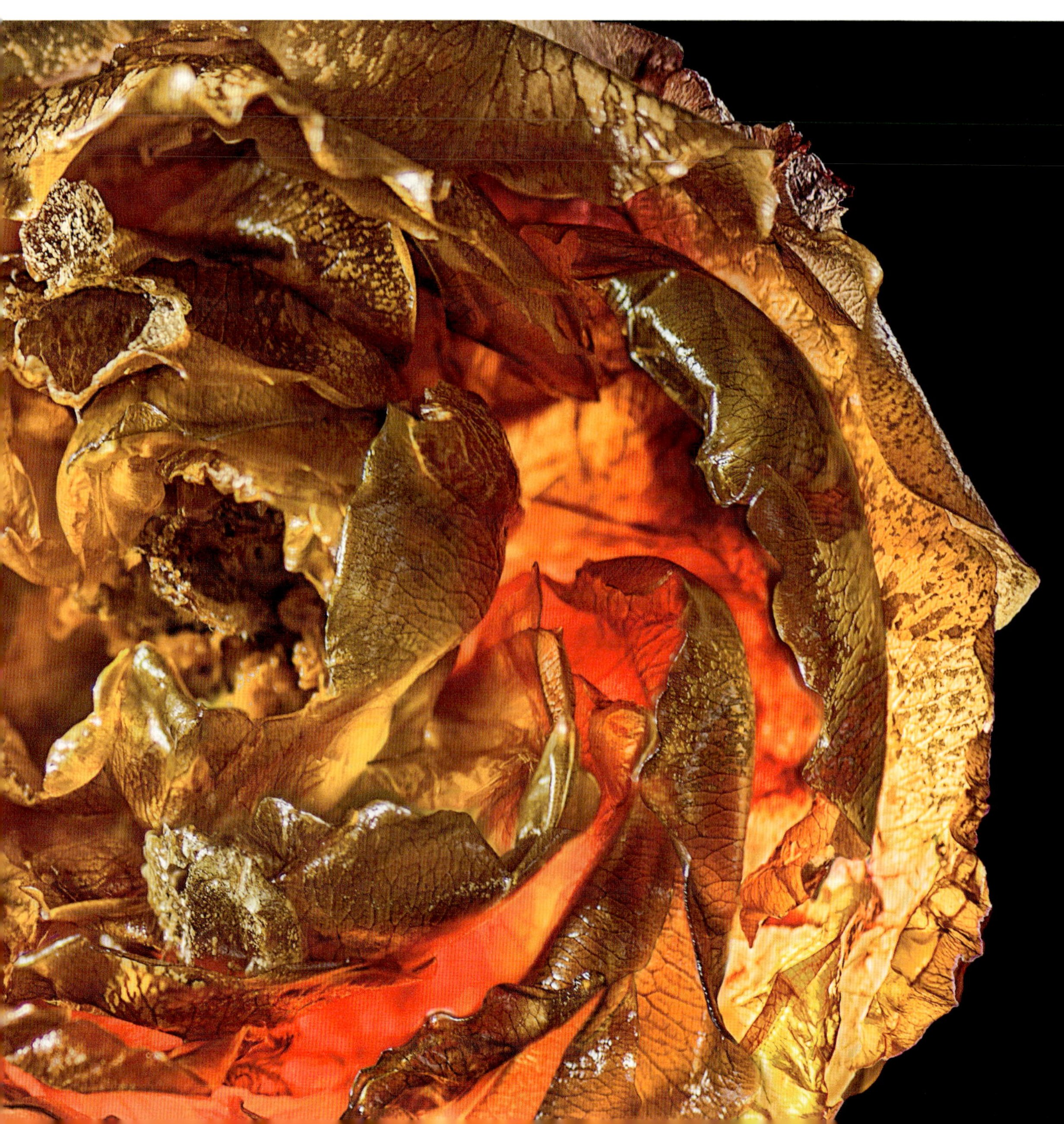

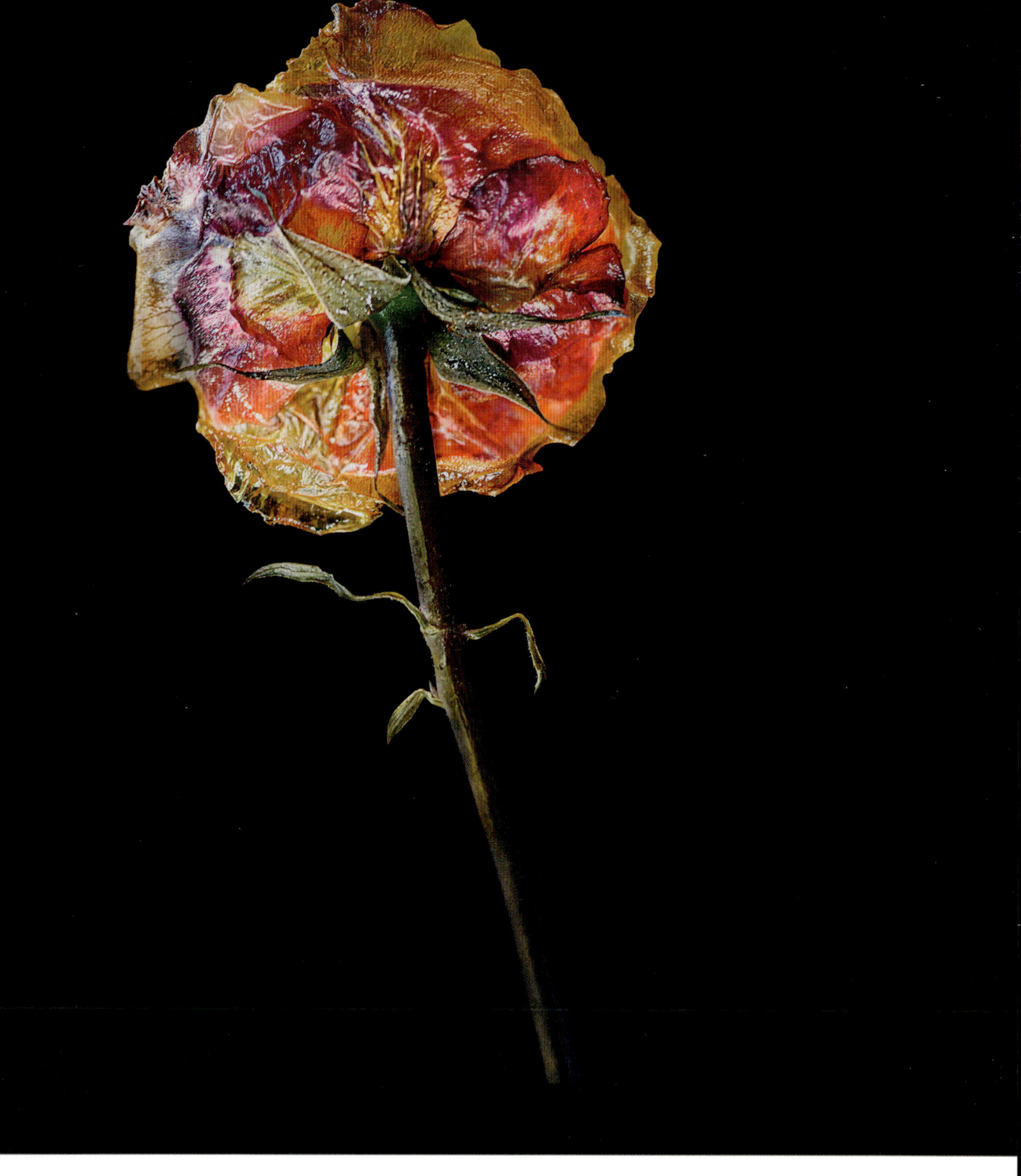

This version of the rose is lit from the side . . .

Focus Stack, then Invert

Continuing on with the dead flowers, I was captivated by the texture of the sunflower, but I wanted to try to make it less heavy. I decided to invert the image, creating a negative, which actually looked like a positive. This is partially due to the fact that I had done a great deal of sharpening and adding contrast. Even with the *focus stacking* some of the prickly spines coming from the spine were not as sharp as I wanted them to be. Using a pressure sensitive-tablet and a very small brush, I brushed over the spines, which made them appear to be in much finer focus.

Maximum Depth of Field

Once word gets out that you are working on a particular series or theme, you'll occasionally have friends and acquaintances donate to the cause. A great friend had a couple of dried poppy pods that she gave to me. I cut the woody pod apart and photographed it with window light and a reflector and, again, using several exposures, which I would blend together in Photoshop for maximum depth of field. It was okay, but a little uninteresting, and I had begun adding foreign parts into the flowers. I had recently photographed a friend who sported a very large and wild beard, so I decided to take the beard and add it to the flower. It's a strange result that requires a second look by the viewer. It also became part of the larger work.

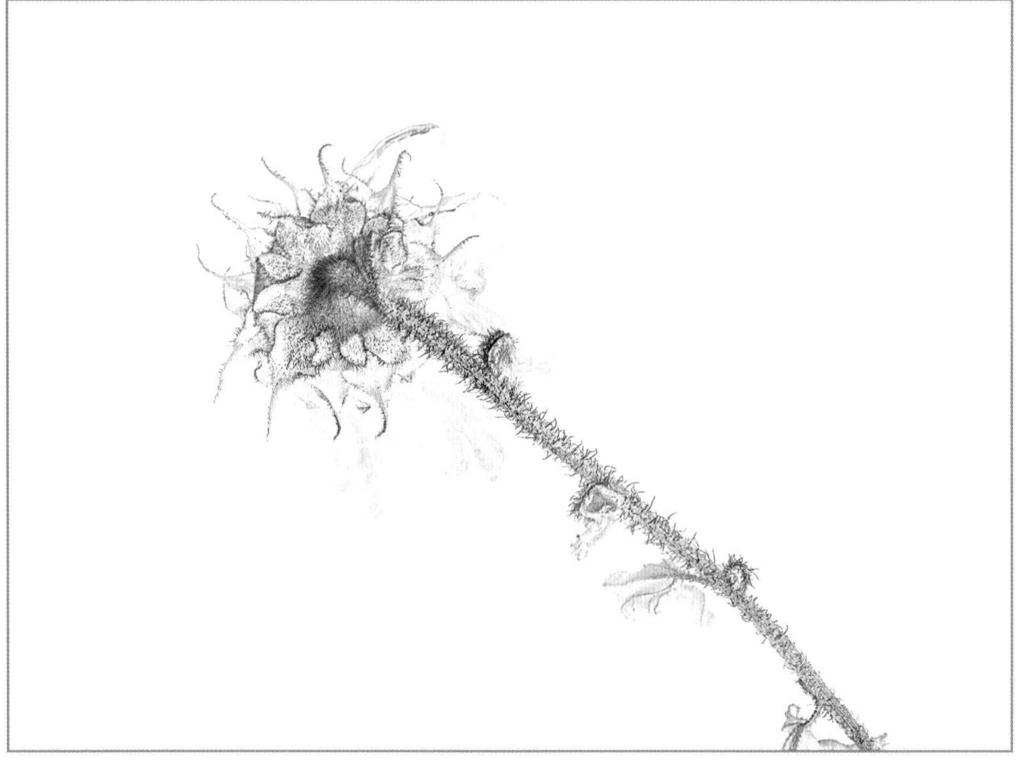

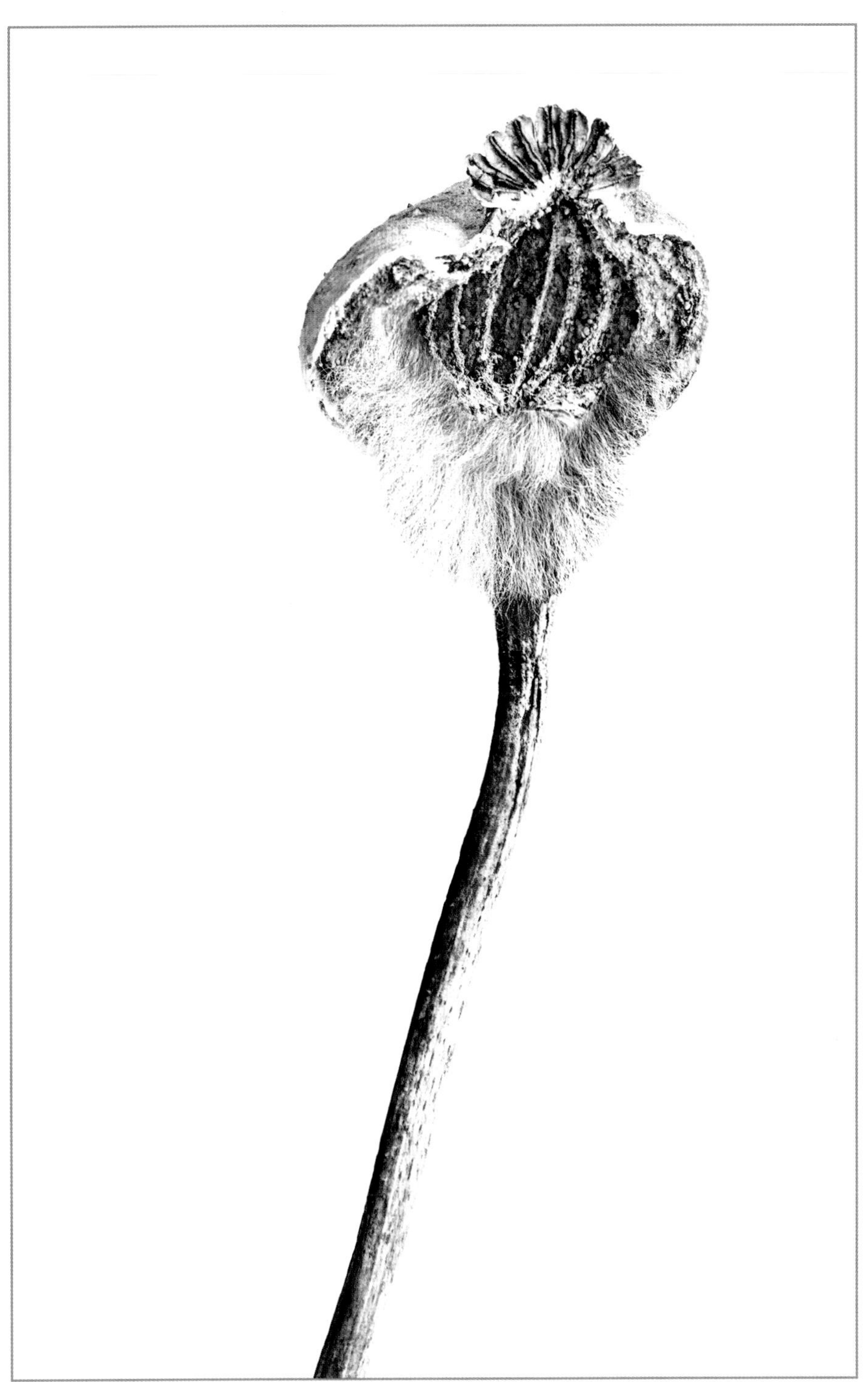

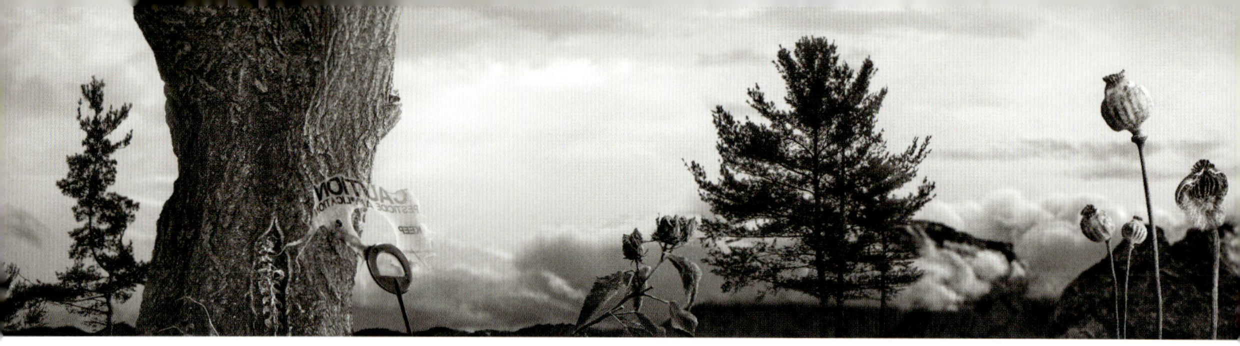

Nothing Goes to Waste

When you are working on a series of images like *Damage*, nothing can go to waste. I found this poor bird, dead, near a tree in my backyard. Of course, it had to become part of the series. At this point, I was starting work on a much more complex piece of work called *Tree Sparrow* that was meant to be a commentary on genetic modification and climate change. I photographed the bird, took it off the background, and melded it with the tree in Photoshop, being careful to blend feather and bark in such a way that it appears that the bird has been devoured by the tree, or flown into it with such force that it nearly flew through.

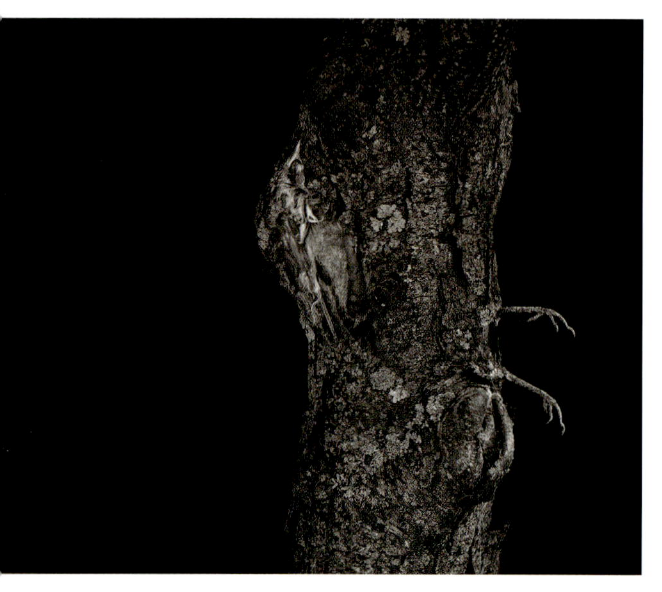

A More Complex Piece

This image is an environmentally themed mural. It was a massive project, not only because of the number of pieces used, but also because the size would make any errors terribly obvious. It was made in about four pieces because I guessed that my computer would have a very hard time with a 300 ppi, 2x15-foot image file. When I got each piece to the point where it was what I needed it to be, I saved all four parts before merging as many layers as possible and then bringing these separate images together into one final image *(above)*.

A Gift

Occasionally you are given a gift when working on a series. The image *Lady in a Tree* is actually not post-processed at all, other than a bit of burning, dodging, and sharpening. This apparition appeared fully formed in a tree and fit neatly in the mural.

Where Things Become the Most Interesting

One of the more important things about working in series is getting to the point

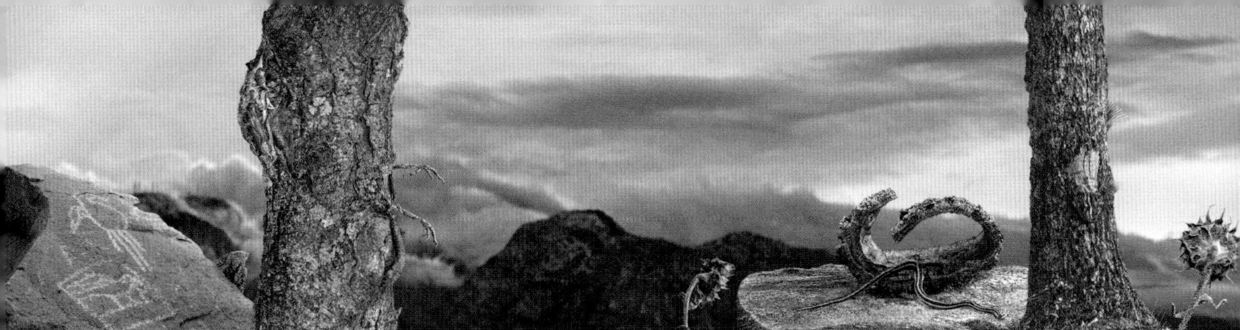

where things become increasingly difficult. You've seemingly exhausted all of your ideas, but you shouldn't give up at that point. That's exactly the point where things become the most interesting and rewarding. Bring in new elements. Work from a different angle or with different lighting, or use what you find on a morning walk.

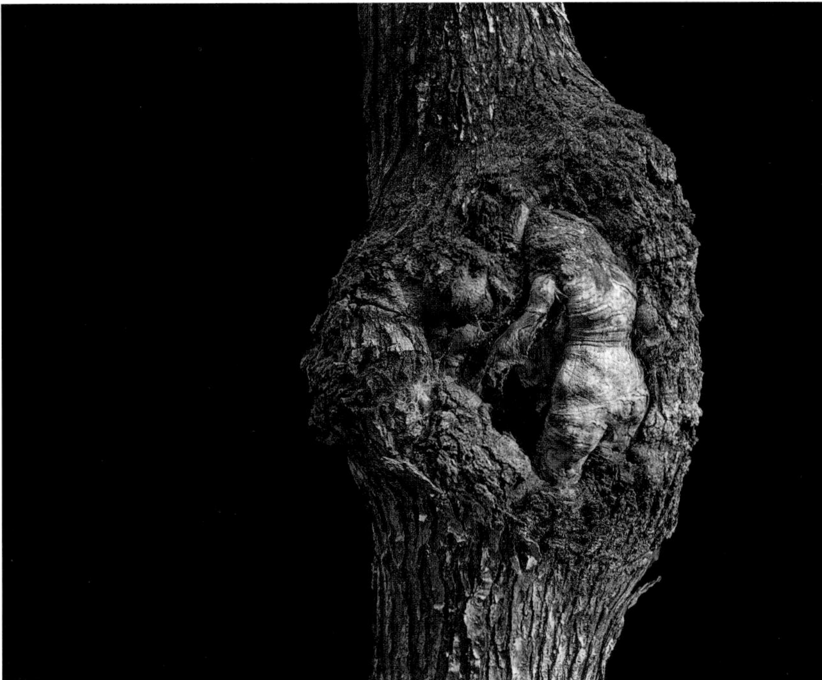

I enjoyed the texture of this oak tree trunk very much, but to incorporate it into my damage series required reaching for something outside of my previous experiences. I found the dead snake and buried it in my garden. Seized by the idea of incorporating it into the tree, I dug it up and found that there was nothing left but the skeleton. I photographed the long string of bones and used it with the tree. It became part of a much larger piece, specifically the 2x15-foot mural.

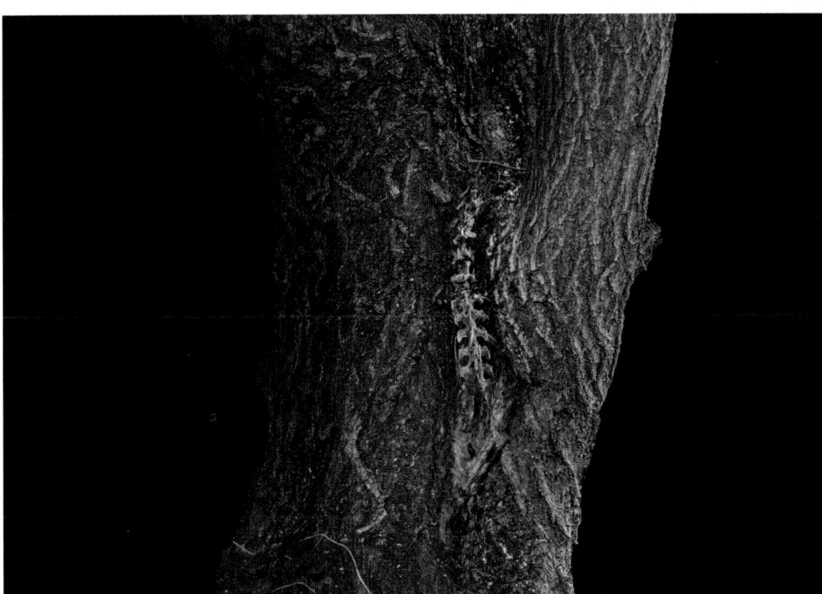

Detritus Series

Ordinary Objects

The mural was the logical stopping point for the *Damage Series*, much to the relief of friends and family who were tired my photographing road kill and dead things. After the monumental mural, I felt the need to photograph something smaller and quieter.

I wanted to examine the subject of beauty. What is it really? As strange as the *Damage* series was, many of the pieces were still considered by many to be beautiful. The dead flowers, the gestural grace of a dried leaf, the unexpected similarity to stained glass in a fried rose. Is there beauty in everything, even the most mundane and ordinary things? Is there beauty in the detritus all around us? Thus began the *Detritus* series.

By photographing ordinary objects and then manipulating the photographs into something new and unrecognizable, I began to explore what makes something beautiful. This image began as a photograph of the cap for a pipe fitting, complete with rust and peeling paint.

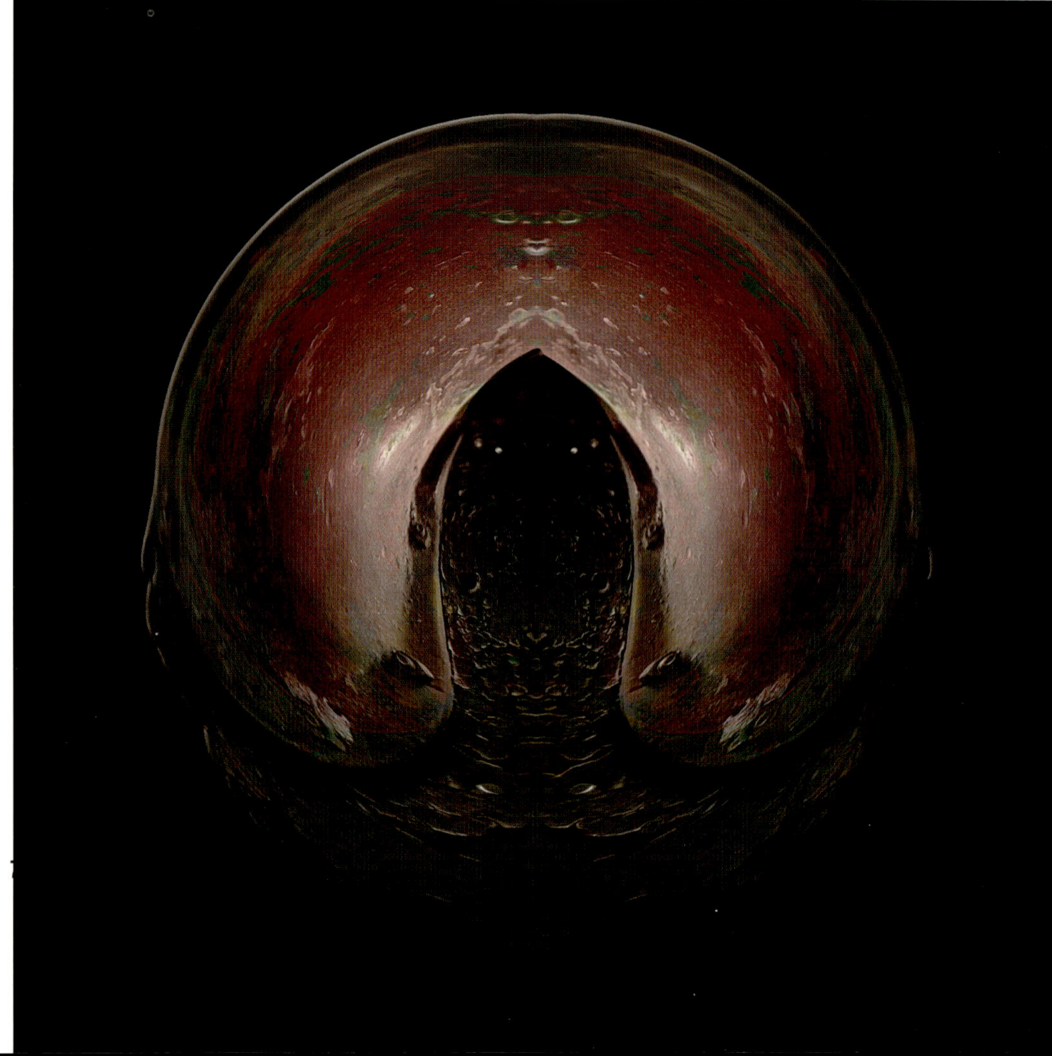

Pure Texture

This image began as pure texture. I saw the texture carved into wood and decided to see what would happen if I mirrored the image and then worked with taking pieces apart. Since we are bilateral creatures, like birds, other mammals, fish, and so on, when an image is cut and mirrored, something similar to a face often appears. Just adding a little extra color or accentuated something that's intrinsic to the photograph makes the face appear. In this one, I see a bird in the center.

The interesting thing about this series though, is that nearly everyone sees something different.

I began to explore what makes something beautiful.

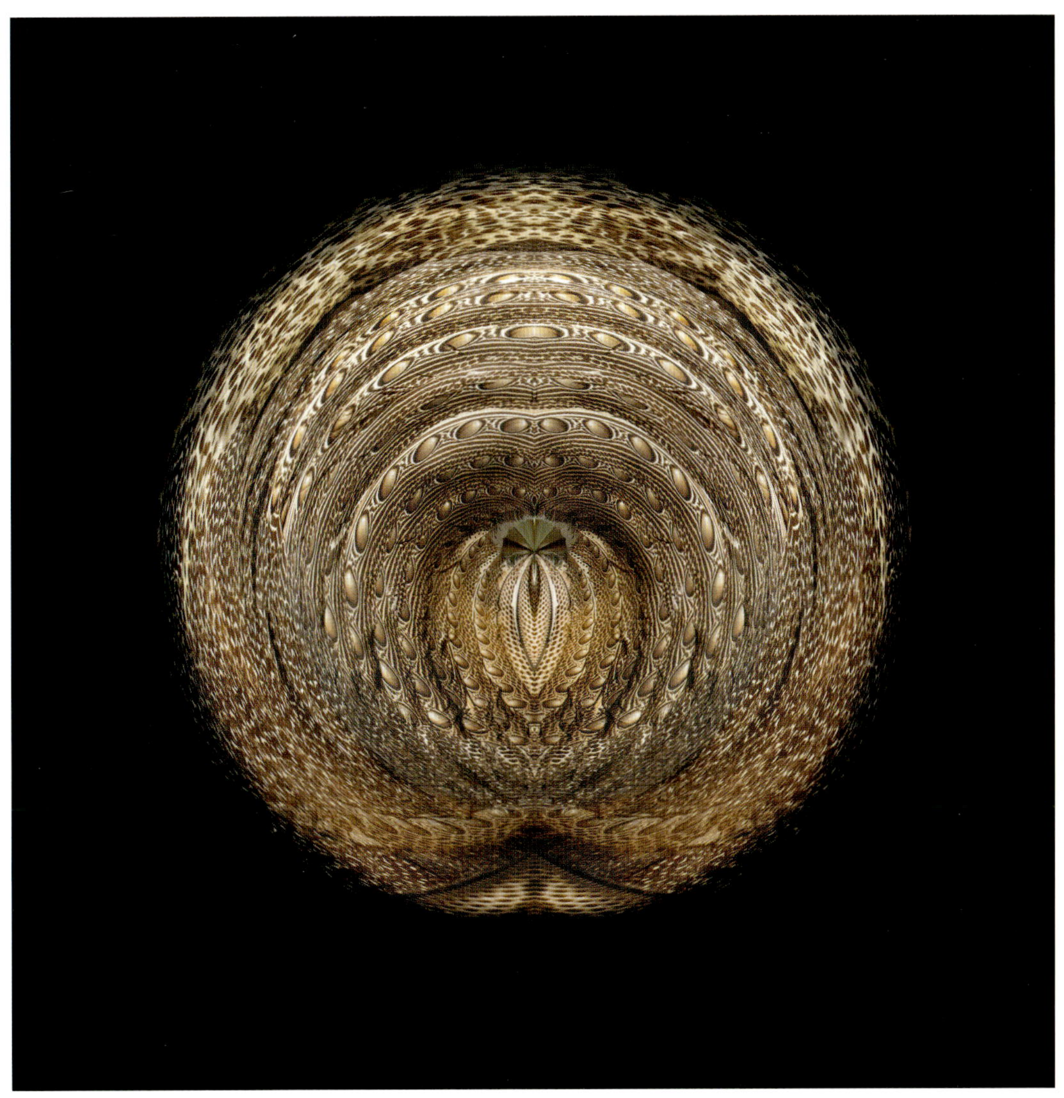

Enjoy Texture and Form

This was created from the pattern of a receding tide left in the sand on a Maine beach. The texture of the sand was beautiful in itself, and the lines left by the water added a depth and configuration that reminded me of an Egyptian relief carving. I enjoy the fact that there is a hint of facial structure in this, but it is not the least bit overt. Sometimes it's just great to enjoy texture and form.

The texture of the sand was beautiful in itself . . .

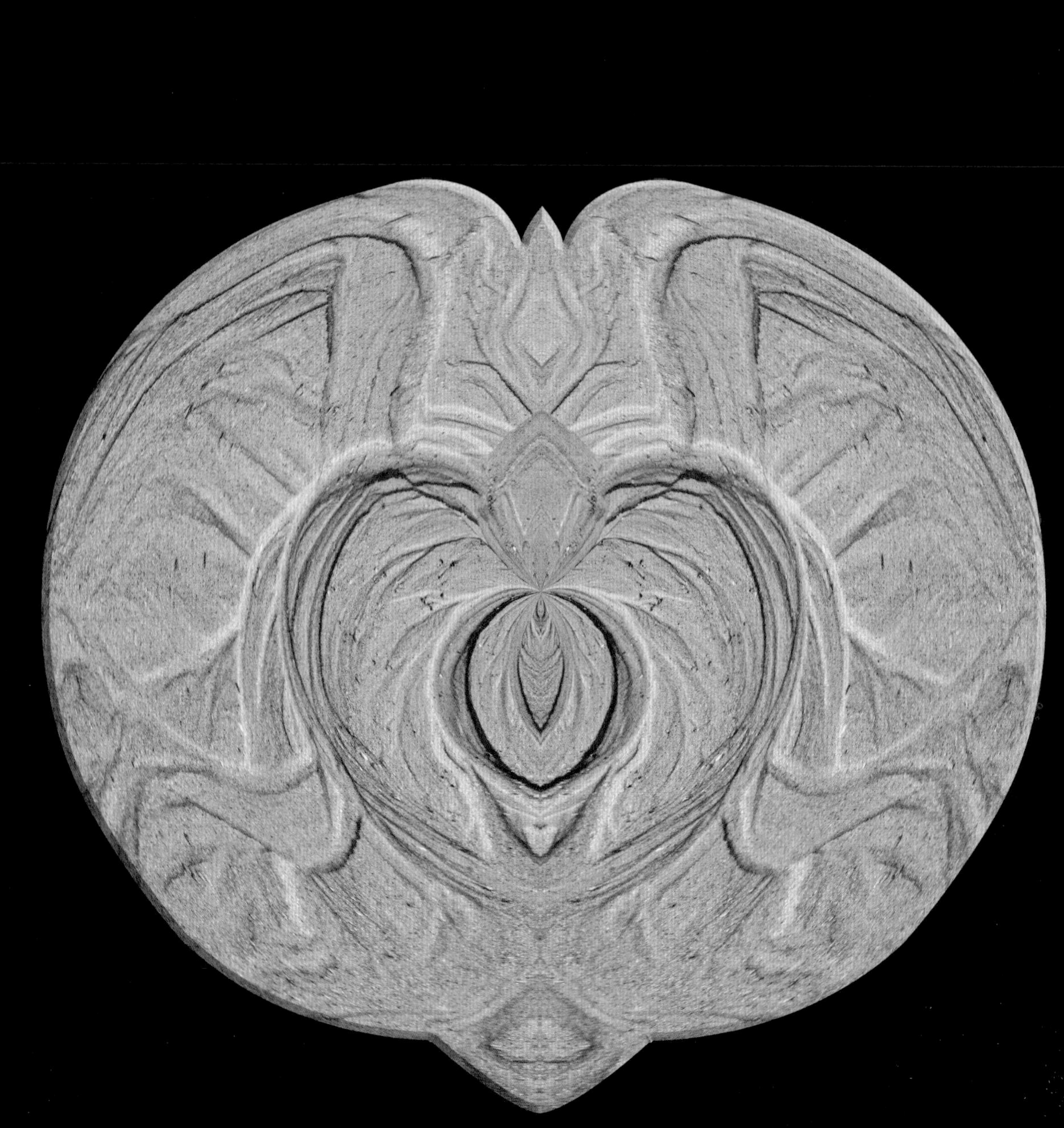

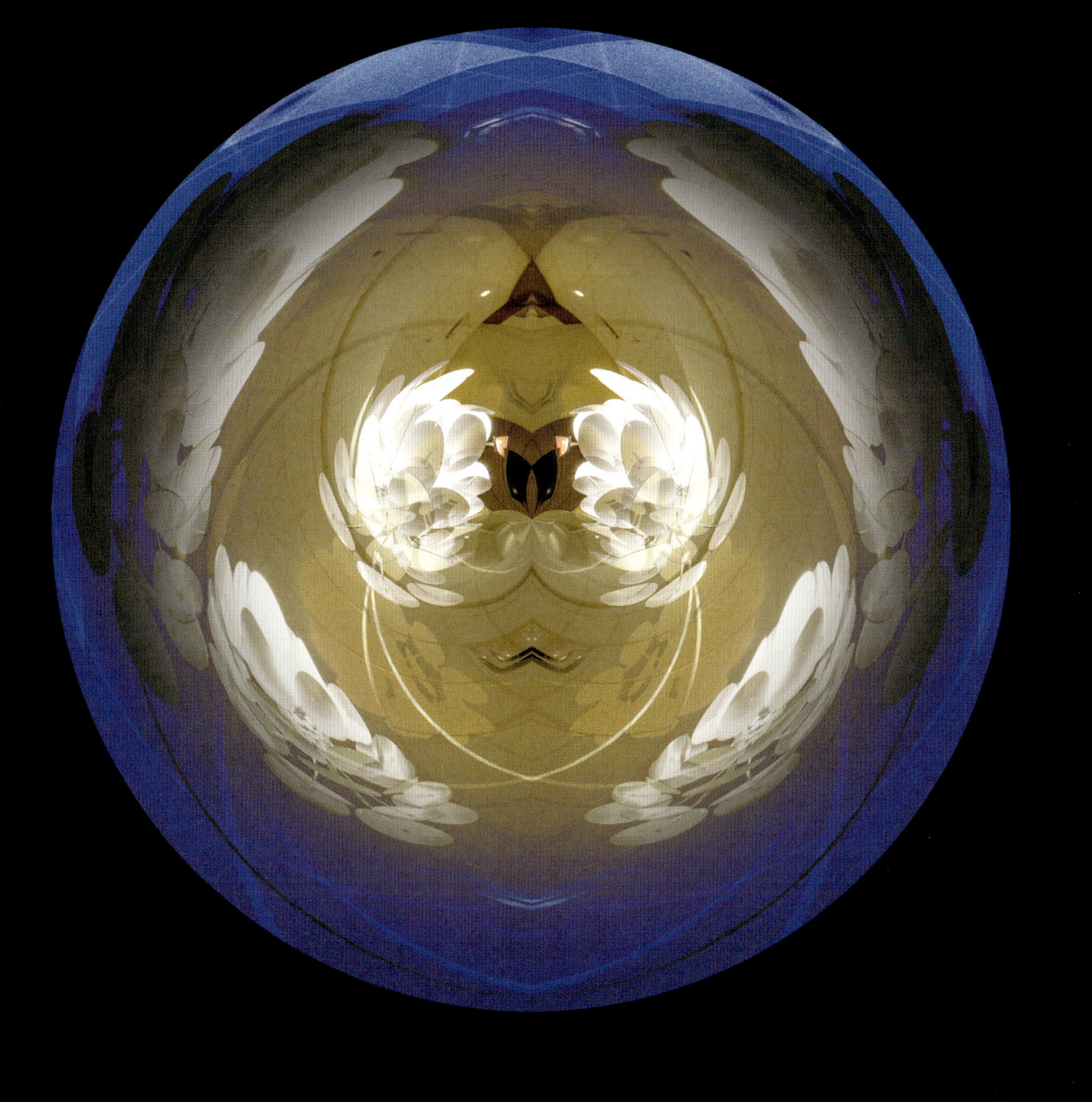

Layer Blending Accentuates the Glowing Characteristic ▲

Beginning as a photograph of a lighting fixture, this one takes the luminous subject matter and, through some layer blending, accentuates the contrast between the glowing characteristic and the edge turning a deep blue.

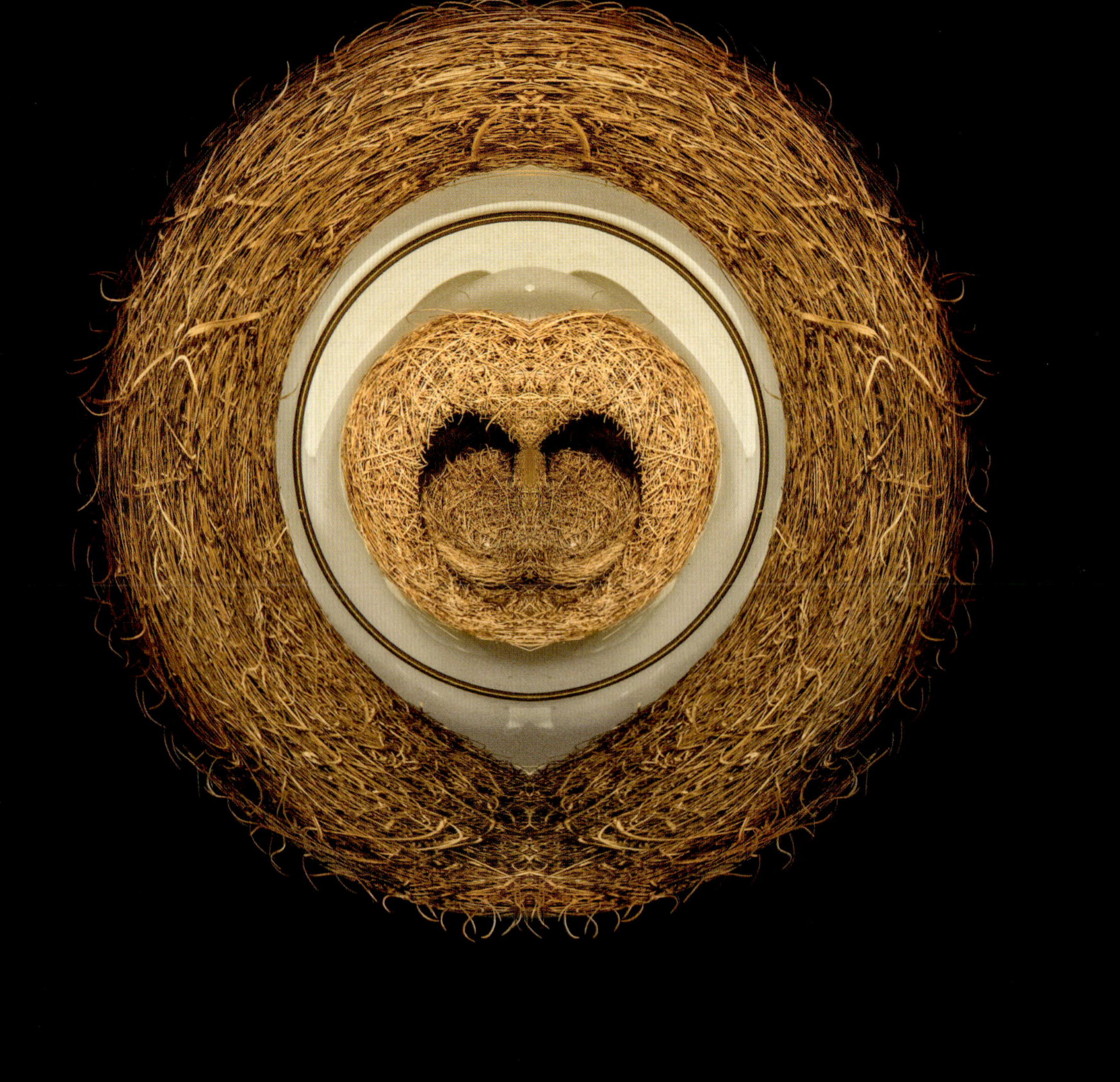

Extending Beyond the Edges

A photograph of a bird's nest was the genesis for this image. The edges of the table upon which it was placed are evident in the white areas. Rather than have the edges of this com-

Adding a Bevel and Emboss layer style gave the new twigs dimension.

position clean and clearly cut, I decided that it needed to extend in a very natural way beyond the edges of the circle. Sampling the color of the nest at the edges, and then on a new, blank layer, painting small, tapered strokes, allowed me to extend the twigs that made up the nest. I selected the twigs by using Select > Color Range, then copied the selected twigs to a new layer. Adding a Bevel and Emboss style layer gave the new twigs dimension.

A Simple Glass

A simple glass in front of a window was the starting point for this image. I used several layers, distorting each a bit differently, inverting the color, trying different blend modes, and finally, used the Elliptical Marquee tool to define a circular shape.

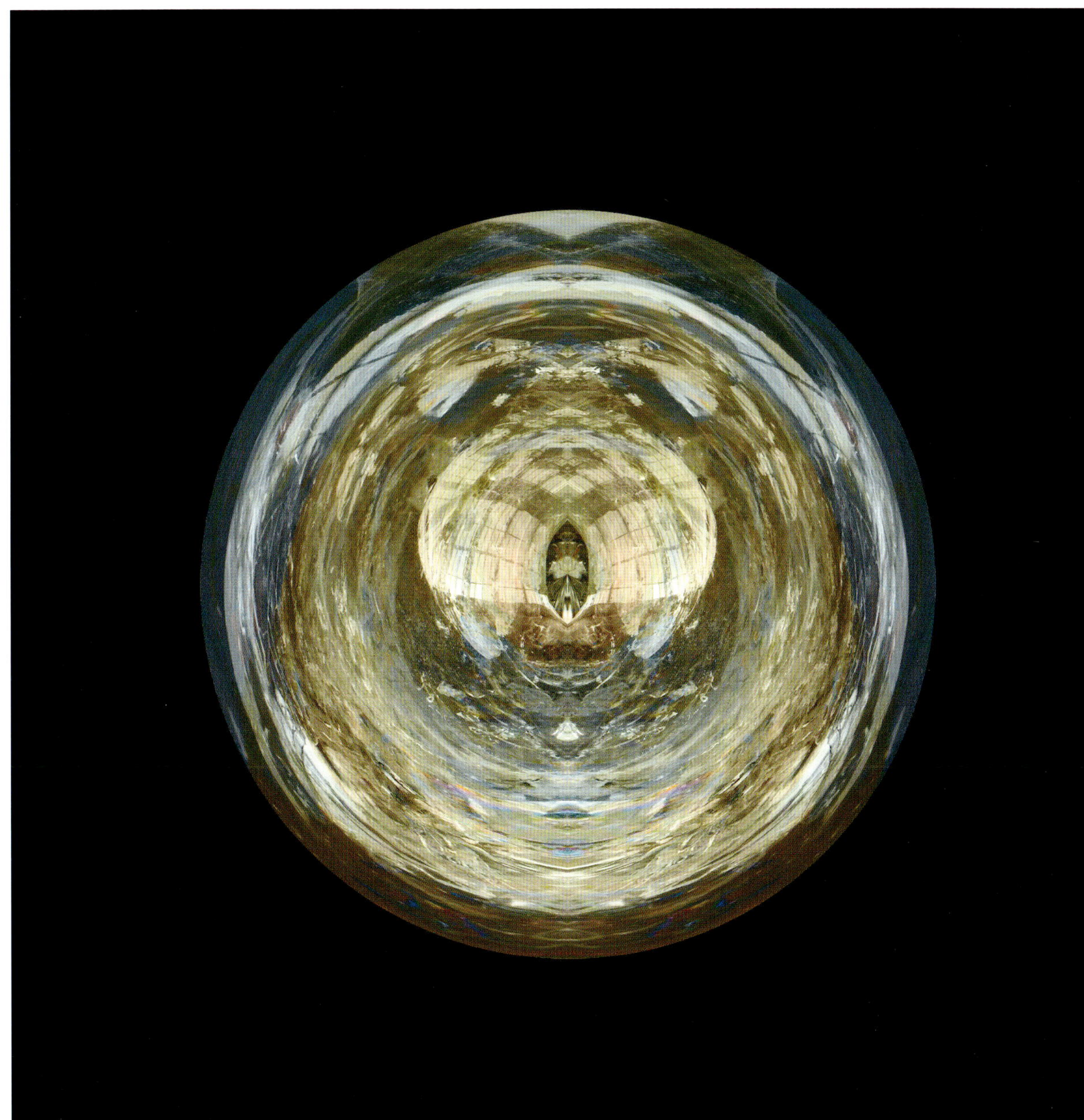

Step and Repeat

This is not a new technique but it's one that can make a very engaging composition. This uses the step and repeat option available through the Edit > Transform > Again in Photoshop's Edit pull-down menu.

Make a selection of what you would like to repeat. Copy and paste it to a new layer and duplicate that layer. Activate the Transform command. The Transform bounding box has a point in the center, which is the point around which any transformation will take place. You can move that point anywhere on your canvas (or off, if you wish) and when you rotate your subject, it will rotate around that point. For this effect, simply put the center point in the center of the canvas and drag your subject to the desired angle. To repeat with a keyboard shortcut (Transform Again command), hold down all three modifiers keys (Mac: Command, Option and Shift. PC: Control, Alt, Shift) and the T key. Repeat until you have the desired number of copies. If you want them evenly

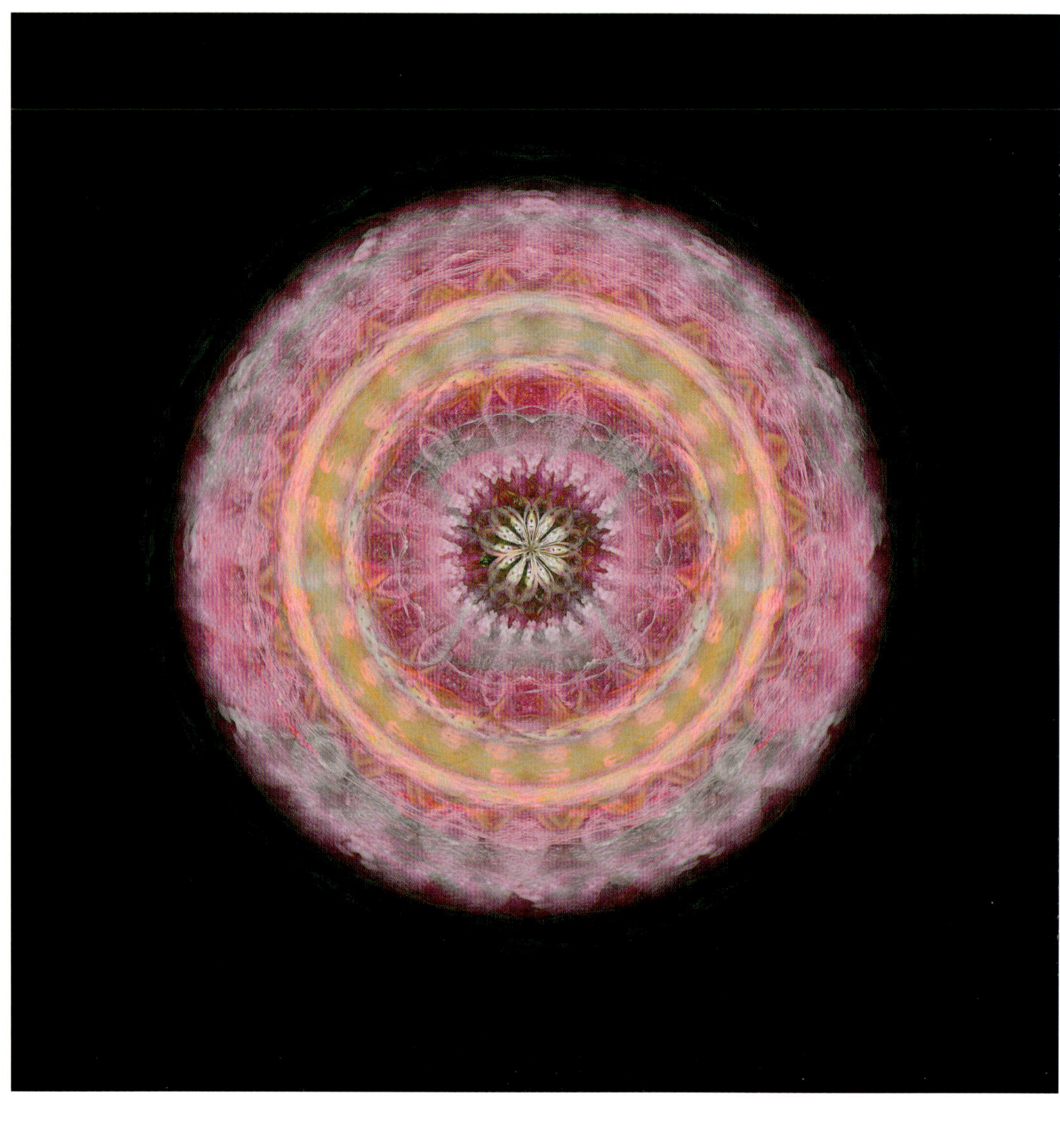

spaced in a circle, use the numerical measurement in the options bar by putting in a number that divides evenly into 360 (for the 360 degrees of the circle). You can now go down to the layer below your copies and put a background color below them.

Translucency and Extra Layers

I found that I was especially attracted to transparent or translucent subjects. This began as a photograph of a trolley car headlight. The translucency lends itself to extra layers that get more interesting and puzzling, as they are copies over each other and then blended together with Layer Blend modes. This was a transitional piece because the *Detritus* series soon evolved with the faces becoming more and more apparent. Before I knew it, these ordinary items were turning into aliens—the extraterrestrial kind.

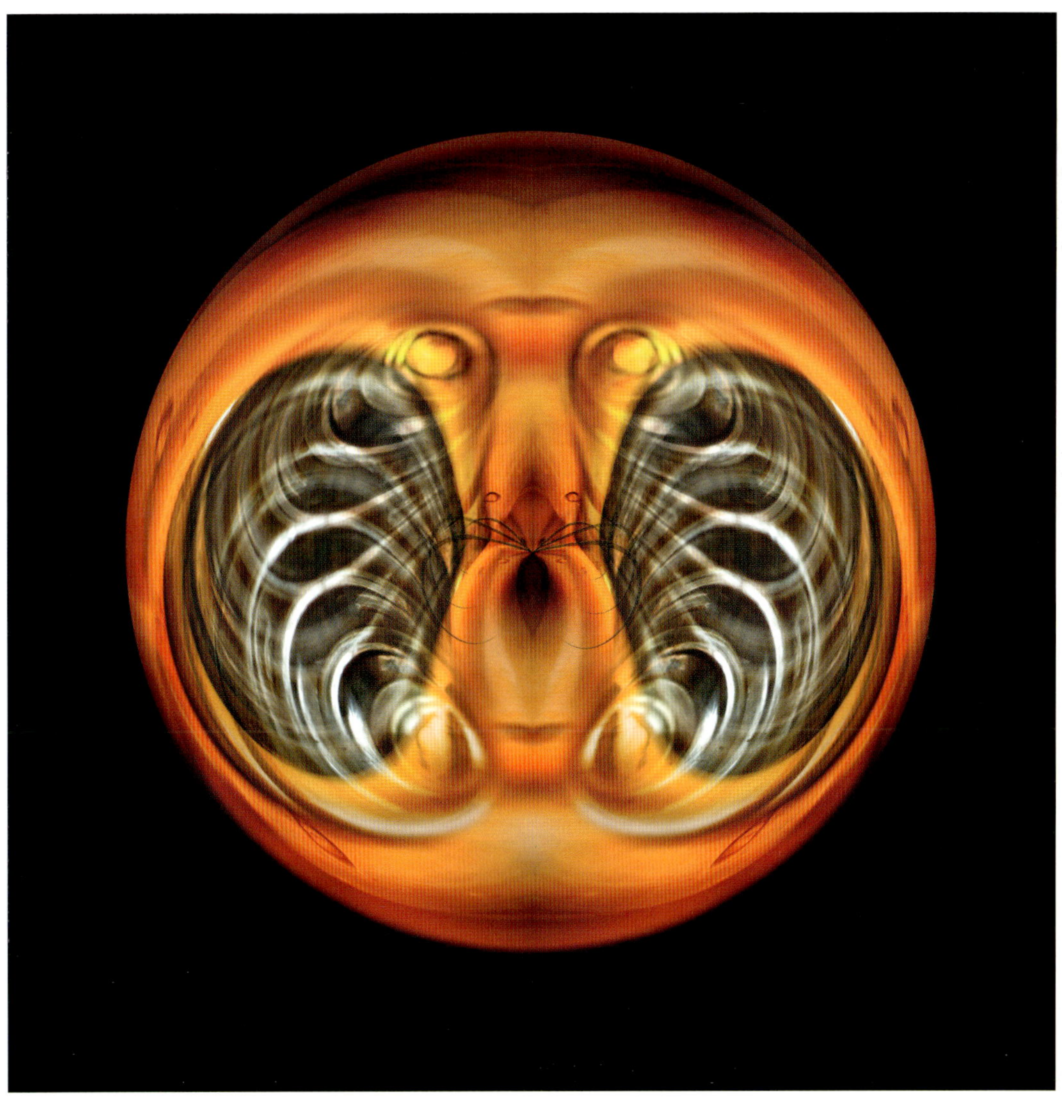

Alien Series

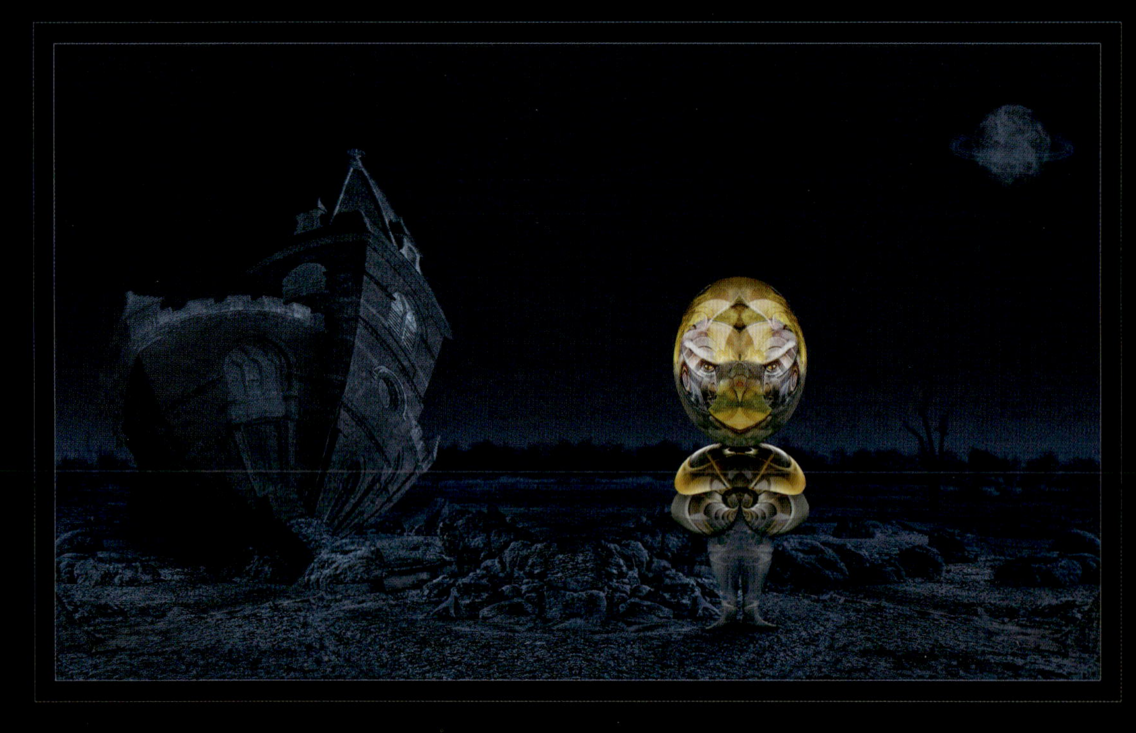

The Challenge

Take Me to Your Leader was the first of my alien series and it began as a result of a challenge by a friend. This friend texted me two photos, one of a bathroom sink and the other of a fish. "Make something out of these!" she challenged.

I brought both images into Photoshop and spent several hours layering, distorting, and then pulling them apart. I spent more time the next day with the nearly complete alien, polishing and then sent it back to her. It's one of my favorite aliens and it was the first.

What began as the response to a challenge became a sort of photographic meditation. I was working on a graphic novel which was quite dark and somber, so I needed something more relaxing and uplifting to work on as a break.

My friend enjoyed the result of the challenge and offered up some background options that could work with my alien. I added a wildly distorted building using polar coordinates to get this effect, and this is the result. For competition, I reverted to the simple image of the alien alone with his head tipped to the side in a quizzical pose.

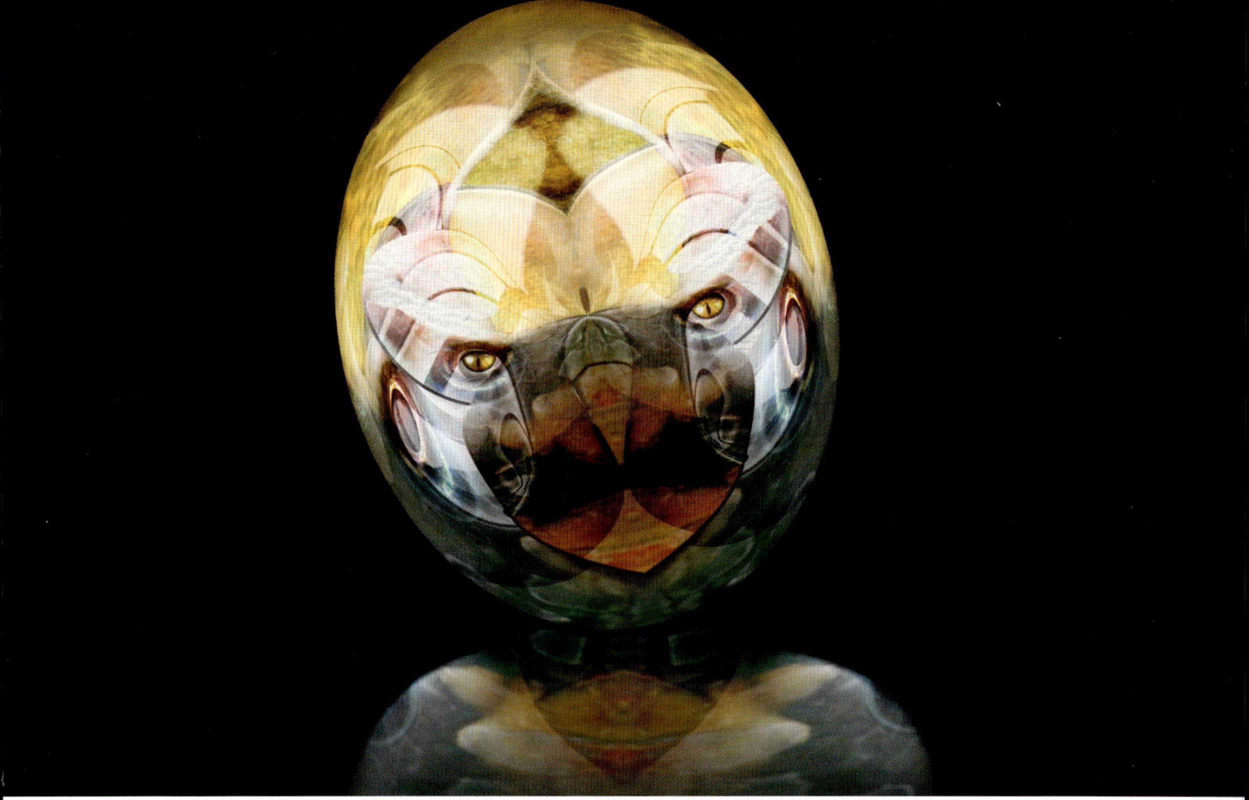

Fine-Tune with Fresh Eyes

I worked on the *Take Me to Your Leader* series for a couple of weeks, each time coming back to it to fine-tune details with fresh eyes. Taking time to step away from your work is vital to *seeing* it with increased clarity.

Once I considered this image objectively—with fresh eyes—I found that by selecting certain portions of the face and copying them to a new layer with layer styles such as Bevel and Emboss or Drop Shadow I had more control over which shapes, forms, and details could be accentuated.

It's important to remember the Create Layers command, under the Layer > Layer Styles menu or right click (PC) or control click (Mac) on the Layer Style in the Layer panel. This allows you to transform or selectively erase effects where desired.

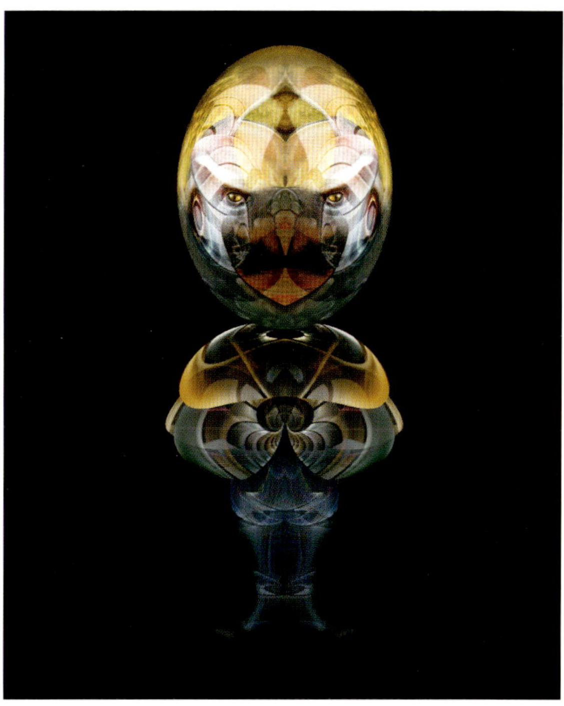

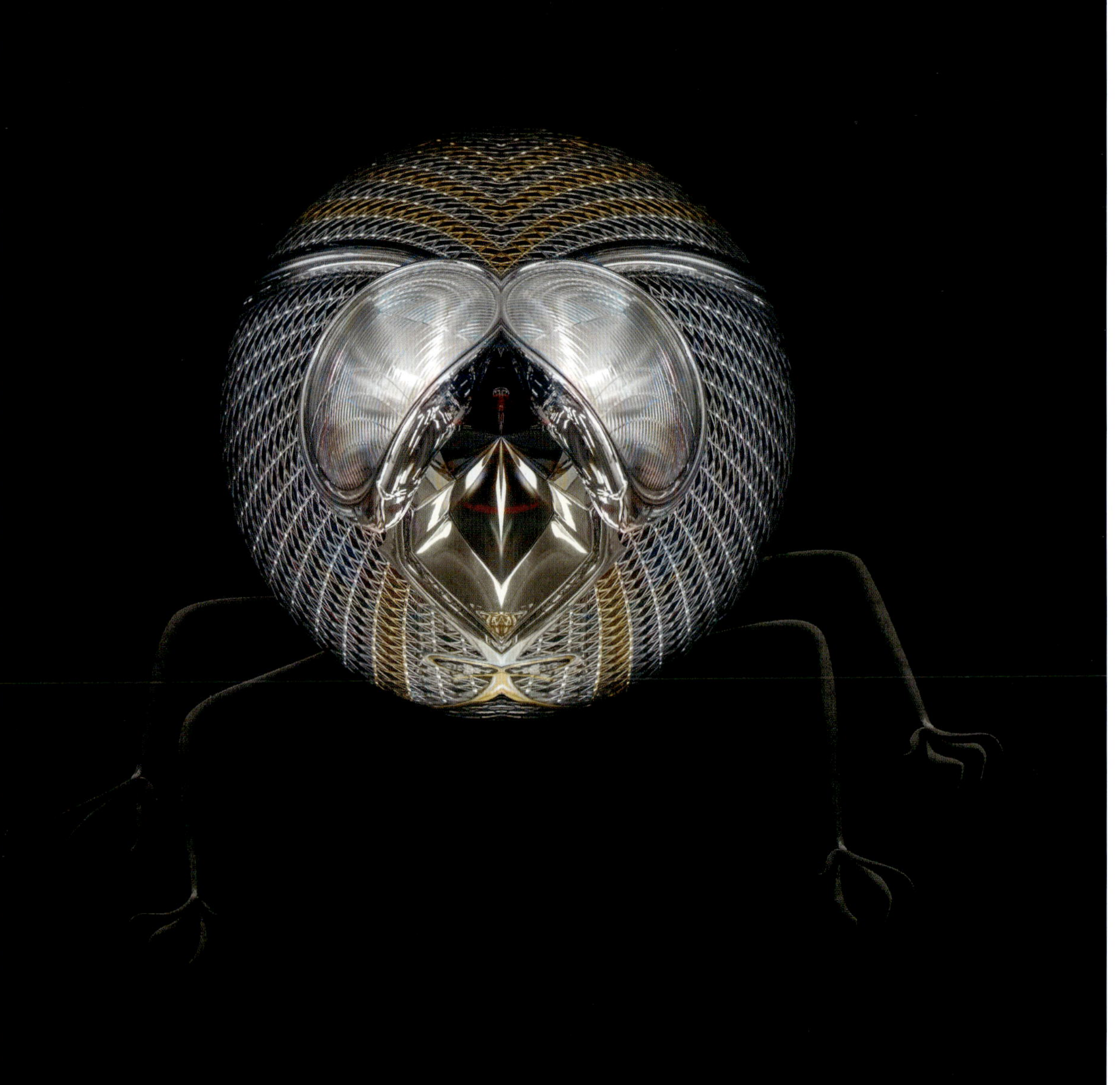

Alien Bug ▲

The image *Alien Bug* began as a photograph of a car grill. I cropped the image, distorted it, and the very bug-like eyes appeared. Using a circular marquee selection, then inverting that selection, eliminated all but the round center. The grill pattern seemed flat, without the dimension you would see in an insect or a face, so burning down the edges all the way around created form and dimension.

The legs were drawn out using the Pen tool, then filling with a gray found within the circular pattern to fill the shapes made with the Pen tool. A Bevel and Emboss layer style with a texture added.

The Pen Tool to Make Specific Shapes

Built from a photograph of a metal wine cask taken during a winery tour, this cried out to be something very mechanical. Again, this image was cropped, then mirrored and distorted. Like the preceding image, a round selection made to isolate the center of the image was placed on its own layer, then the edges were darkened slightly. This time I copied sections of the circle, using the Pen tool to make very specific shapes that would appear as legs. I then made another, more triangular selection for the creature's feet.

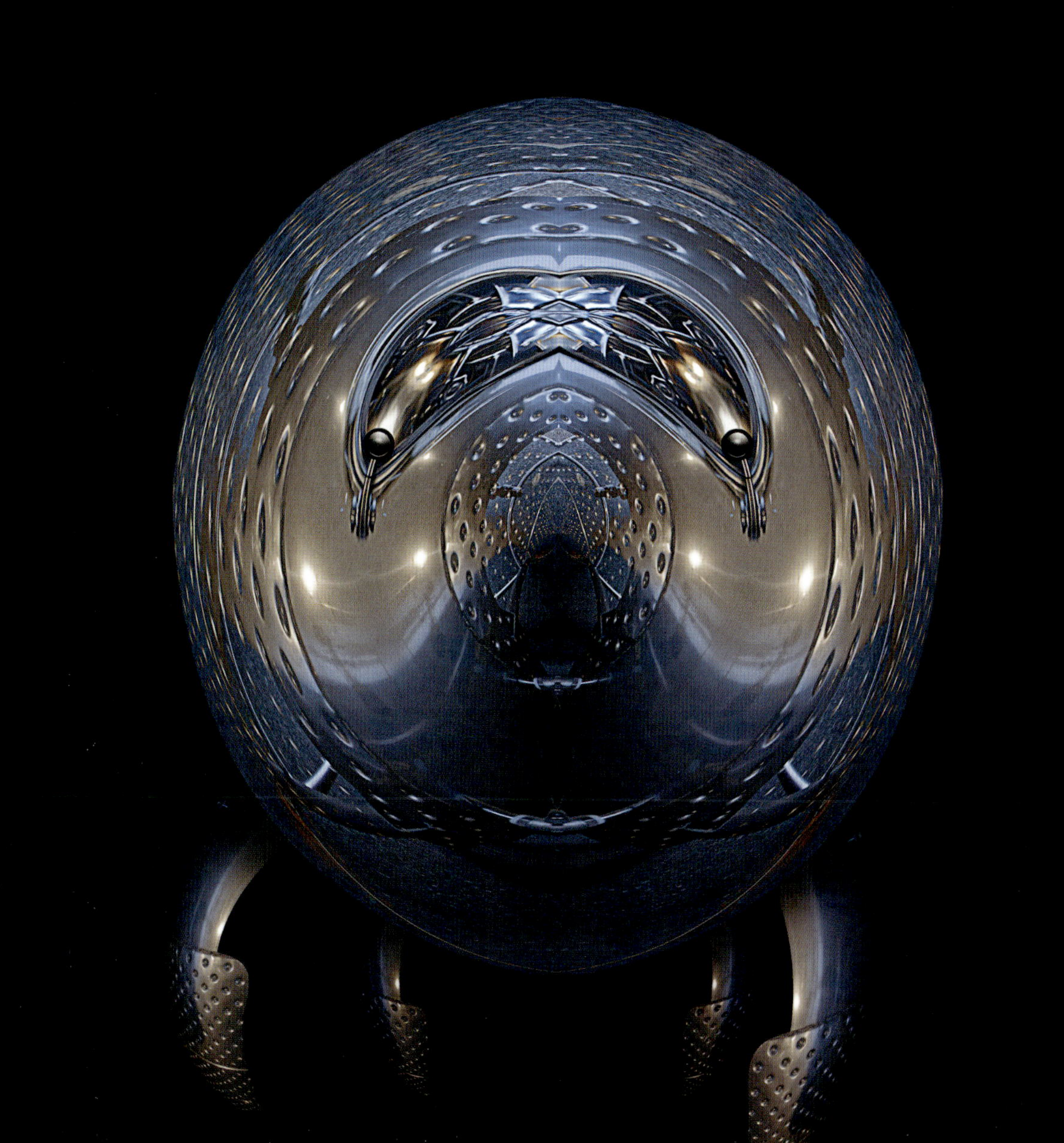

Mirror and Distortion to Make Eyes

The original photograph from which this creature was constructed was of a glass of ice tea. It wasn't at all apparent that anything would result from this image until I experimented a bit with mirroring and distortion. It needed eyes to come to life however.

I often make eyes to go with the creatures. To do this, I copy a section of the original image that has the color I wish to have in the eyes, but also has some pattern in it. I make a circular selection of it and bring it to its own layer. Make sure the circle is still selected. (Use command or control click on the layer's thumbnail to load a selection of anything on its own layer.) Use the Filter > Blur > Radial Blur with the Zoom option selected. Experiment a bit with the setting in order to get the right effect since this is resolution and size dependent and will vary with every instance. This should give you a pattern which spreads out from a center point. Next, make a new layer and select just the center of it for the pupil of the eye. Feather the edge just 1–2 pixels and fill with black. It's going to look strange until you add a specular highlight. Make a new blank layer and use a hard-edged white brush. Add just a dab of white paint at the junction of the pupil and iris in the direction from which you want to have your light source. On another blank layer, repeat with a slightly larger brush just a bit further from the center of the eye. Blur and adjust opacities down to taste. Edge with black.

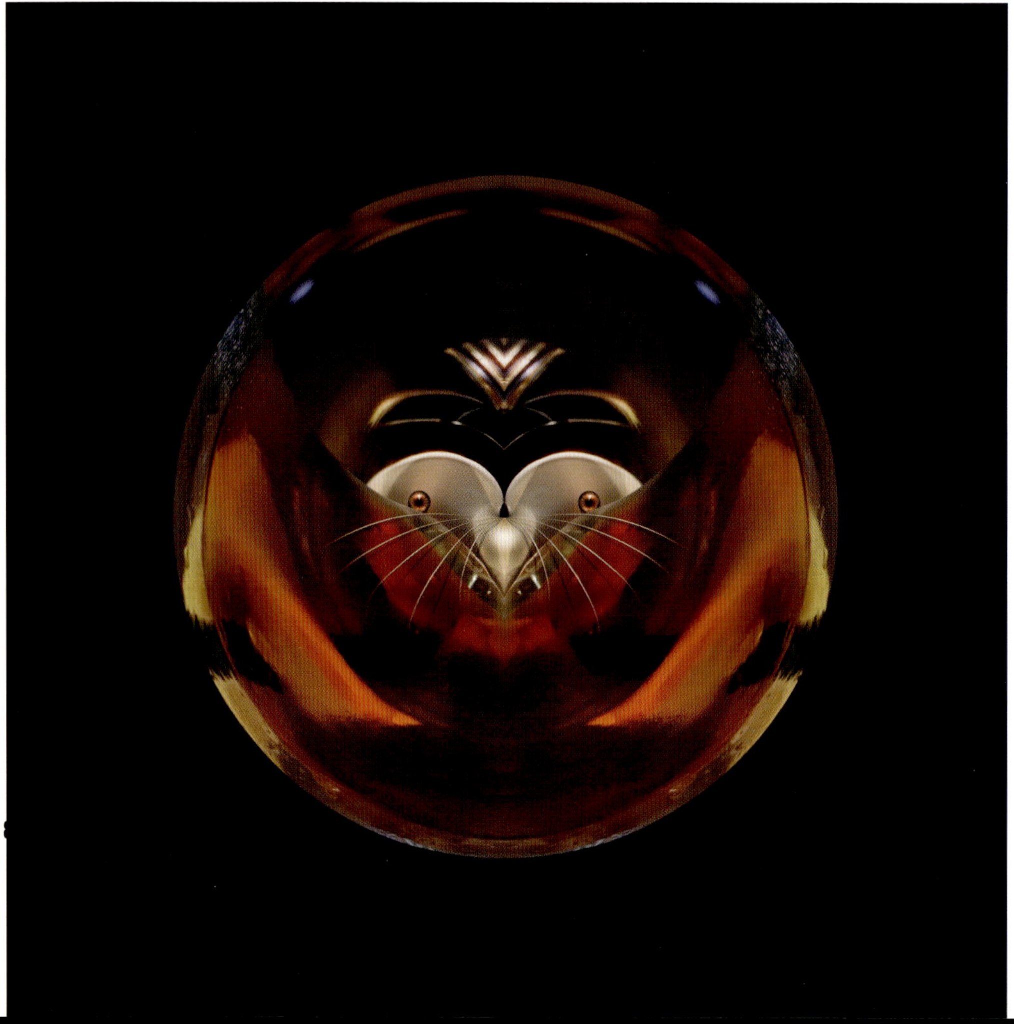

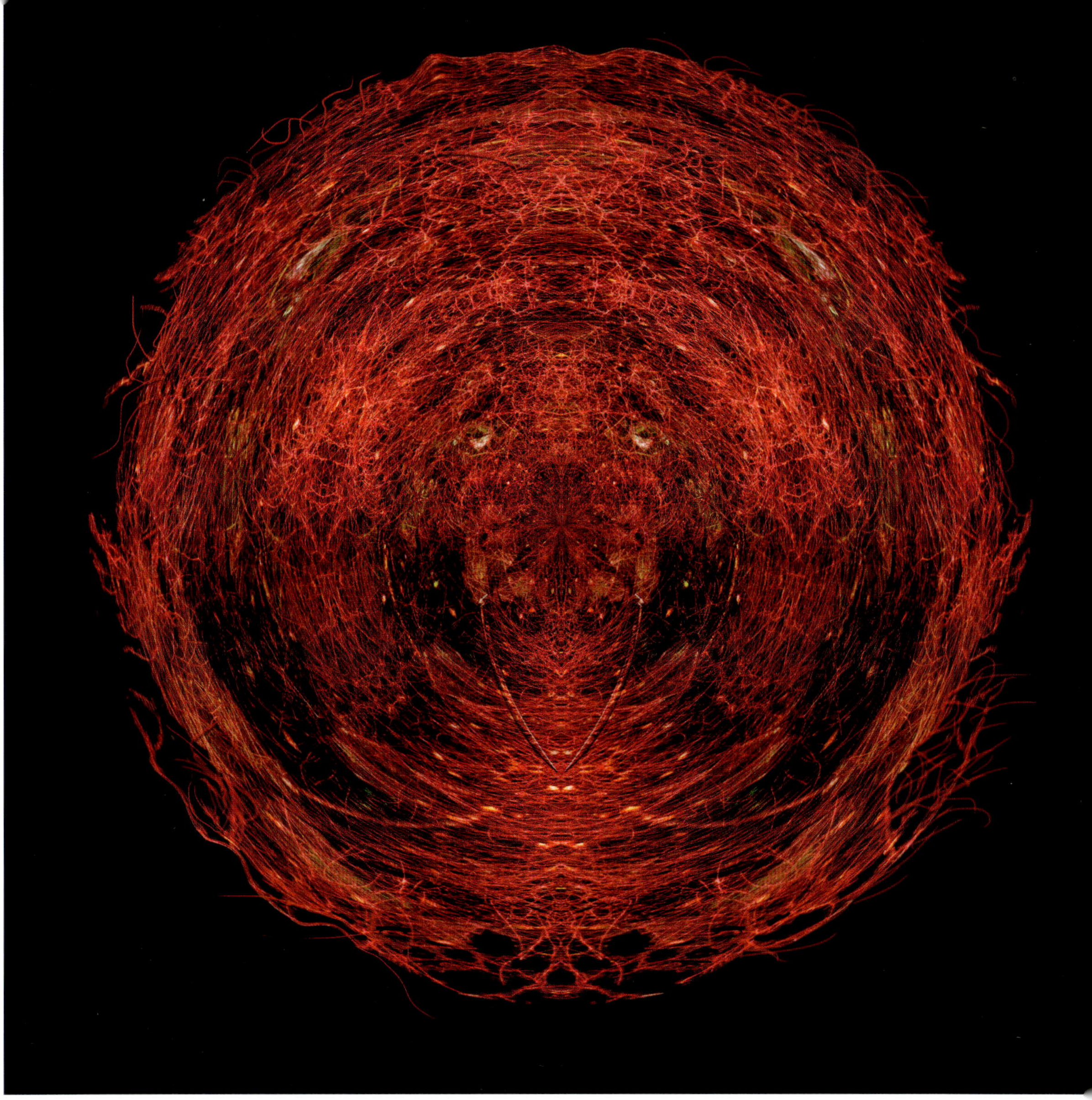

Giving an Appearance 

This tangle of red foliage reminded me of a lumbering, stuffed toy. Once I mirrored and distorted him and trimmed the result down to a circle, the edges needed to be wild and twiggy. So on a new, blank layer, I painted tapered strokes, which extended out past the edges. I made small eyes for it, but it still needed more. I copied some thin, crescent shapes from the existing layer and added a Bevel and Emboss layer style to these tapered pieces to give him tusk-like structures. I also decided that his eyes should be obscured by the wild mane of red twigs, so I made a selection (using Select > Color Range, in this case) which allowed me to put the red twigs in front of the eyes I'd made. It gives the creature a doleful, sappy but shyly-friendly, appearance.

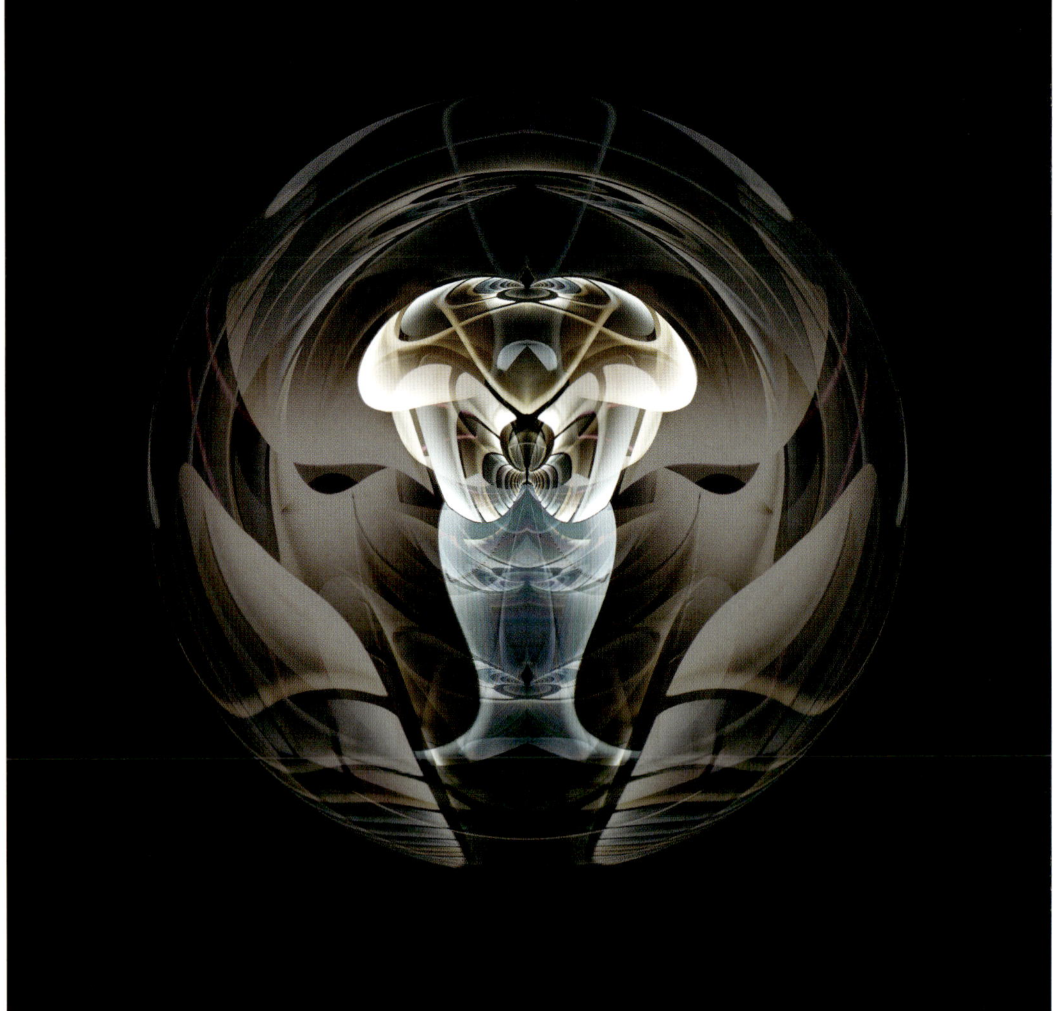

Create a Sense of Dimension ▲

This image appeals to me because of the way the light creates a sense of dimension. The original image is a shot of windows at the border of a hall's wall and ceiling at a convention center. Again, using mirroring and distortion, I had some interesting lines. However, I decided not to make a circular construction this time. I used the Pen tool to cut out shapes vaguely reminiscent of shoulders, then a body, then legs. Only one side needed to be defined for each piece, since that layer, once cut out and brought to a new layer, can be copied and transformed using the Edit pull-down menu, Edit > Transform > Flip Horizontal. To make the transformation happen from a center point of the composition rather than the center point of the item being transformed, drag the center point of the transformation bounding box to the mid-line of your composition.

The circular background came from the same image, but the opacity was lowered.

The Channels Panel

A jellyfish at an aquarium was the original image for this piece. Before beginning my piece, I needed to select the fish out of its background and into a new file. Selecting a jellyfish by mechanical methods, such as the Magnetic Lasso or Quick Selection tool, would be incredibly tedious and not discerning enough. Instead, I used the following selection technique.

Activate the Channels panel. Look at each channel (Red, Green, and Blue) in turn and decide which one has the most contrast between the object and the background. Make a copy of that channel by dragging it down to the Create-new-channel icon (left of the trash-can icon) at the bottom of the Channels panel. Now open the Levels panel by choosing Image > Adjustments > Level. In the Levels dialog box, use the arrows at either end of the Input histogram, dragging them toward each other to make the darks blacker and lights whiter. Once you have enough contrast, select OK, closing the dialog box.

Next, switch from the Channels panel to the Layers panel. Now, load this same channel as a selection by choosing Selection Edit > Load Selection, and then in the panel choices, select from the pull-down menu the channel that you had duplicated.

Finally, once you have your marching ants (flashing dotted line that indicates the perimeter of your selection), you are ready to copy and paste your image component into a new layer.

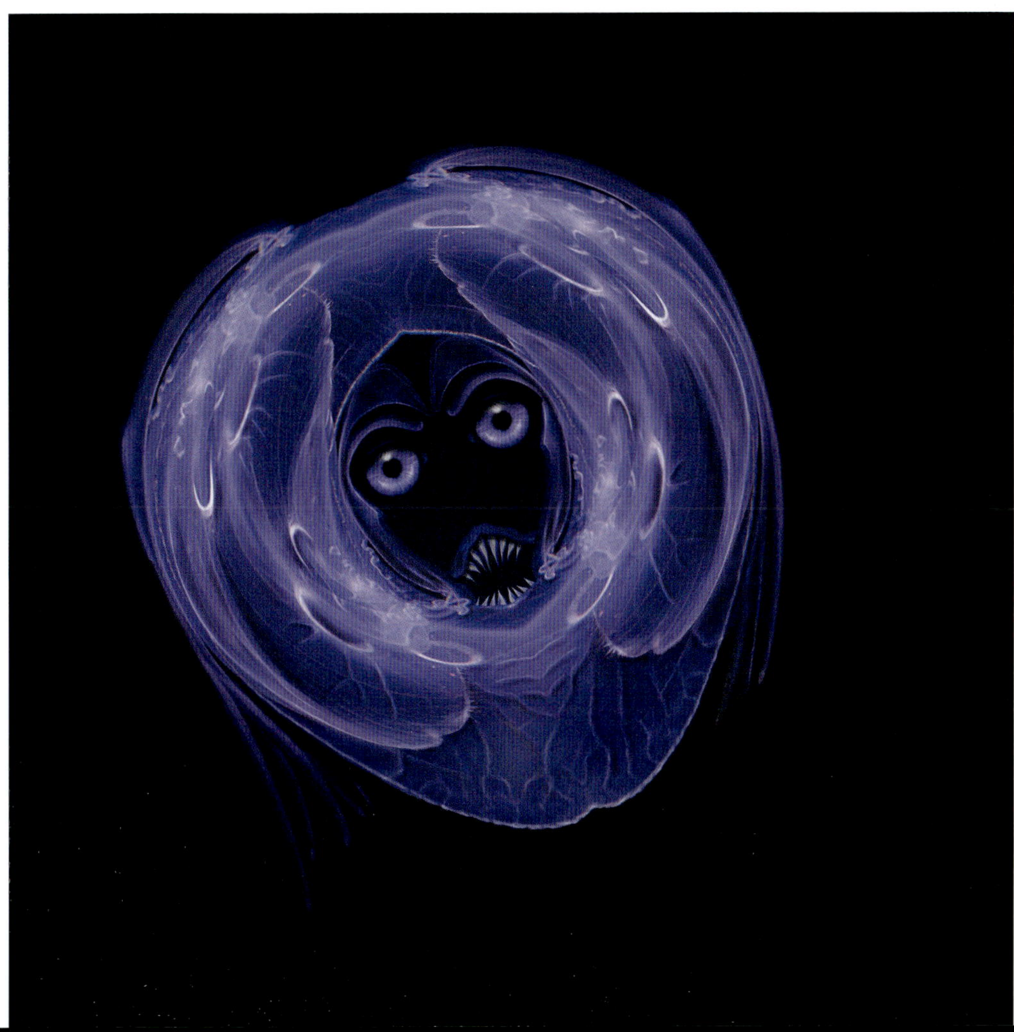

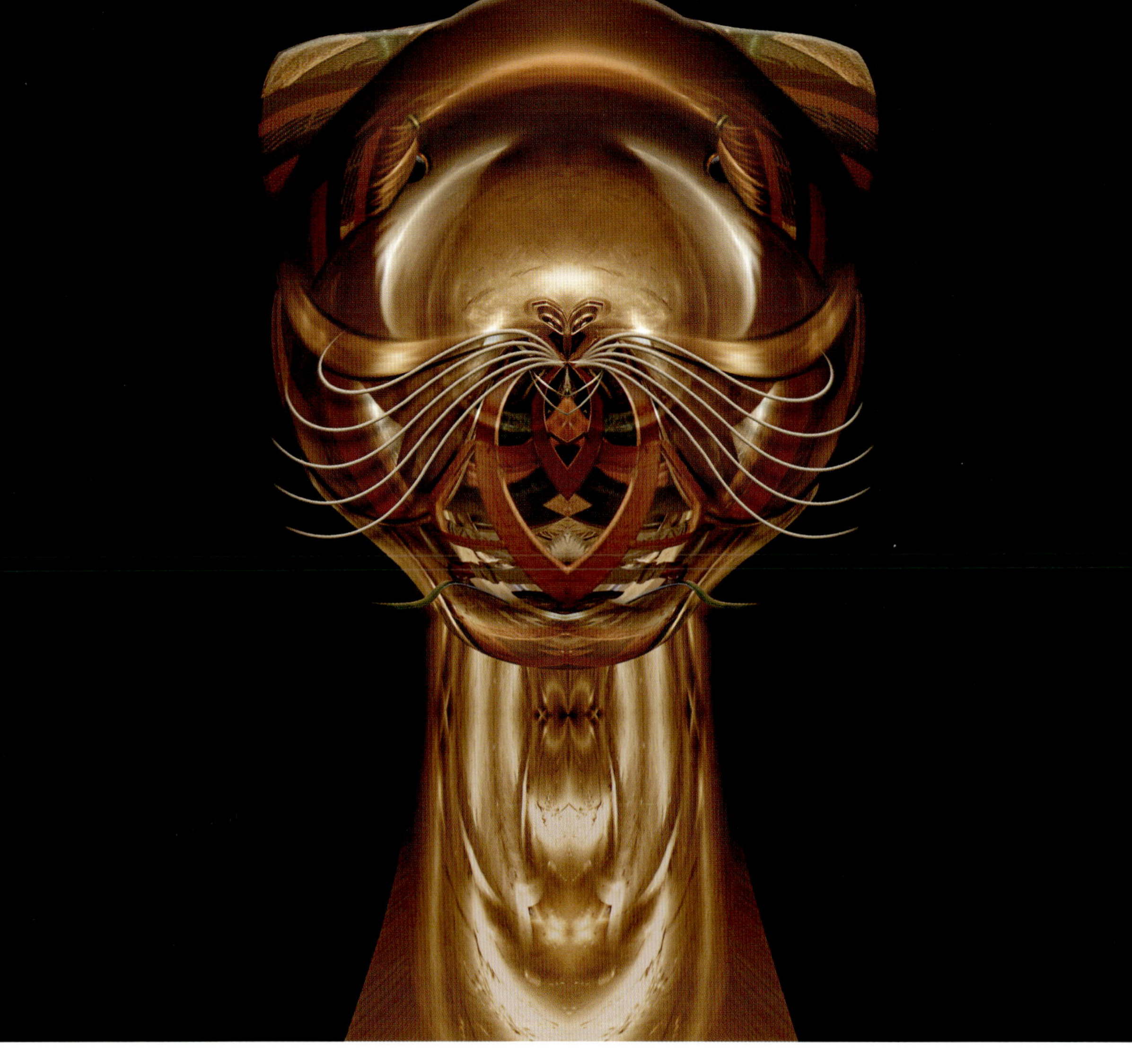

Creating the Cat-like Appearance ▲

Another original image from the winery, this time a warmer-colored, less-textured metal wine barrel. Once mirrored, distorted, and cut to a circular shape, the concentric shapes made me think of a cat. To make the ears, cut a triangular shape from the body, copy it to its own layer, and then use the Warp tool or the Liquify filter to give a bend to the new ear in its center. Once you have it shaped, copy and paste it to a new layer. Then, from the pull-down menu choose Edit > Transform > Flip Horizontal to create the second ear.

The bands are just strips of the cat's face copied to a new layer and then blurred. To keep the blur from blurring the edges, too, click on the first Lock option in the Layer panel to lock the transparent pixels. This will keep all the pixels that are transparent clear of any color or information.

The whiskers are strokes of the Pen tool, stroked with a hard-edged brush in gold. A Bevel and Emboss layer style was then added to the layer.

Mundane to Jewel

Continuing with the idea of creating interesting and appealing creatures from mundane items, this jewel-type object began as a bathroom sink. I used multiple layers with different blend modes to get this look. Then I cut the circle shape. I cut a smaller circle out of the center, and used the Liquify filter to curl the top ends.

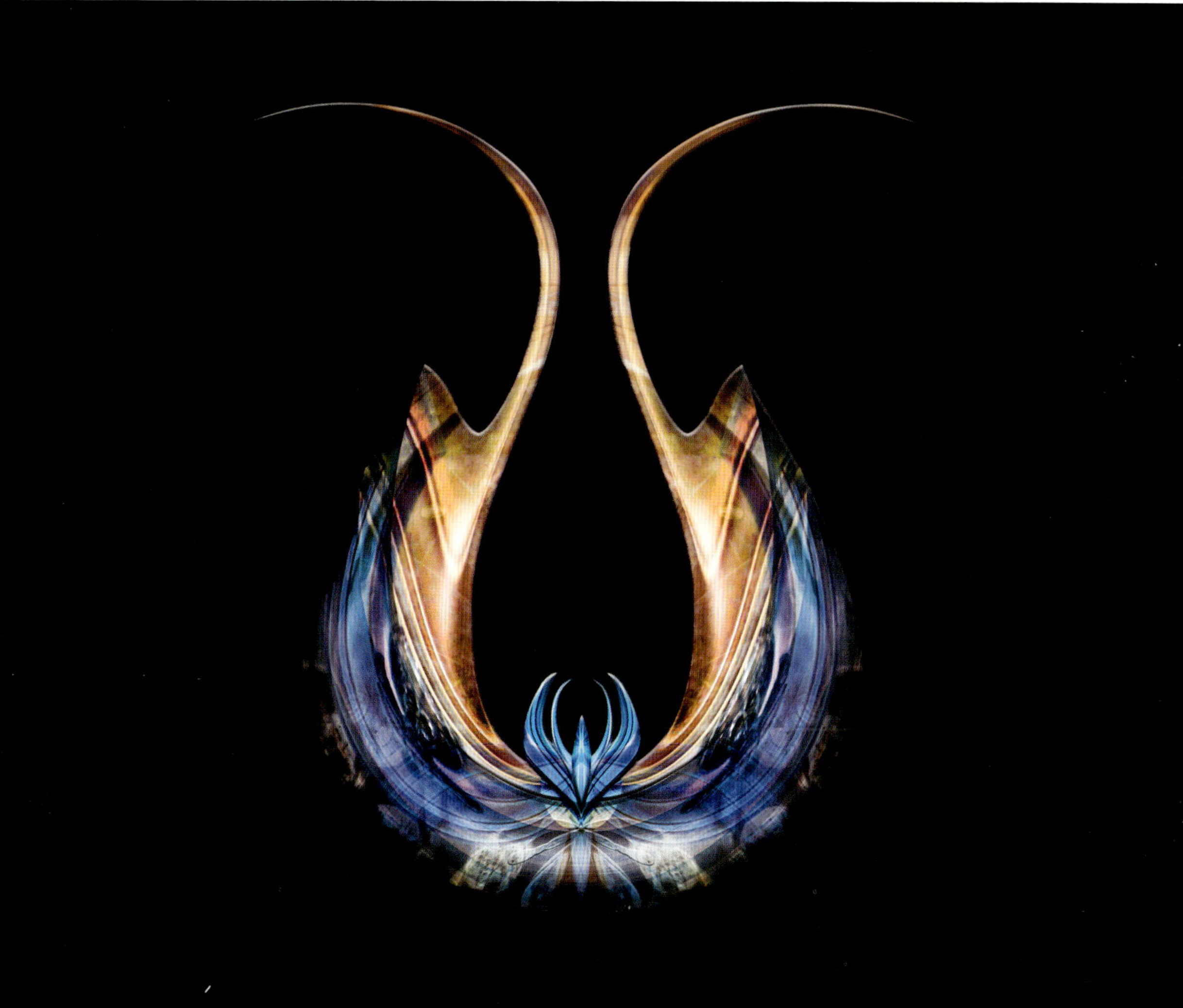

Polar Coordinates

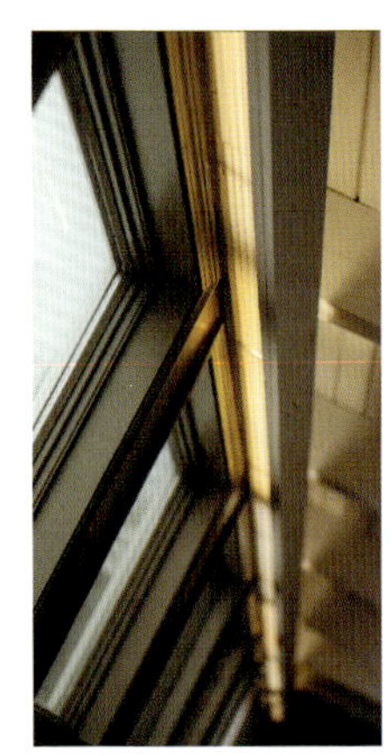

This alien was made from a photo of a hallway with windows. By selecting from the pull-down menu, Filter > Distort > Polar Coordinates, I curved the lines of the hallway. Pieces were then cut off in arched shapes and layered on top of each other. I created eyes in the method described earlier and placed them in a layer behind a smaller arch.

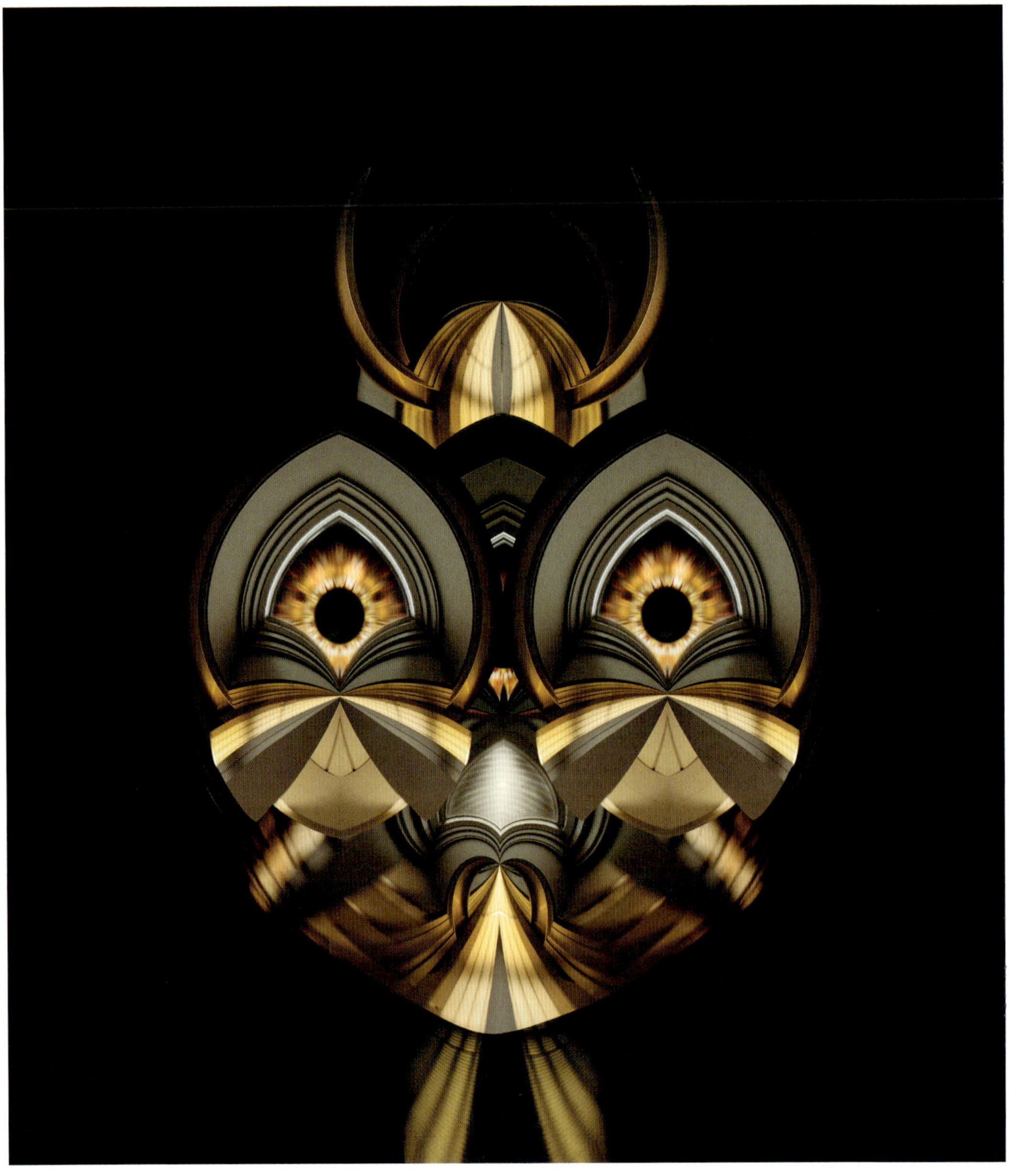

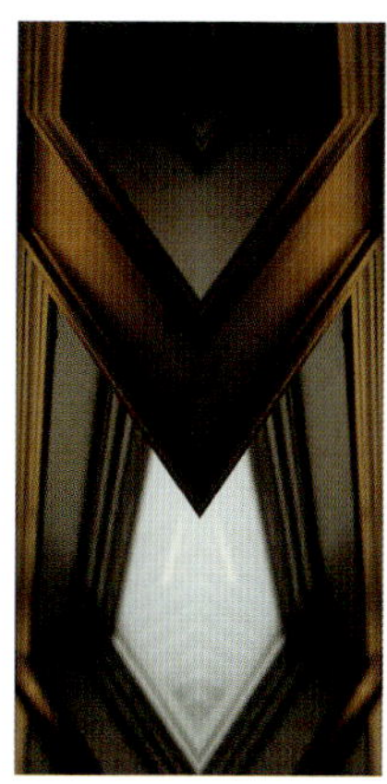

A Different View

A different view of the same hallway with lights was the basis for this alien. The image was first cropped, mirrored, then cropped again, and again mirrored, and then distorted using Polar Coordinates. Then parts of the resulting shape were cut out and layered together. Rather than human-type eyes, the triangular shapes made perfectly appropriate eyes for this creature. The hair on top is made from pen lines (paths) stroked with the Brush tool and then textured using a Pattern Overlay in a layer style.

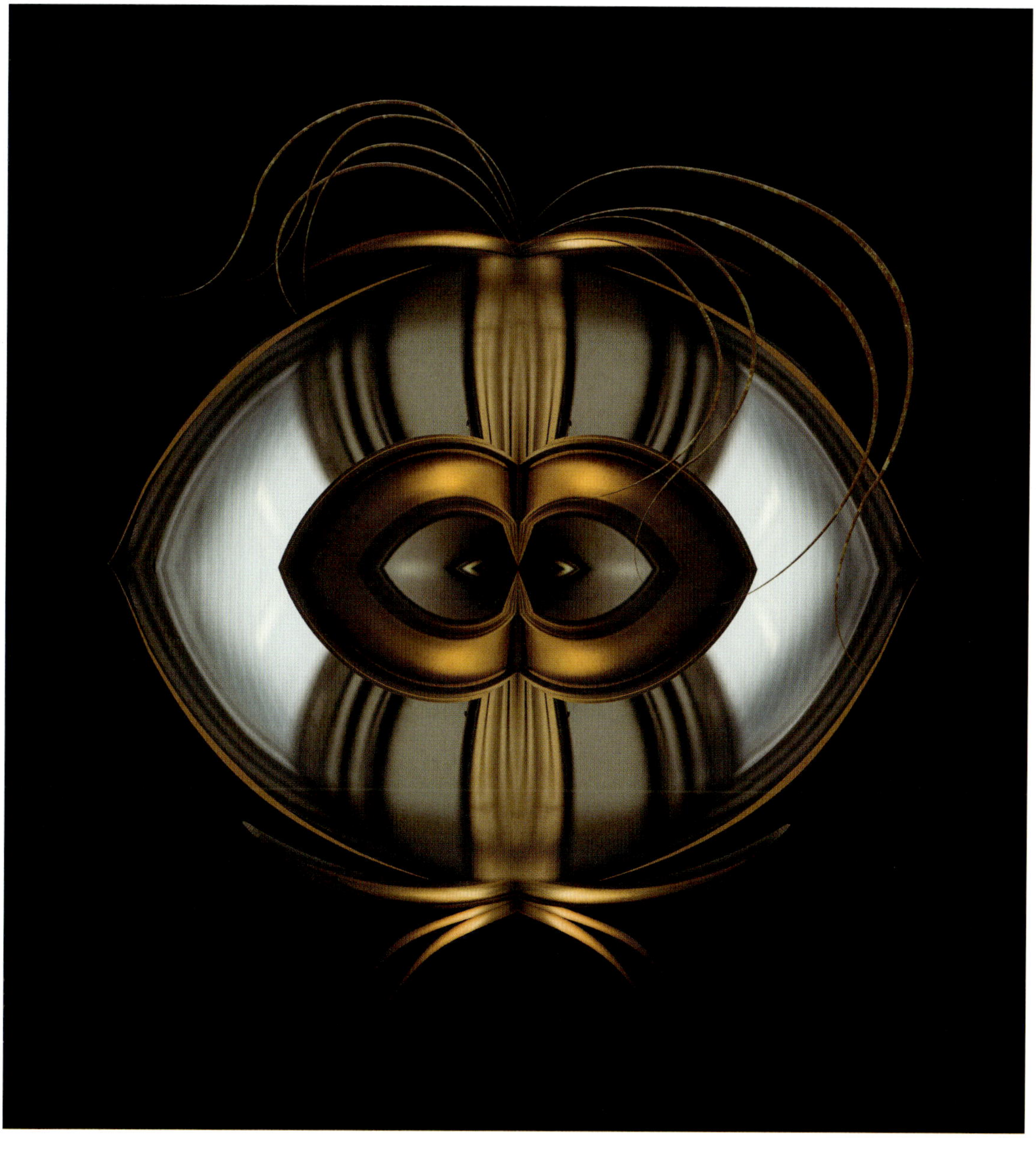

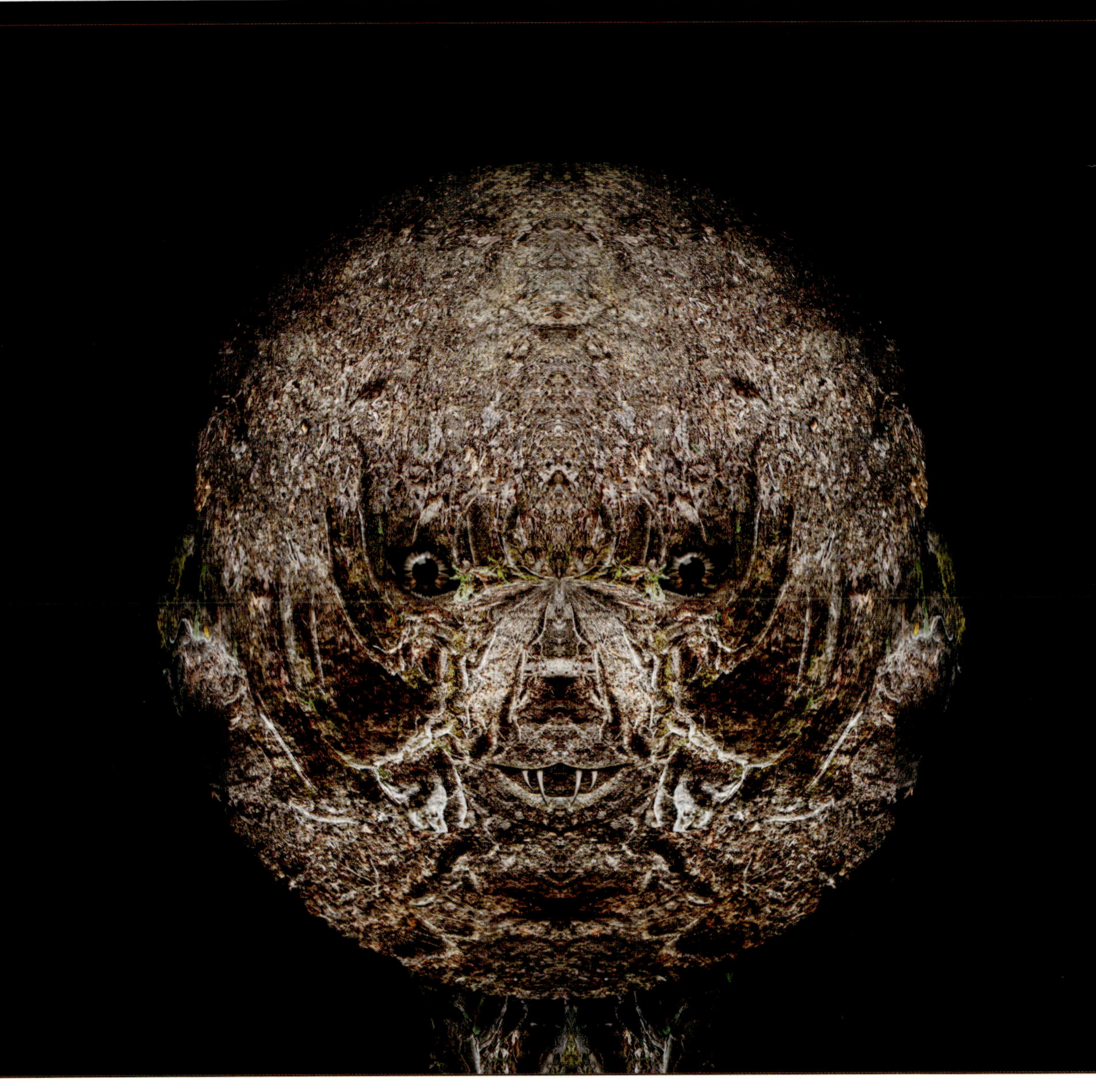

Natural Shadows and Highlights ▲

Architectural elements make for one kind of alien, organic structures are the basis for a completely different feeling creature. This is made from a photograph of tree roots. The natural shadows and highlights of an interesting root structure can make for a very intricate composition.

From Nest to Frondeca

Another composition from very natural materials, *Frondeca* is created from an abandoned wasps' nest. The leaves that naturally stuck out of the nest created eyebrows and other indentations formed nostrils and eye sockets. I photographed a twig for the top and extended them using the Warp tool. To taper the ends, I used the elliptical marquee tool to take away much of the twig and end the twigs in a tapered shape.

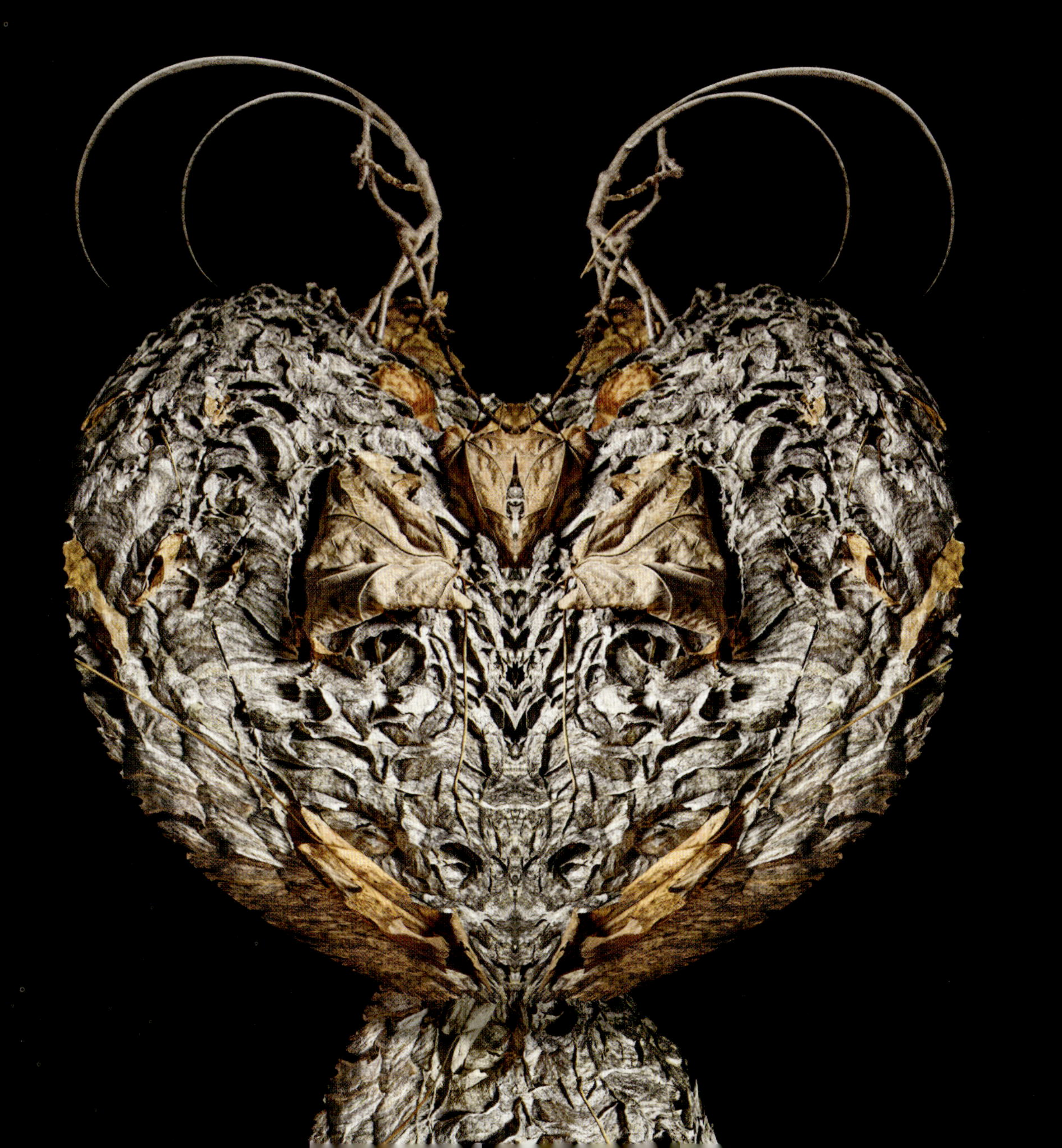

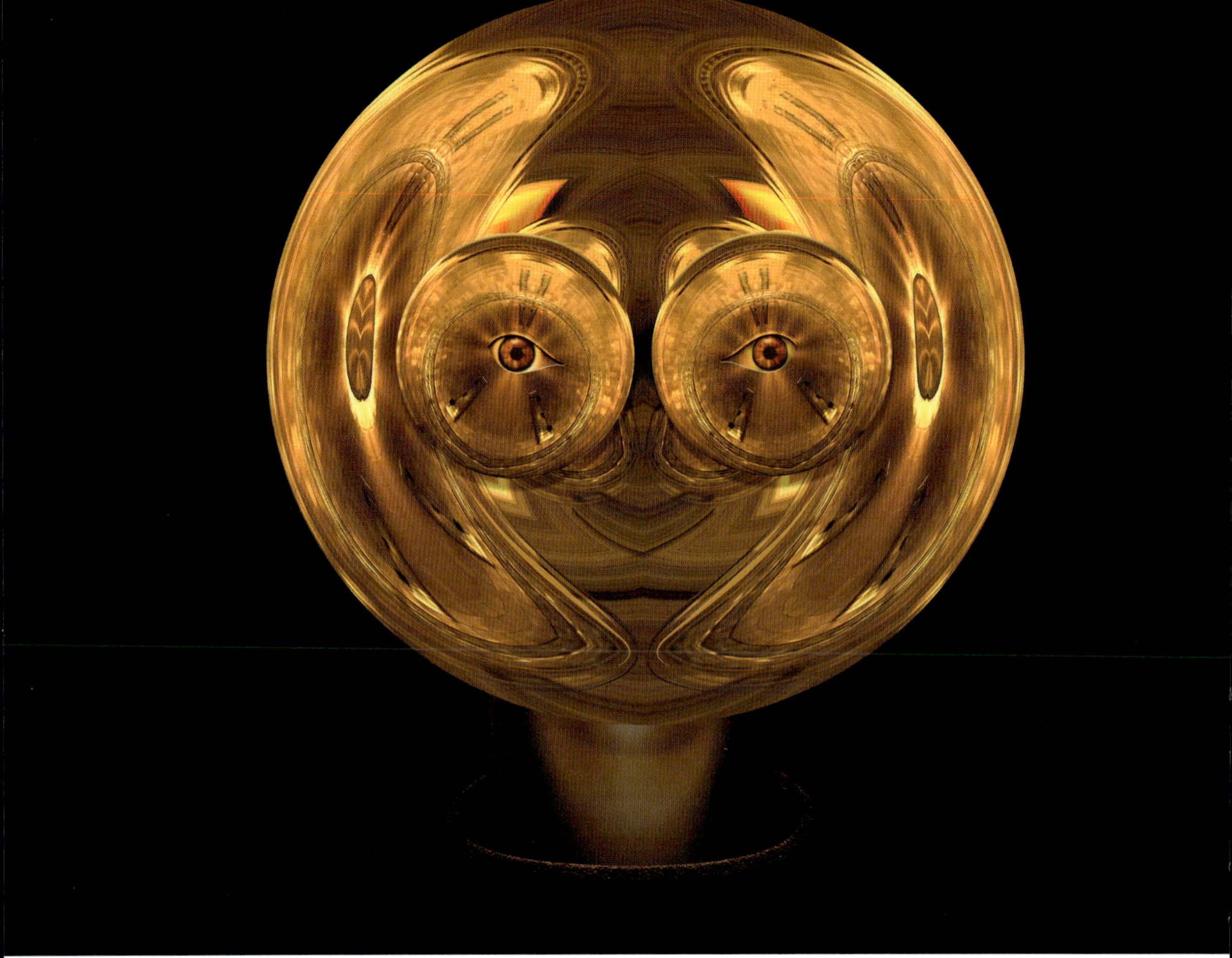

Drop Shadows Add Dimension ▲

Golden Alien is a circle on top of a circle. Ellipses are cut out to show eyes made from scratch. Drop shadows add dimension. The original for this image is a blue car fender with some reflections, which added texture. The color was inverted to make this gold color.

The neck was made by making a rectangle from the gold color and darkening it at the edges, dodging to lighten it at the center and leaving the top shadowed, since that would naturally be shadowed by the chin. The Transform > Warp tool was then used to taper the neck at the sides.

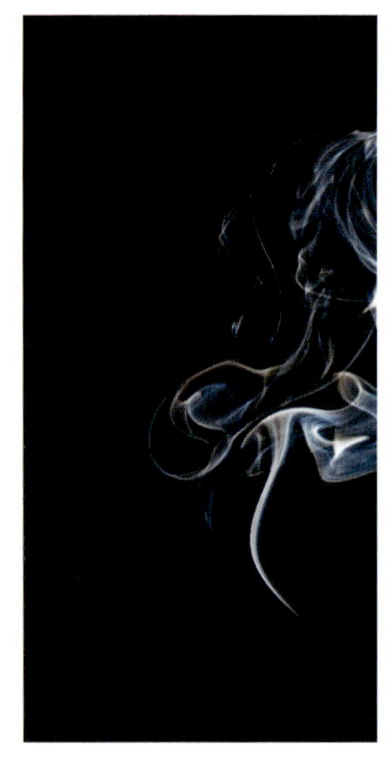

Making Brushes

Making brushes is fun and amazingly easy to do. A smoke brush was used to make this creature. To shoot the smoke *(facing page)*, use two lights, one on either side, slightly behind the subject and pointed at the subject. Use a black backdrop (paper, fabric, night– it doesn't matter), but make sure the backdrop is far enough removed from the lights that no light will fall on the backdrop. Use an incense stick to create the smoke. It's great to have an assistant move the stick around while you photograph it so that you get some interesting movement.

To make a brush from the smoke, open the image and invert it so that you have a negative version of your original. The smoke should be black to dark gray on white now. Open the dialog box for Image > Adjustments > Levels. Using the White Eyedropper, click on the background to make the backdrop completely white. Next, use a Rectangular Marquee tool to select the smoke. Go to Edit > Define Brush Preset and give it a name.

If your smoke extends to the edge of the canvas, simply use a white soft-edged brush to taper the smoke off before it reaches the edge of your canvas.

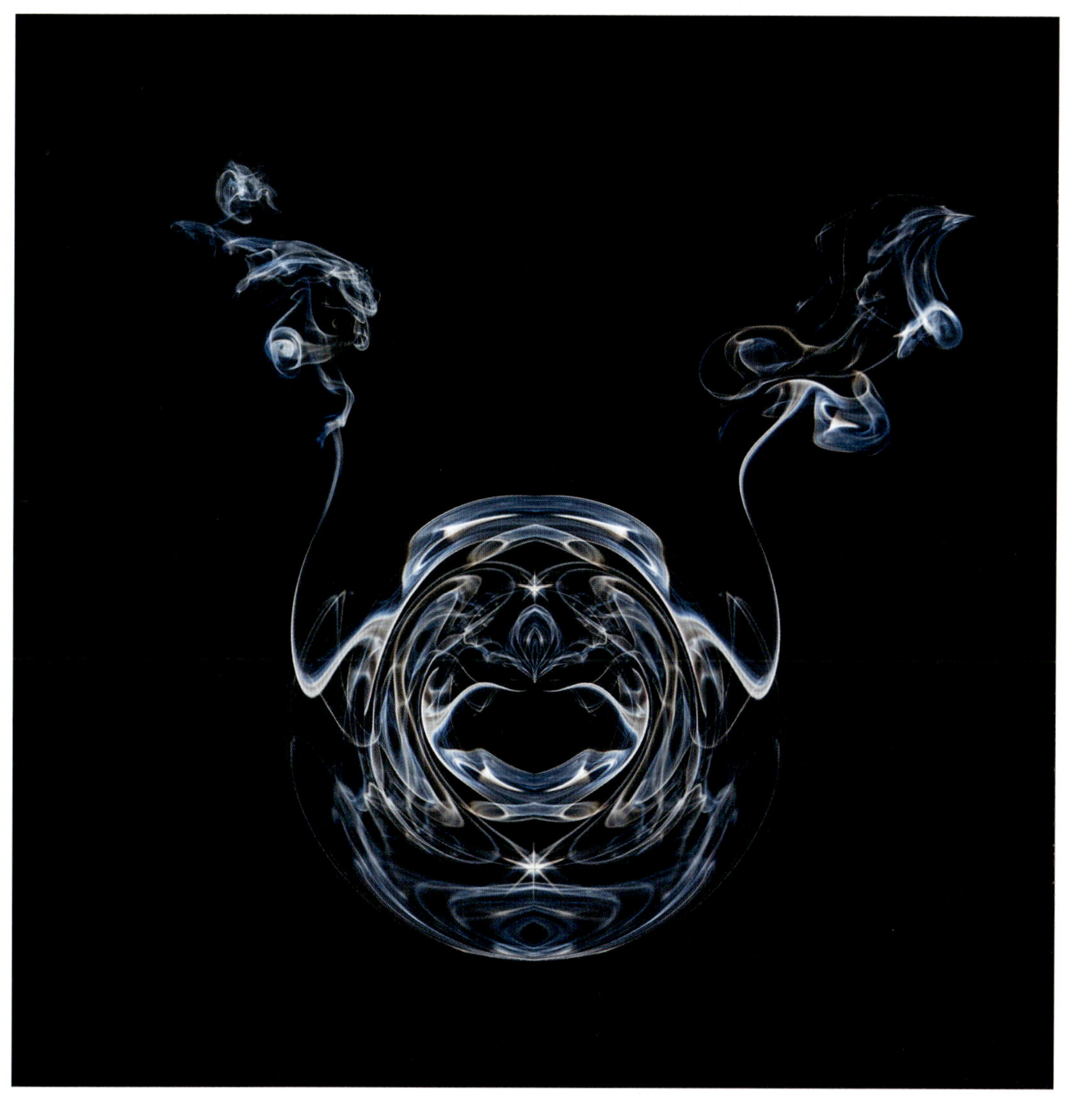

Composition from an Antique

For this image, the photograph I worked with is from another car fender. This time I photographed a really great antique car. I cropped into the hood ornament and a bit of the car's grill to make this composition, which had a great deal of color and intricate detail before I started. Mirroring it and then distorting it made it look almost like stained glass. I found some natural shapes within the distortion and used them as guides for cutting, discarding parts, and layering other parts to make the scarab shape here.

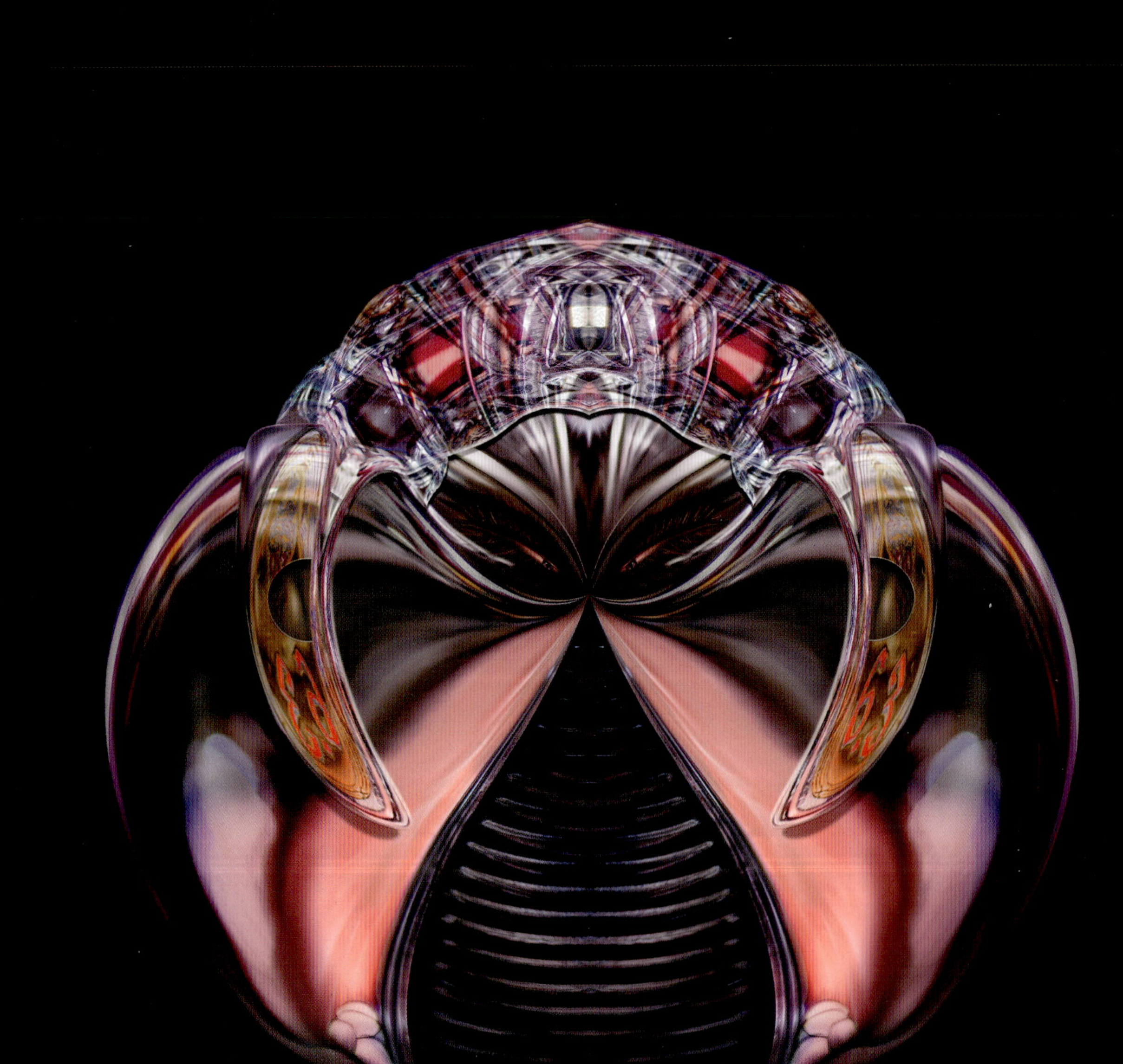

Beginning with Mirroring and Distortion

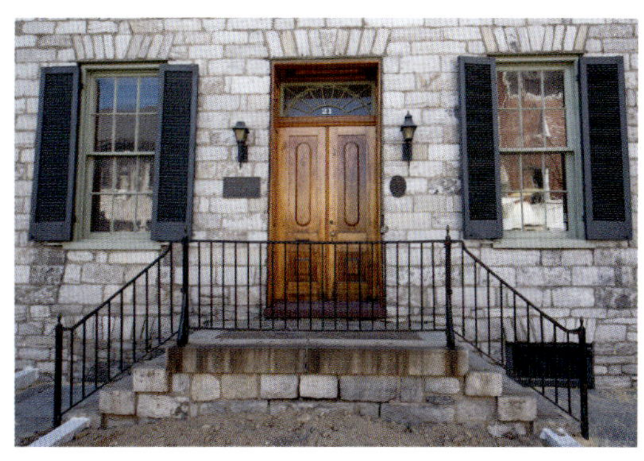

This began as a photograph of the side of a building, with three windows and a staircase with a wrought iron railing. Mirroring and distortion were just the beginning. Layering and copying layer over layer, then changing the layer's blend modes created what appeared to be a snake. I took that further by adding eyes and tendrils to the piece to complete the look.

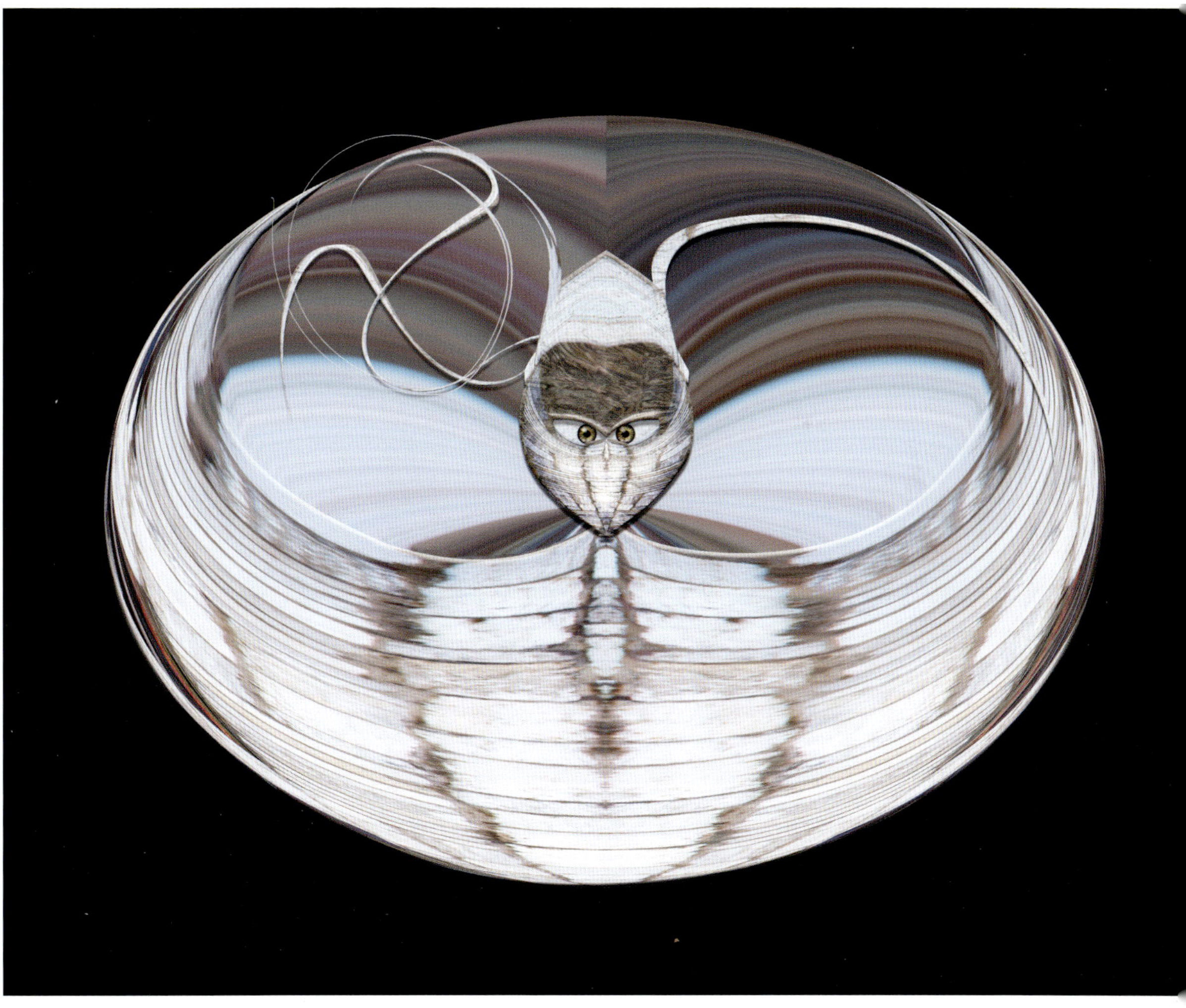

Tea Reconsidered Series

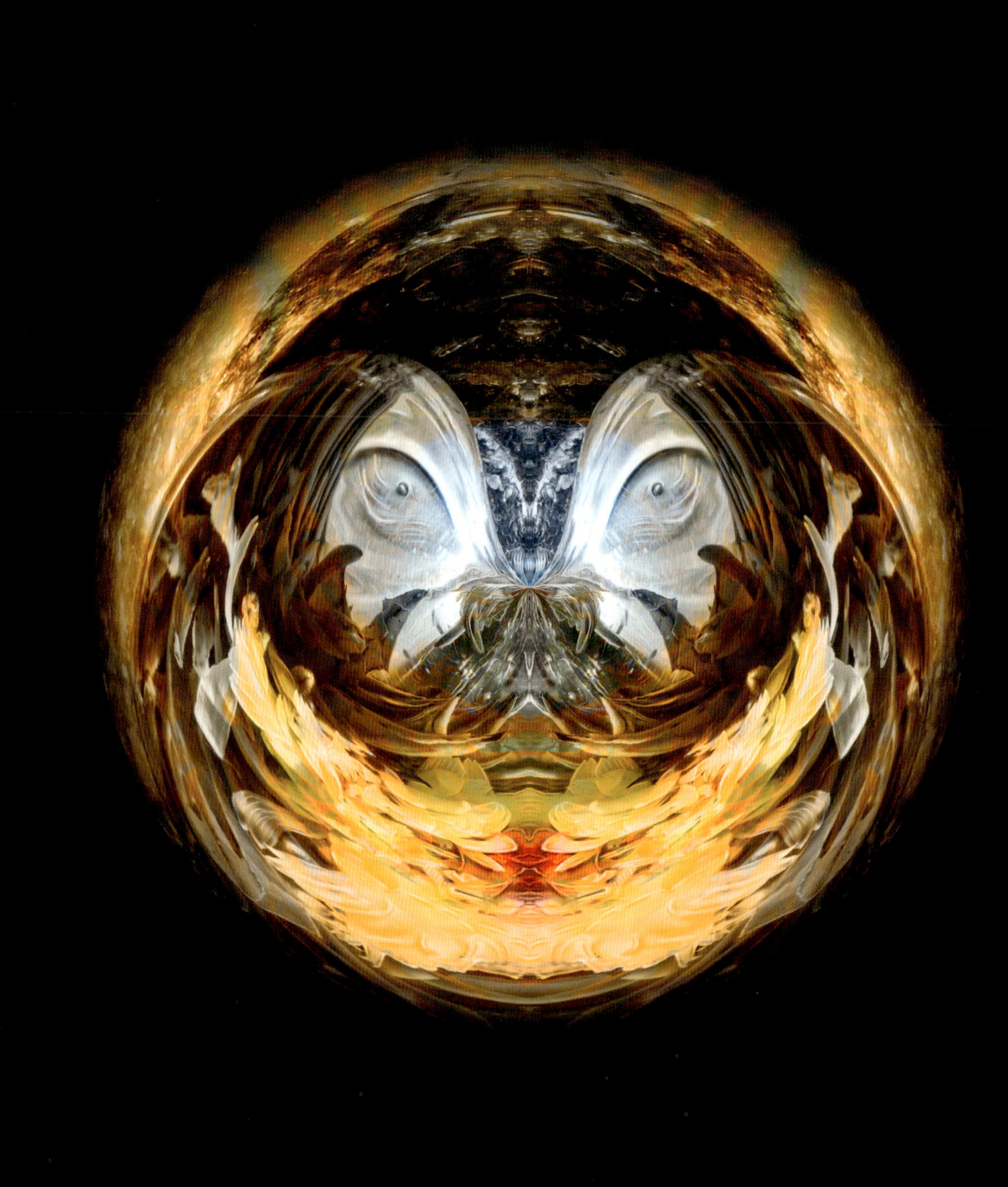

Reimagine the Subject

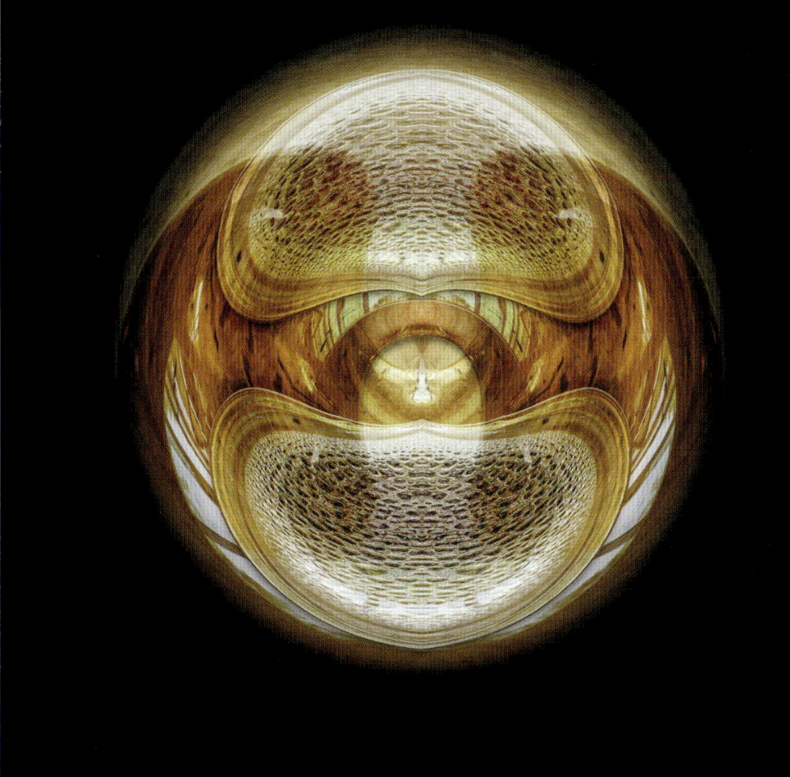

The aliens were a photographic meditation. They were an exploration of using ordinary objects, and some not-so-ordinary objects, to create very unique imaginary creatures. It occurred to me that it would be even more interesting to photograph a single topic or subject and explore all the ways in which I might be able to reimagine that subject. A friend happened to know I was a tea lover and gave me a glass teapot as a gift. I began photographing that teapot and the various ways in which I could brew tea with it. The next series of images are simply tea, reconsidered.

This piece *(facing page)* is a transition piece. It still holds the essence of the *Alien* series in that there is something that resembles a face, at least eyes, but the evidence of tea leaves is there.

By cropping into different sections of the images and then distorting and using layers in different blend modes, very different results can be achieved. This image *(bottom)* is the beginning crop for this composition.

Through the Glass

Since the teapot was glass, the backgrounds often showed through and became integral parts of the image. In this case, the teapot was sitting on a wooden surface. I felt the distortion of the wood grain curling around a central point happened in a very pleasing way. Water bubbles are also evident in this.

The wood grain was so lovely in this beginning image, I decided to make it the focal point of the composition. The bubbles are simply a counterpoint or contrasting element that gives the viewer's eye somewhere to land within the texture and swirls of the wood.

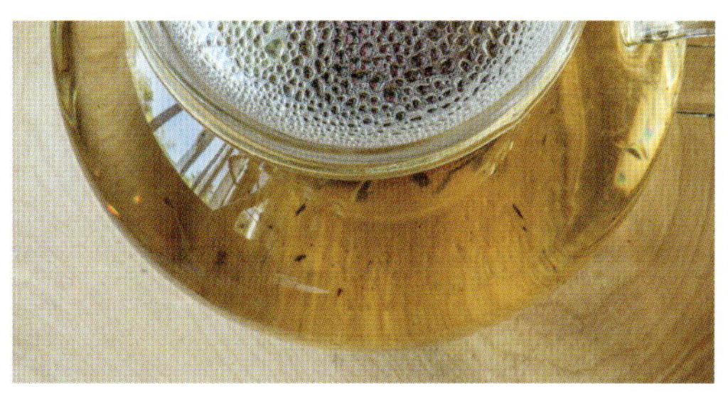

Choosing Graceful Lines

More bubbles appear in this composition. Inverting the color from the original gold of the tea created this blue color. The distortions options I used for this image were Polar Coordinates and Spherize, both of which are reached from the pull-down menu Filter > Distort, and often yield some surprising results. In this case, when I distorted the teapot, the glass spout made a very pleasing shape. I chose to crop into this part of the original photograph because of the graceful lines.

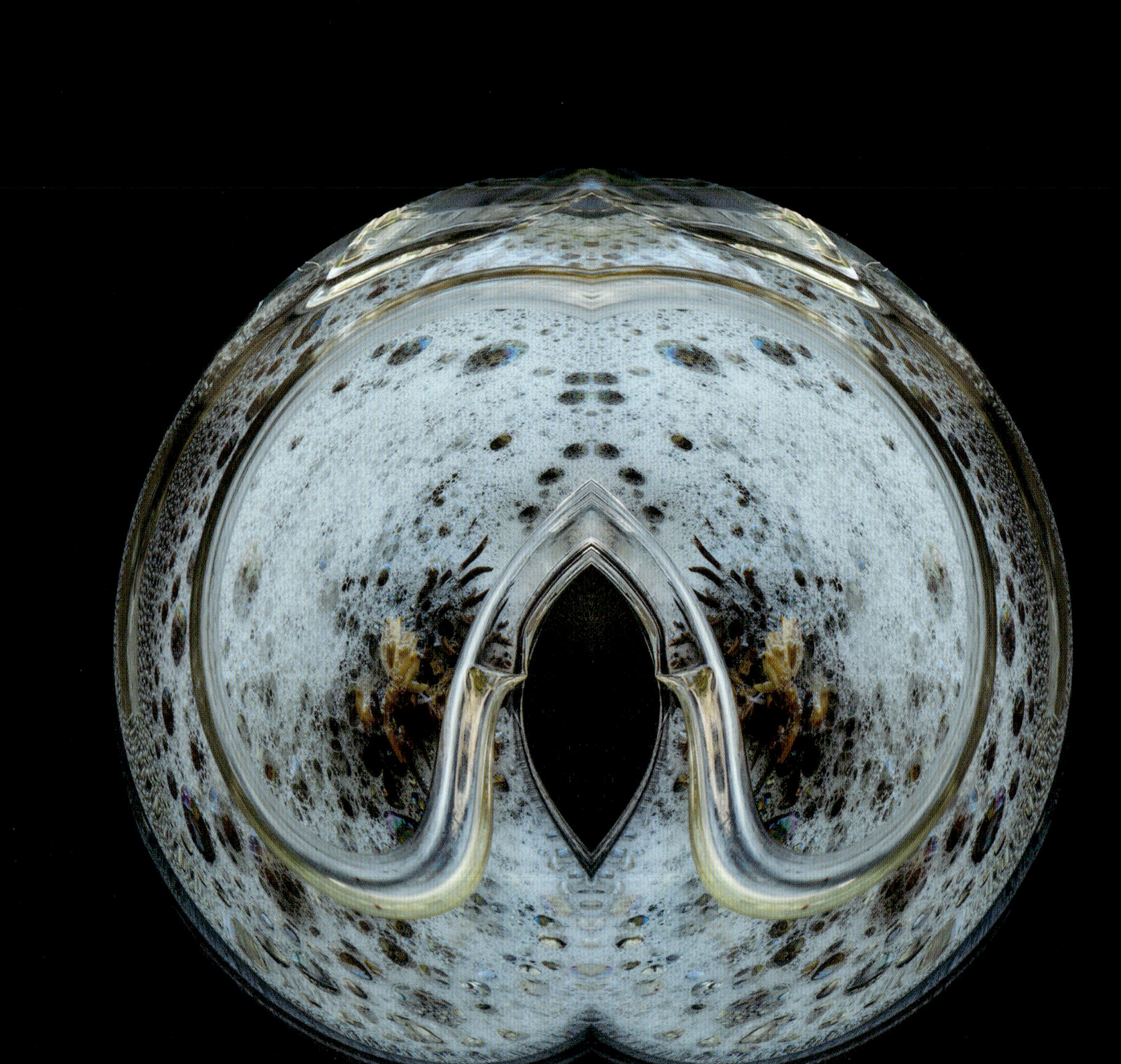

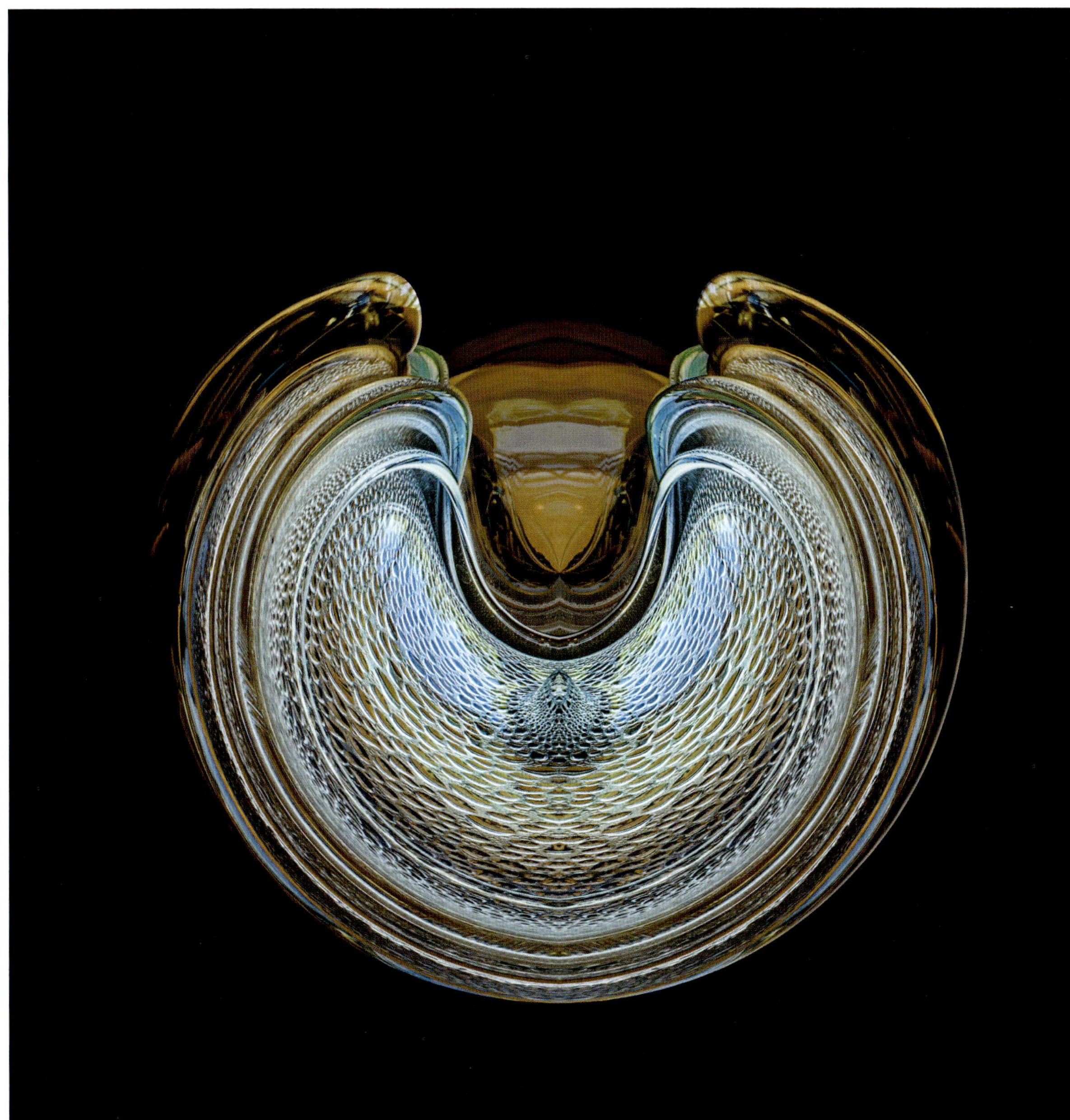

Graceful Layered Shapes ▲

Along the same idea, this is distorted differently and was taken from a different section of the original photograph. I used Layer Blend modes to layer the graceful shape over itself several times so that the composition almost looks like translucent seas shells stacked one on top of the other. Of course, that's what I see. Everyone sees their own stories in these images.

Using the Pen Tool

By using the curving lines of the teapot's spout as a starting point, and then selecting those sections and putting each on their own layer (using the Pen tool), this very dimensional image came to be. A composition of complimentary colors was created by combining the subtle, natural golds of the tea with a layer of these same colors inverted to become blue and the reflection of some of the background.

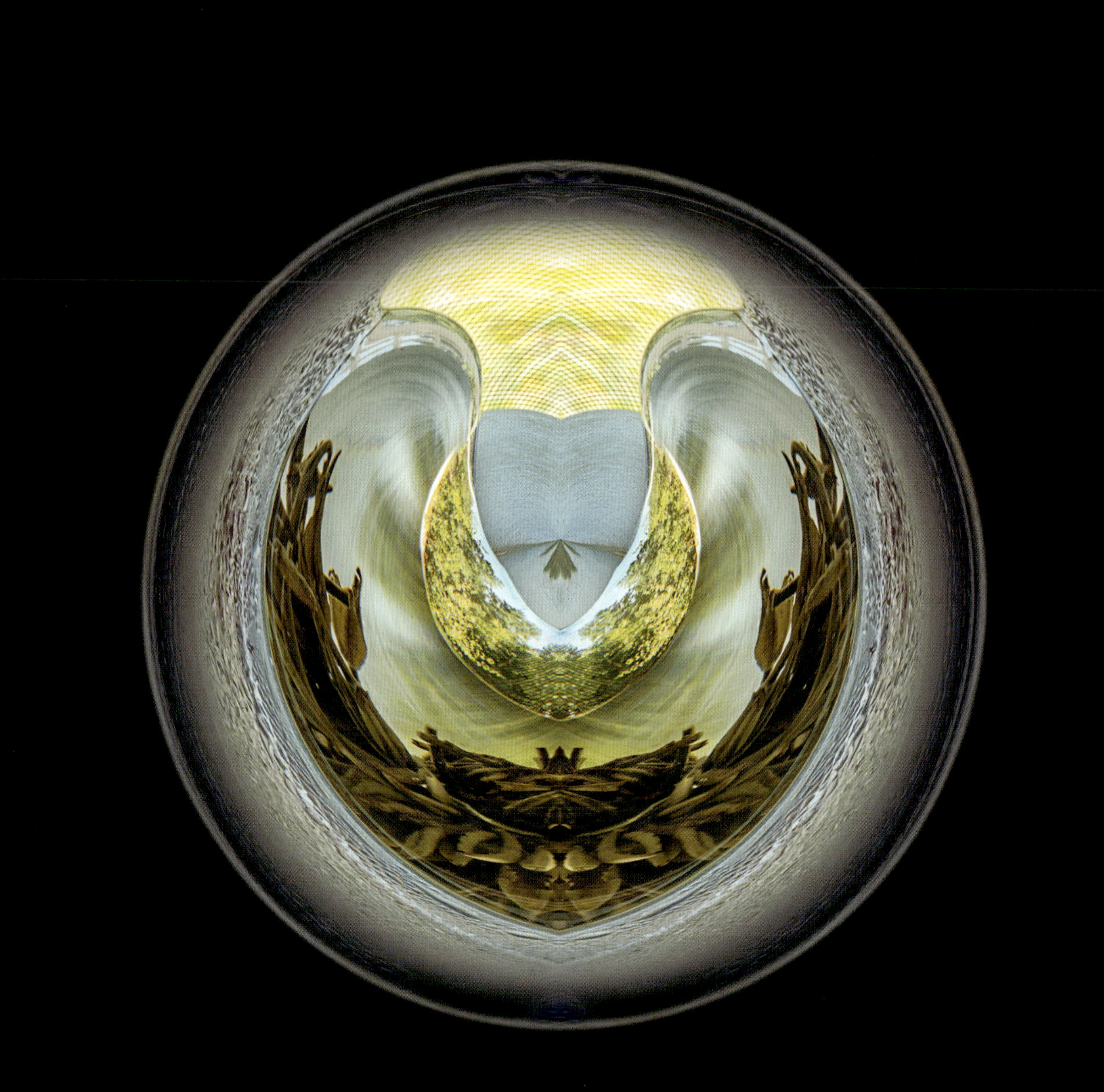

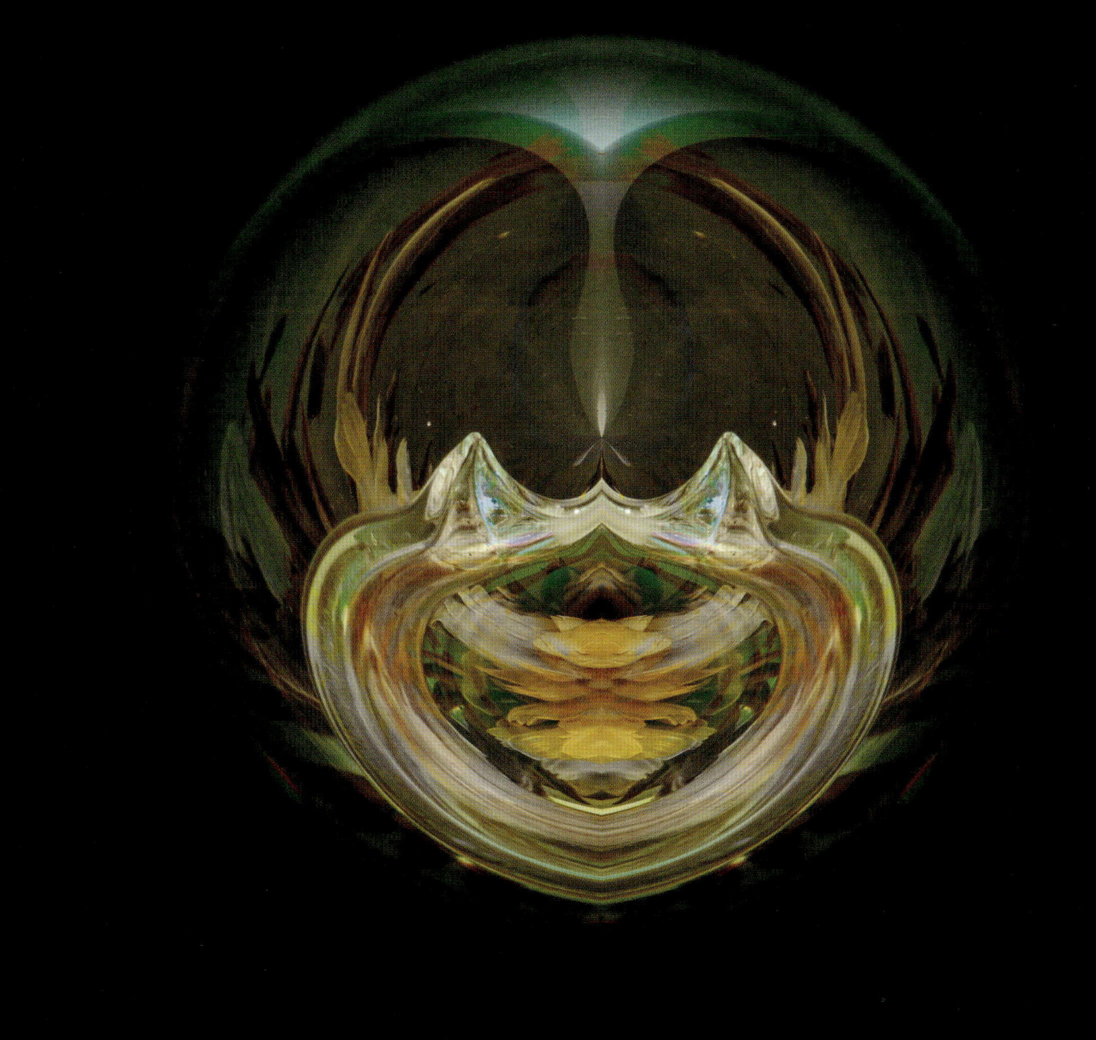

Enhancing the Contrast ▲

The shape of the spout and its glassiness really appealed to me as I wanted to keep its characteristics, but enhance the contrast between the spout and the rest of the image. There are several layers use to create this. There is one in Multiply Blend mode which darkens all but the spout, which is on a layer above the rest. Changing the blend mode of the spout to Dodge can lighten and brighten the glassy characteristic, but adjustments to the opacity may be necessary to keep the effect from being too harsh.

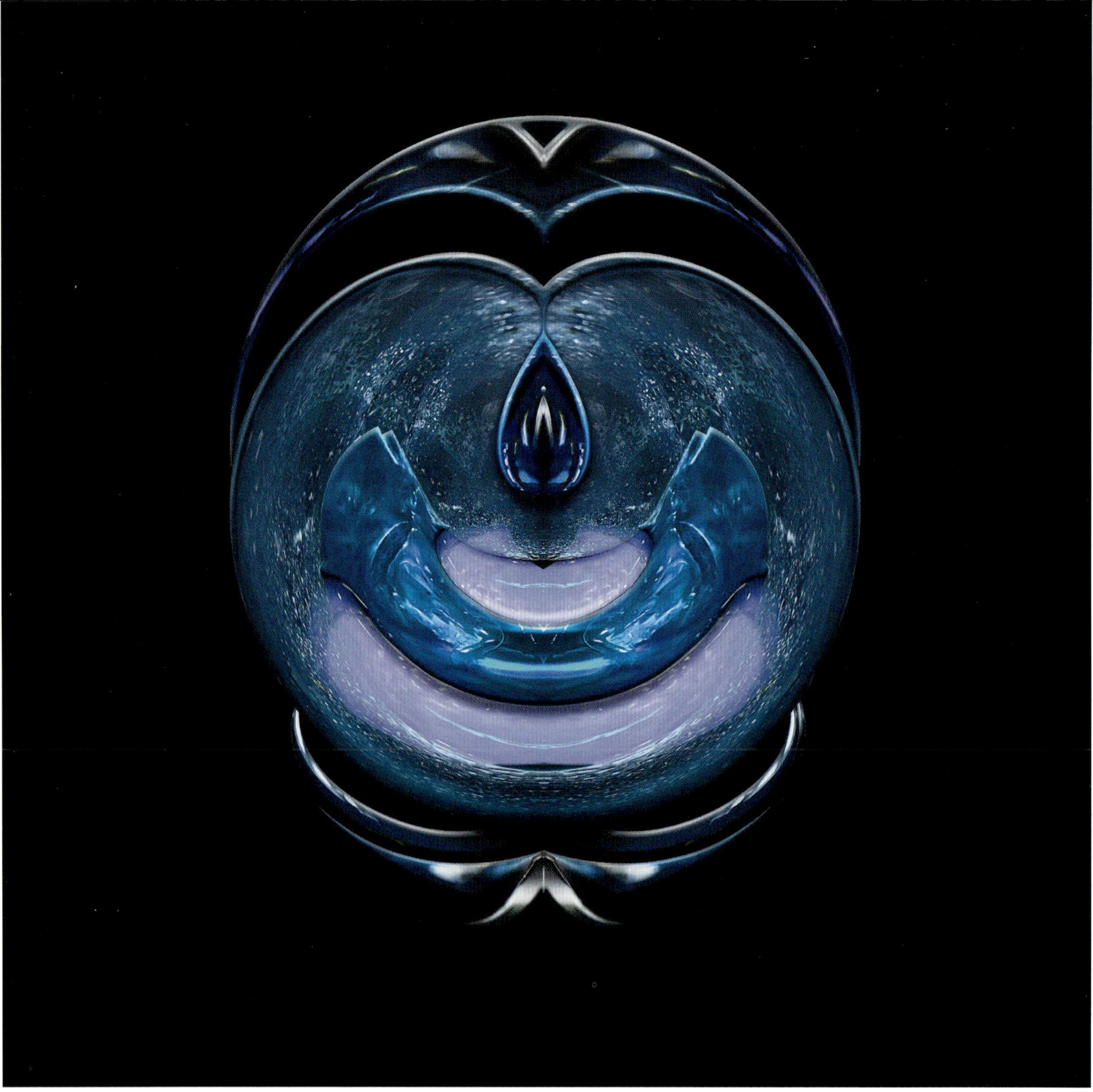

Going Beyond

The idea of going beyond the circular shape for the tea series was an important step. Often, working on a series, part of the process is to make rules. These rules might be as simple as "confine the work to a single subject," or far more complex. I found myself working almost exclusively in a circular format for the *Tea Reconsidered* series, however it wasn't one of the parameters for the project. I began to disassemble the pieces, add more shapes to the circles, cut into the circles and pull them apart.

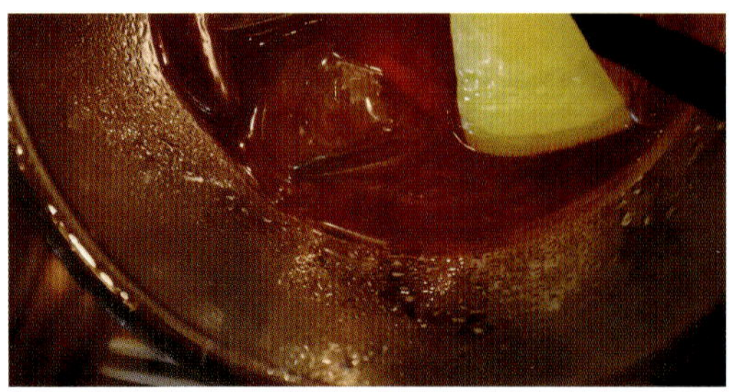

This crop of a glass of ice tea is the beginning point for the very blue image above. Inverting the color turns the gold into this beautiful, luminous blue.

Keeping Effects Subtle

Often it's a more interesting result when the applied effects are kept subtle. I really enjoyed the deep, rich gold color of this image, which also used Multiply mode on one of the layers to deepen the color. Working with the Dodge tool and the Burn tool at the edge of the tea leaves gave them a three-dimensional look that seems to escape the glass boundaries of the teapot.

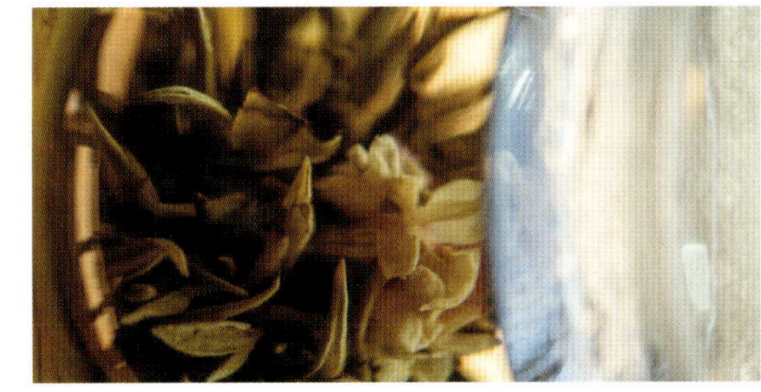

Varying the distance from the subject, as well as the depth of field, results in the wide range of visual opportunities from a single subject. This close-up of the tea leaves, when turned on its side, copied and distorted, results in the gold jewel-like composition below.

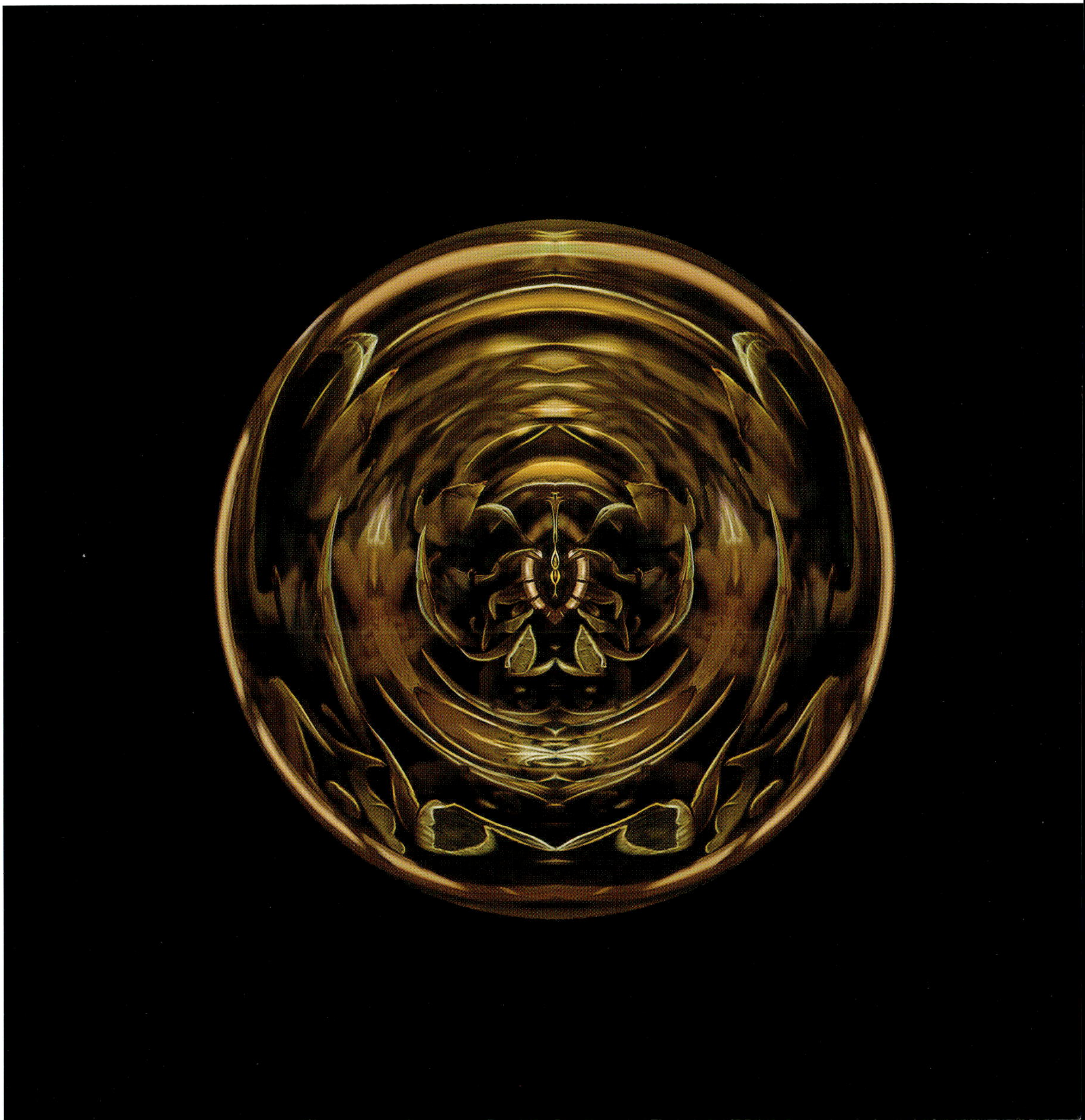

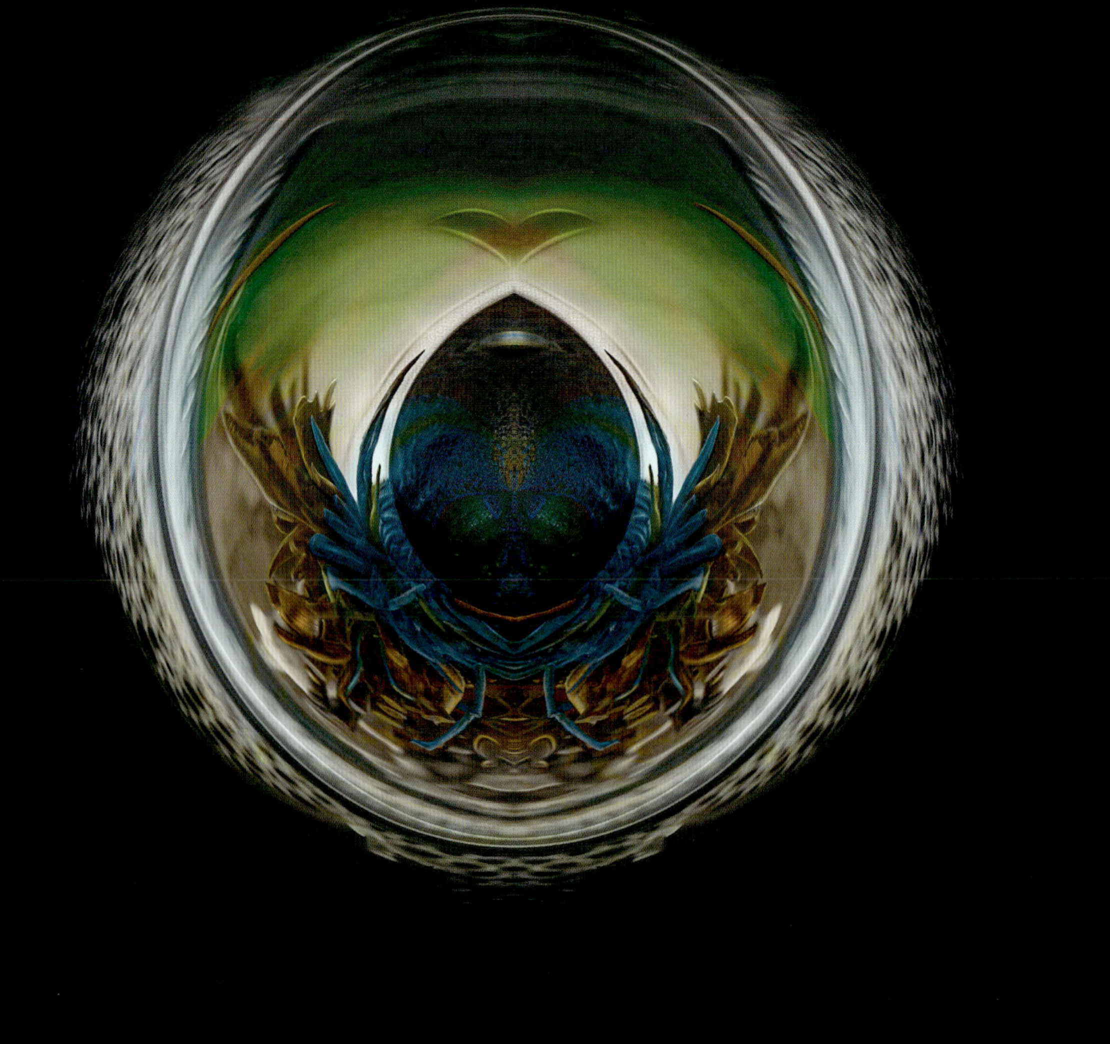

A Natural Border ▲

The bubbles in the tea ring the edge of this composition. Selecting just the center ovoid shape and inverting the color contrasts well with the light area surrounding it. The edge of the teapot makes a natural border to separate the two areas. I accentuated that boundary by selecting that area, copying it to its own layer, and using the Bevel and Emboss layer style to emphasize the dimensionality of this part of the composition.

Concentric Circles

One of my favorite pieces from the *Tea Reconsidered* series, this was created by mirroring and distorting, like many of the other tea images, but concentric circles were then selected and the Blend modes of the layers were changed to create the gold ring, the greener ring and the subtle outside ring. The little alien in the center was only hinted at in the initial mirroring of the image, but hand dodging and burning brought out the details just enough, and not too much.

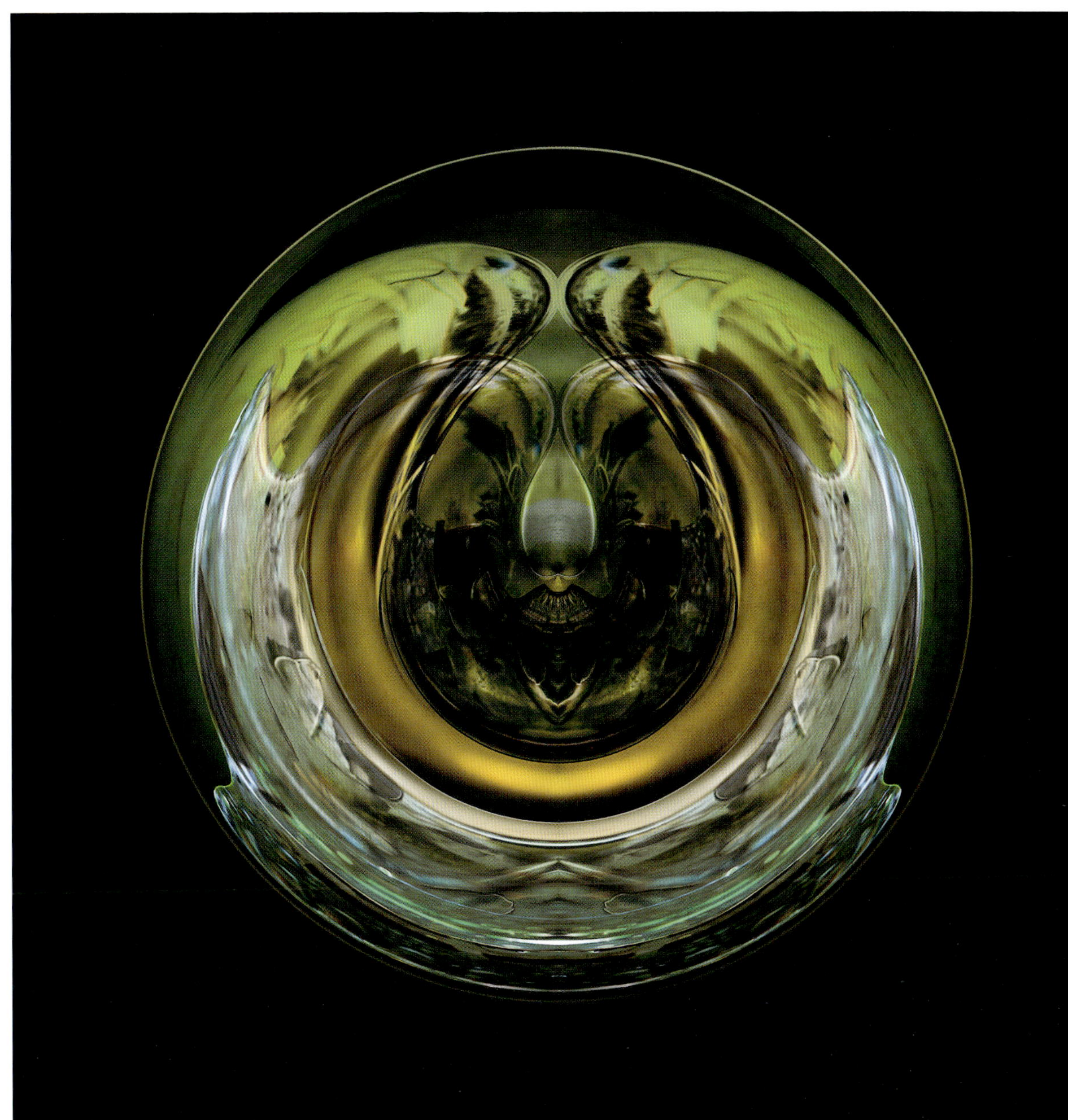

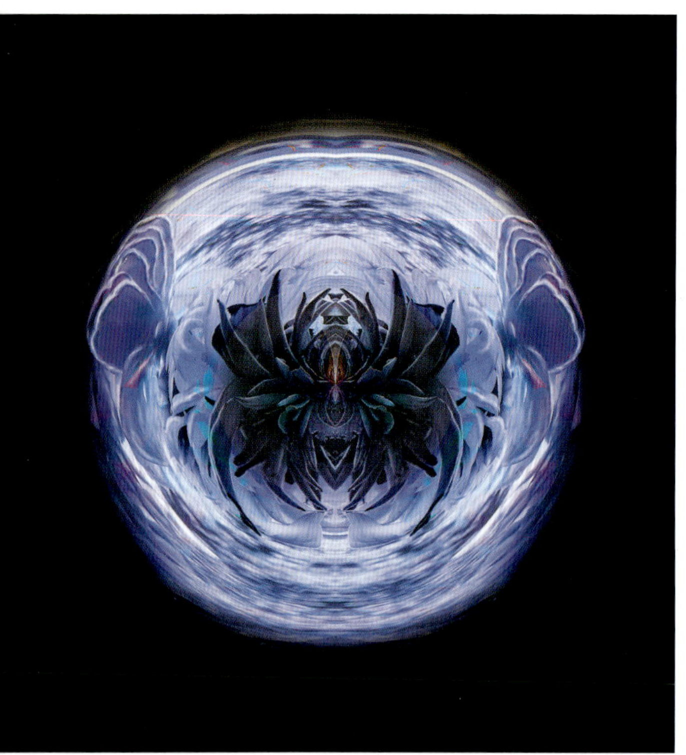

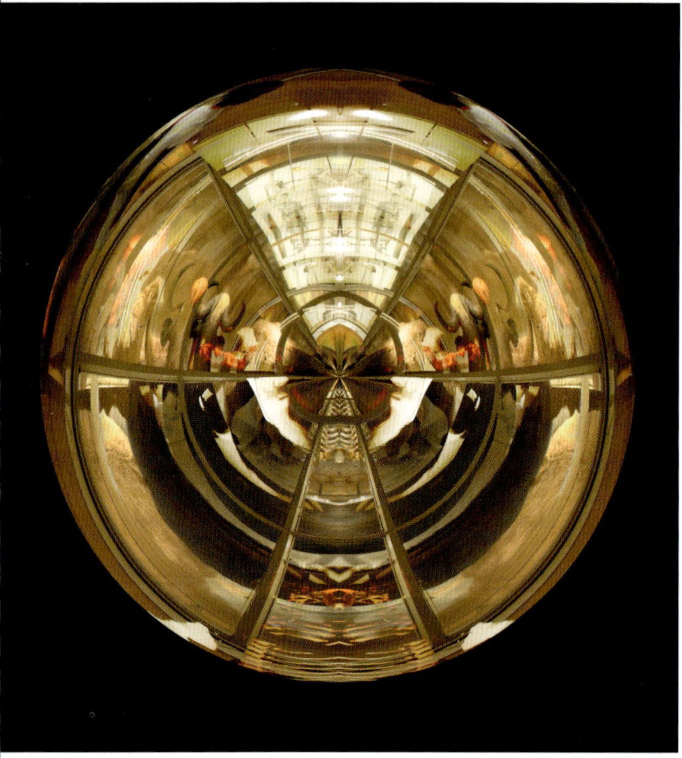

A Voyage of Discovery

The interesting thing about working on a series is that as you produce more and more work, you begin to broaden your thinking, which makes you a better and more engaging artist. If you take images and create one photograph of Cinderella you recreate a story that has been told thousands and thousands of times. If you create a hundred images of Cinderella, you have to really get to know your subject in a whole new way, and you will find that even a story that's been told that many times can lead the maker—and the viewer—on a brand new journey.

What happens when you select the leafy shapes and layer them at the boundary of the image? What strange, seemingly real creatures appear, as if magically, from a mirrored image? What happens when layers are stacked and bend modes changed and pieces subtracted?

The *Tea Reconsidered* series has over six hundred images in it so far—it has become far more than a photographic meditation. It is a voyage of discovery.

From the same original image, this image *(bottom left)* is a completely different result, obtained by using a different crop as well as different layer blend modes and keeping the original color rather than inverting *(top left)*. This piece speaks of geometry where the image to the right is wildly organic.

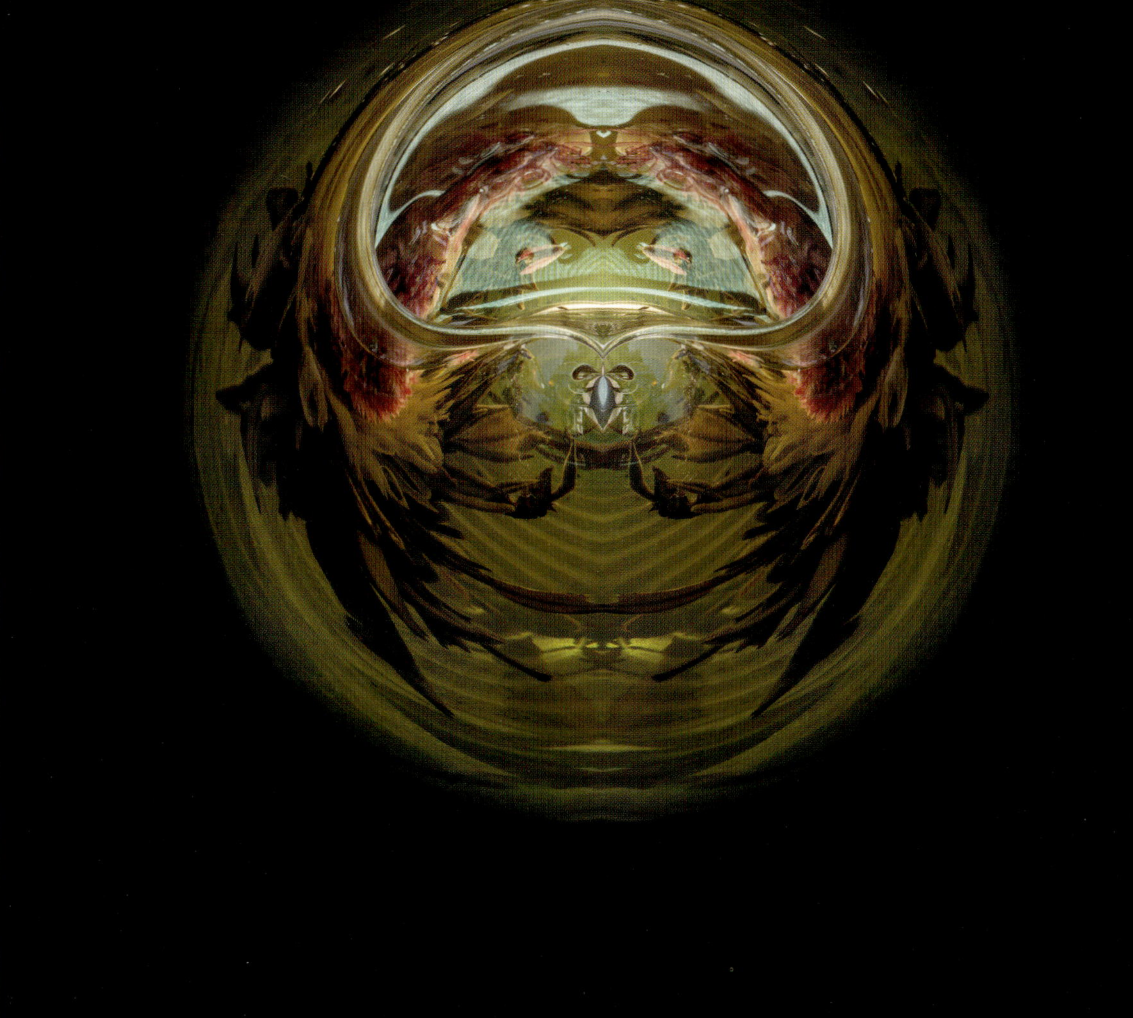

Portals to New Places ▲

While I found many creatures reminiscent of life forms—like the insect or spider-like creature in the previous image—the *Tea Reconsidered* series created just as many new worlds or objects that seem very much like portals to new places, or even planets. This is one of those cases. The light area near the top appears to be an entry point to a fairy tale, inviting the viewer in for a closer look at something that cannot, but does exist.

Empty Teapot

The empty teapot was the starting point for this image. I find transparency very compelling. Layering images of a transparent subject can either destroy the characteristics of the transparency or enhance it. Layer blend modes, especially Soft Light and Overlay blend modes, are the key to retaining the delicate features of a transparent subject through many transformations.

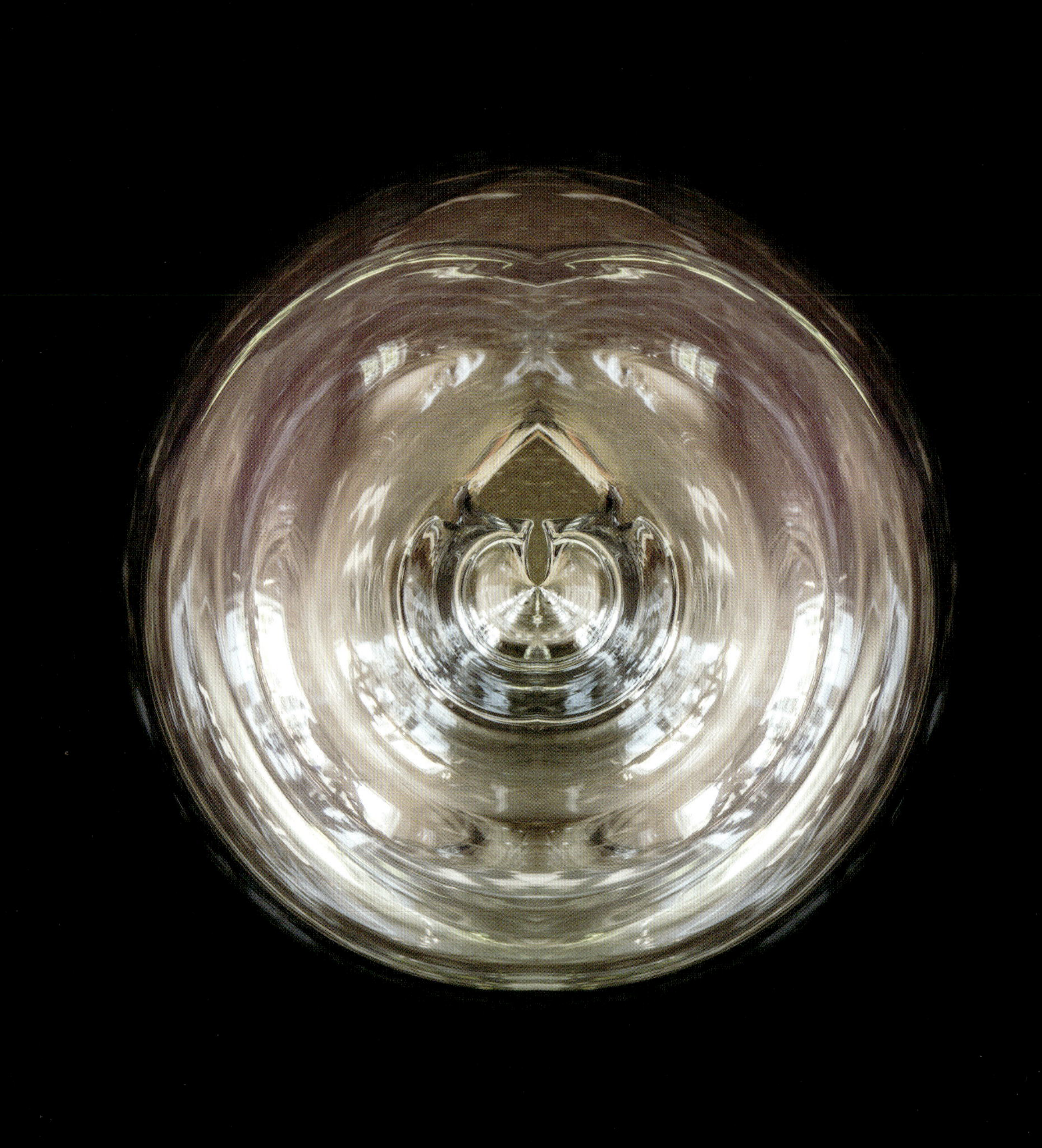

Counterpoint

As a counterpoint to the previous crystalline composition, this one is nearly overwhelmed by the tea leaves. The flowering tea was a new experience for me. Not loose tea leaves, the flowering tea is bundled into a neat, woven seed about the size of a plump thumb. When you immerse the tea in the hot water, it literally blooms in front of your eyes. Small flowers, sometimes yellow, sometimes red, even white grow out of the packet of leaves. They are beautiful and fascinating. I photographed the process continuously as the flower developed and then stood erect while the tea brewed. If the flowering tea was left too long in the teapot, it only took a day or less for the tea color to stain away those reds, yellows, golds and whites, leaving a small stand of vegetation in monochromatic browns.

The original image for this composition was taken very soon after the tea bloomed, while the colors were still vibrant and defined.

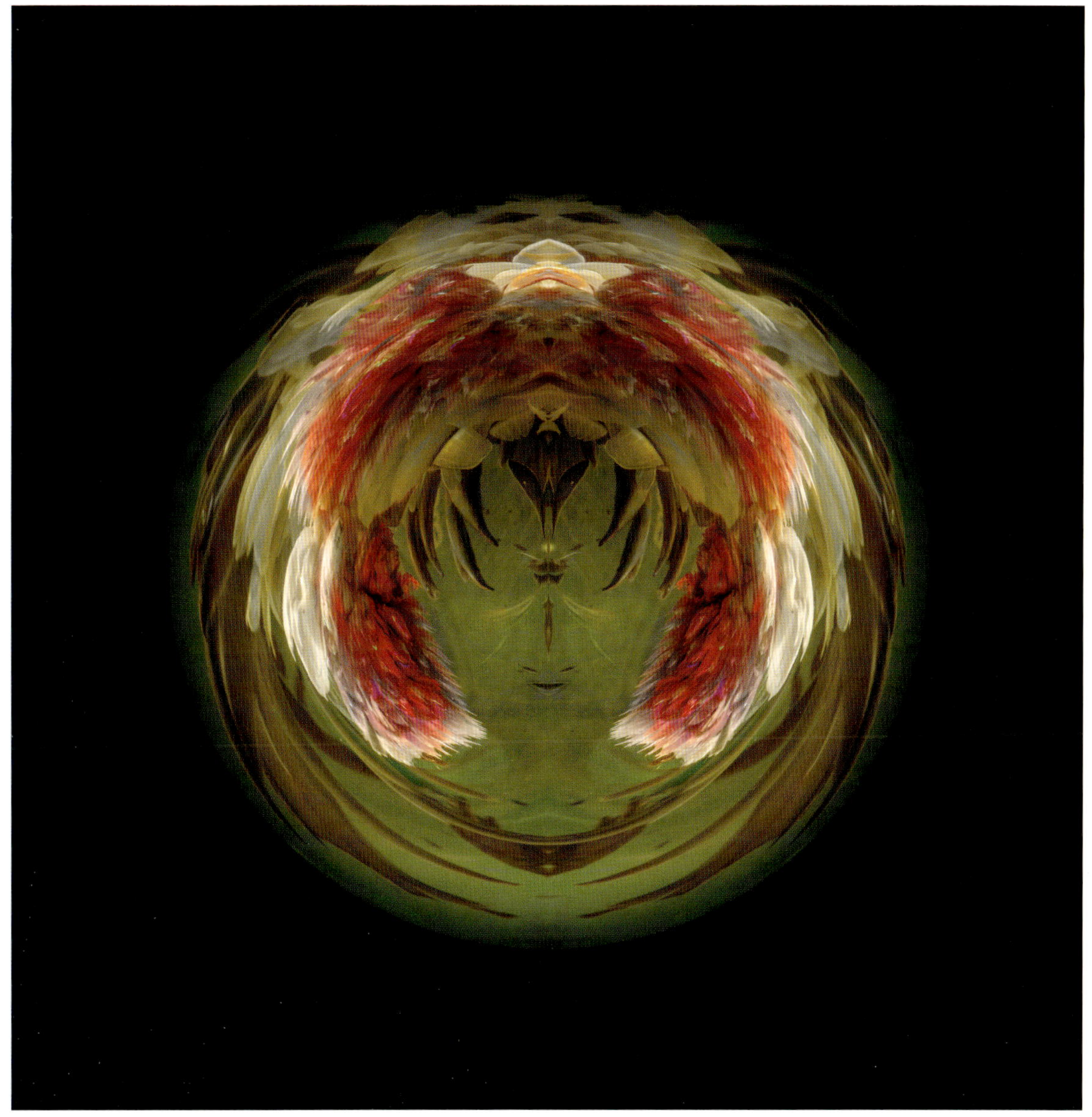

Happy Accidents

Happy accidents almost defined the *Tea Reconsidered* series. In fact, the accidental inhabitants of these pieces are so personalized to each viewer that I wonder if they couldn't function as a more elaborate and colorful version of those old ink blots tests. In this one, I see a wonderful, flying bird as it dives down to pick up a bright red object. It was so clear to me that I added a few delicately painted feathers, simply because they called out to me for their existence.

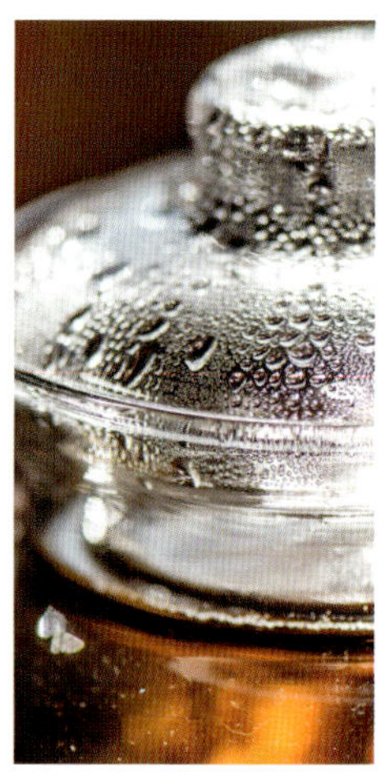

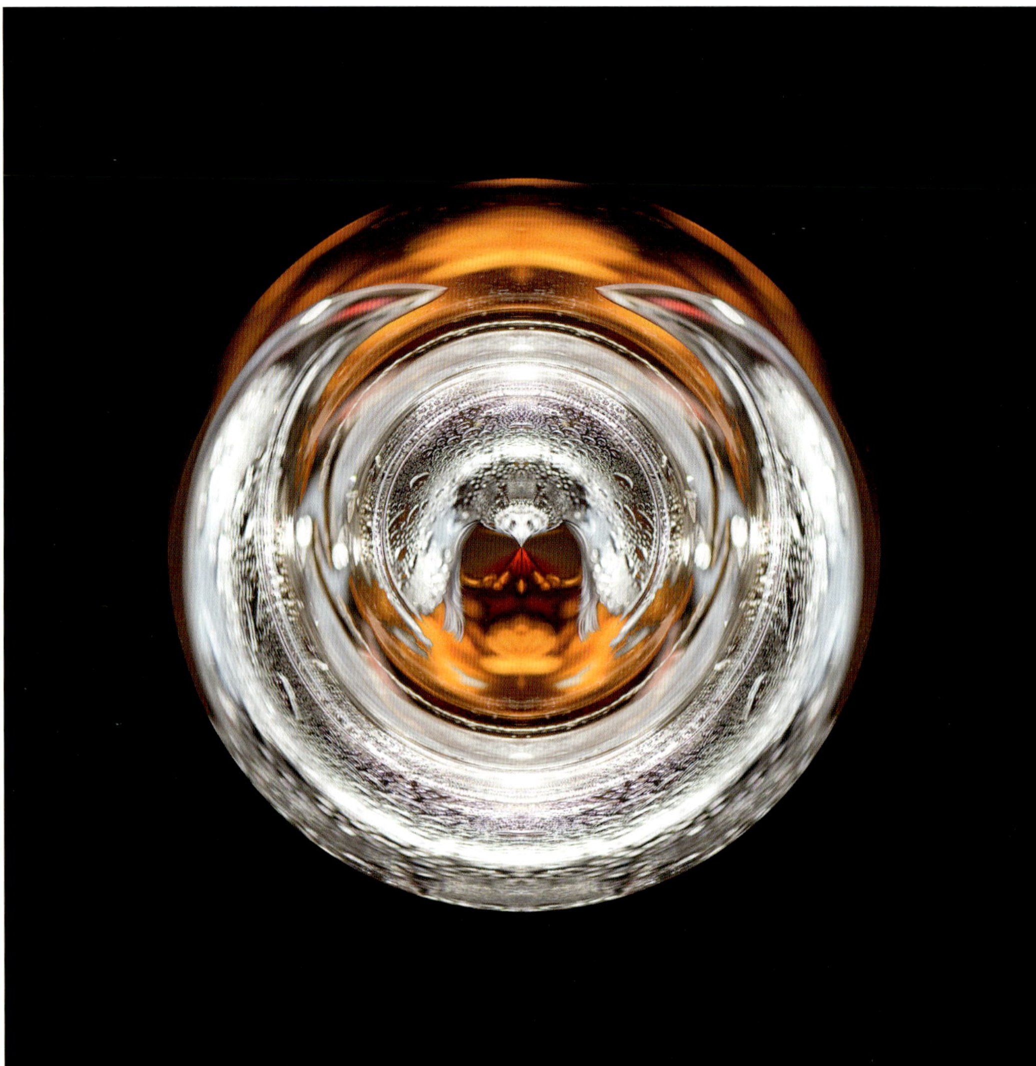

Island of Watery Color

It is hard to imagine how one subject shot from a different angle then cropped differently (all before the manipulations) could result in an image that appears to have no ties to the rest of the images in the series. The same subject is transformed into divergent results. These flowery creations remind me of embroidered flowers from the late 1800s or early 1900s. The slightly muted colors, the bubble and flower motif, the center island of watery color in which the white flowers float, all seem to call to me from a time long ago.

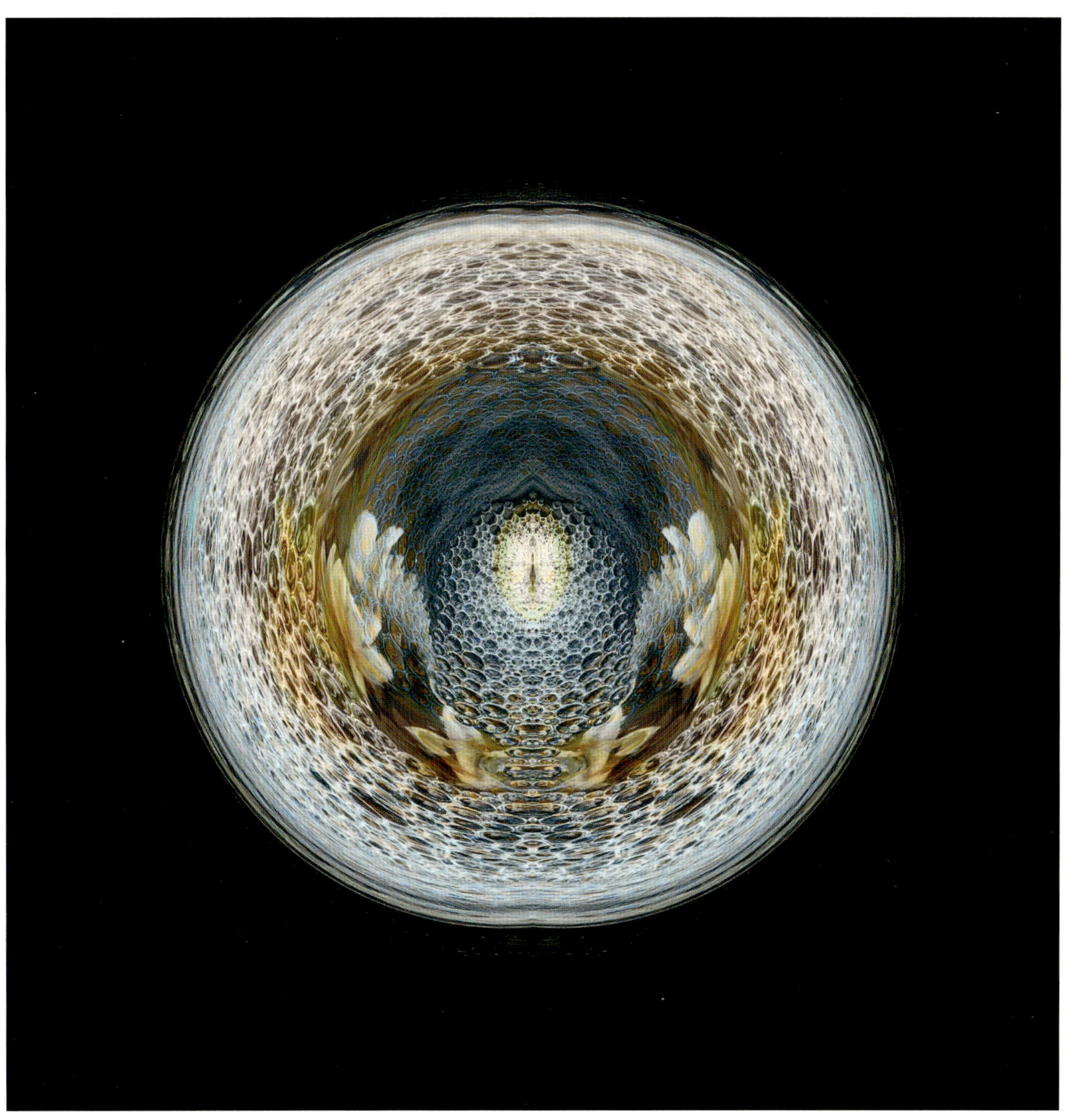

Two Pieces Together

Initially, much of this image just didn't go with the rest, but a similar image fit beautifully. I stripped away the lower portions of the circle and found that lovely heart in a related file. They went together so perfectly. The added heart is an echo of the heart on the top of the circle. The two pieces come together in a happy marriage.

Abstraction is basically the process of elimination. Pulling away sections of the composition . . .

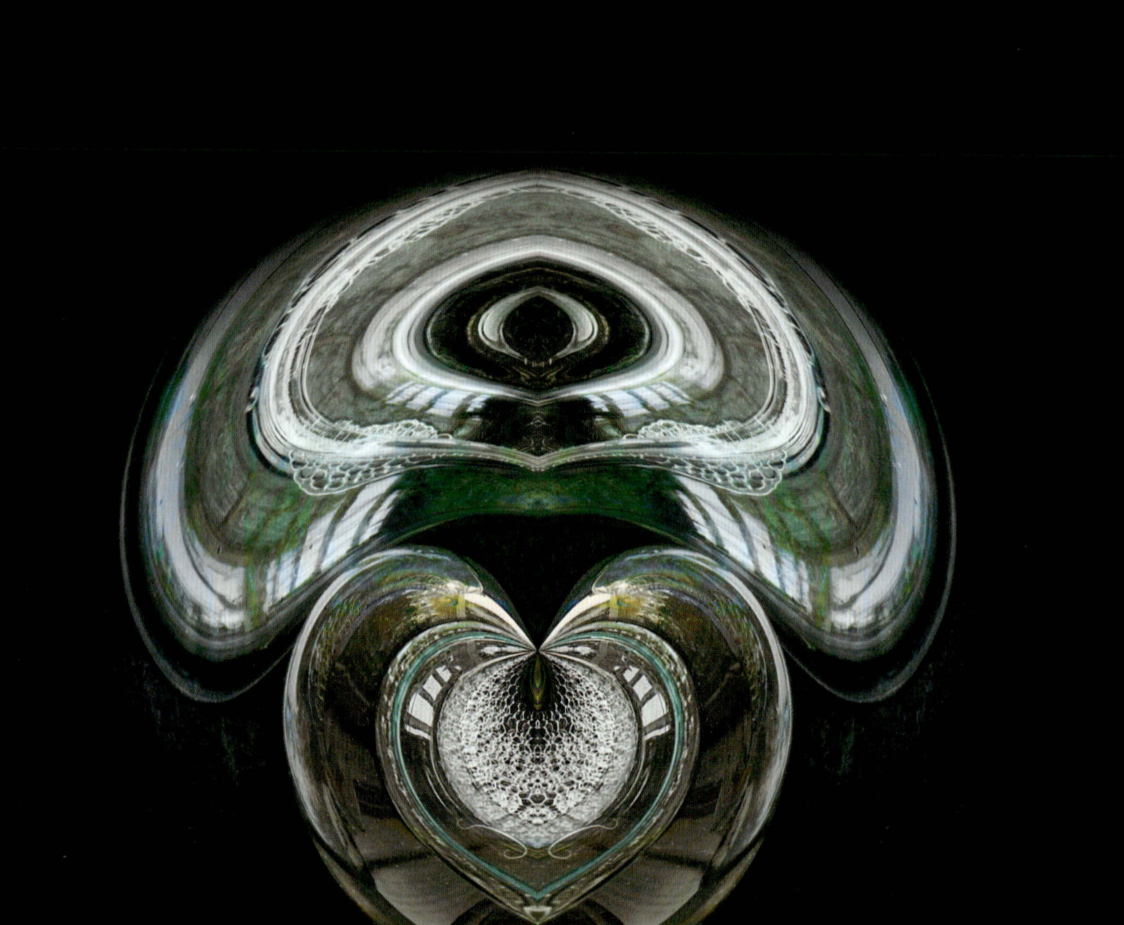

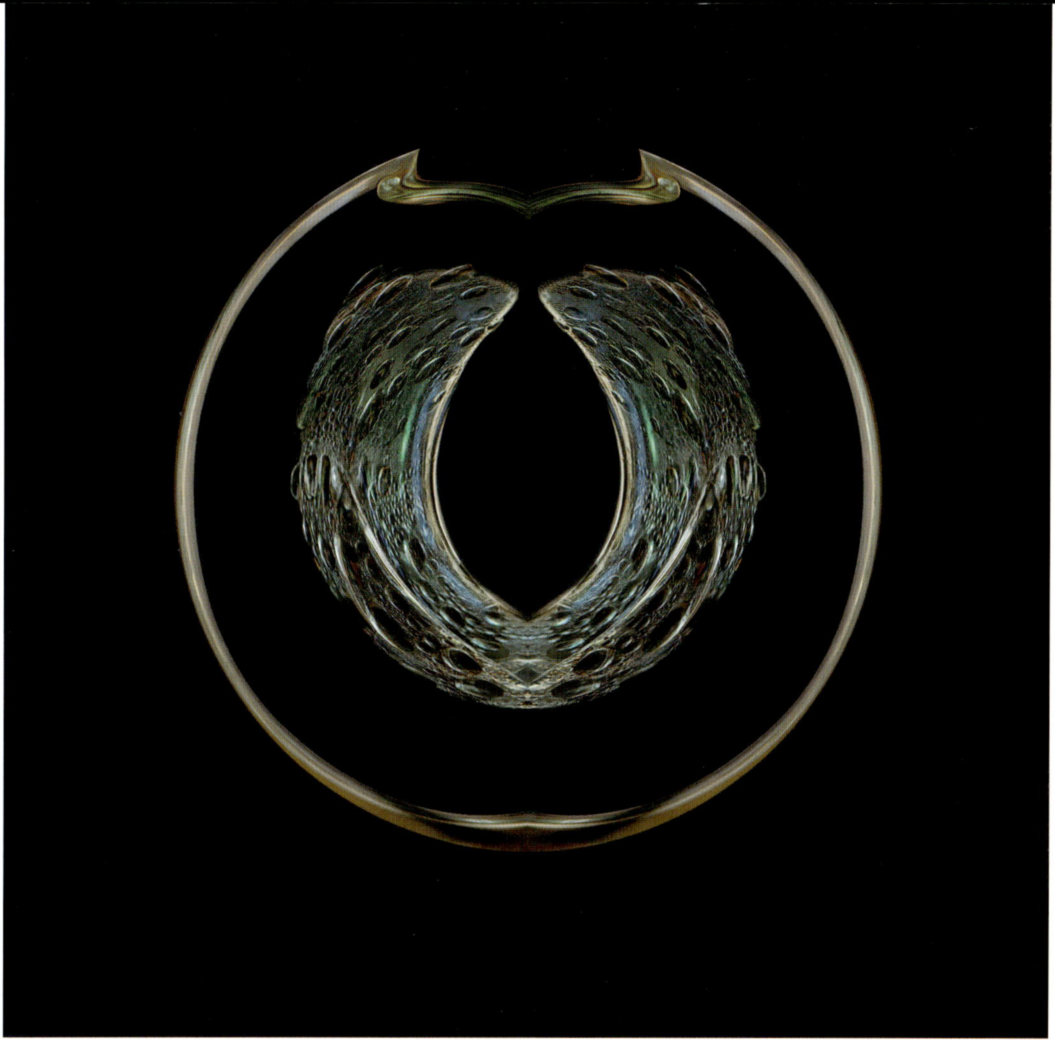

Abstraction by Elimination

Toward the end of the *Tea Reconsidered* series, I began working with the idea of abstraction. One very simplified definition of abstraction is art from which much has been stripped away. That makes this a fairly abstract piece. I used the Pen tool to select the edge and make a necklace of the edges. The central bubbles are selected using a freehand Lasso tool, just lightly following the bubbles here, cutting into them there and making a random edge. The two pieces stand together, disconnected, but functioning as frame and subject framed.

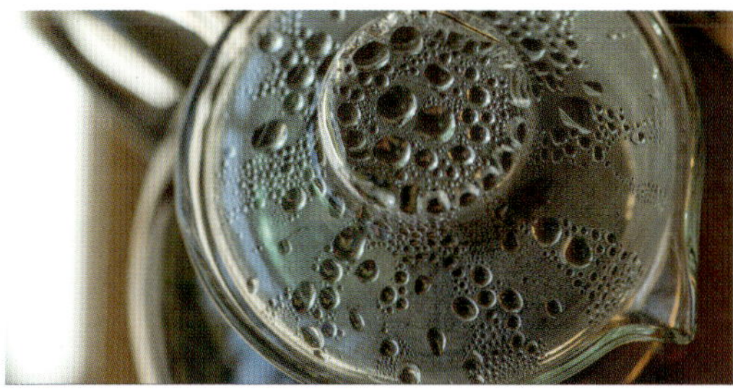

Abstraction is basically the process of elimination. Pulling away sections of the composition, there remains an allusion to the story. This composition asks questions rather than answering them.

Collaboration and Beyond

The Most Illuminating Thing

One of the most illuminating things you can do as an artist is to collaborate with another artist. I began working on a very serious graphic novel project. While chatting with a friend, Alison Miniter, about my work and showing her some of my early work, she offered some of her images as background images for my characters. I've used her backgrounds for several of the spreads, including this one.

I did a good deal of image adjusting, including more clearly defining a light direction by burning and dodging. I added the black elliptical frame to the right side, which is meant to give the impression

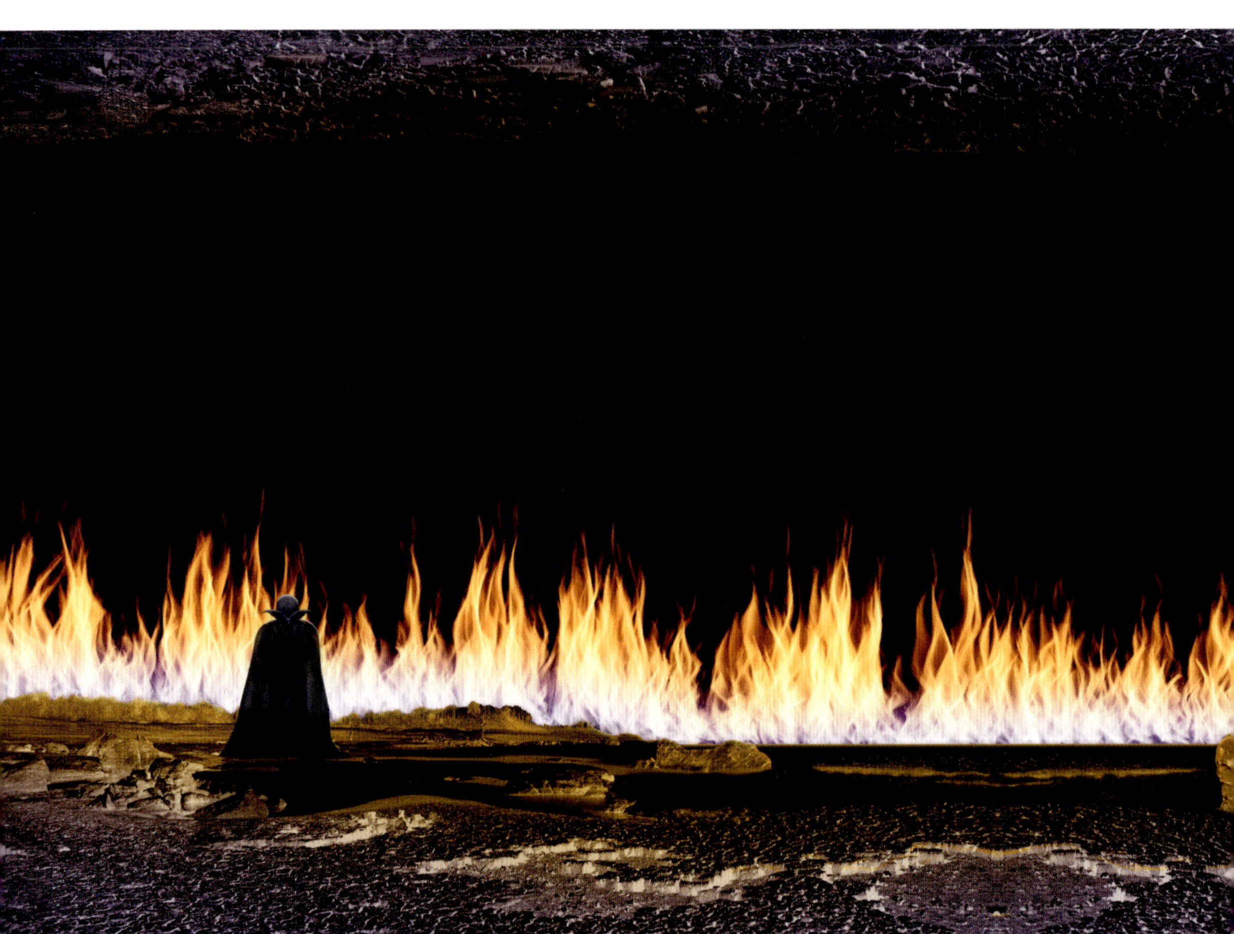

of an eye opening on the scene—like a movie transition.

Making Image Components from Scratch

Photoshop has some fun, recently added tools for making things from scratch. One is the Fire filter. It's under the Filter > Render menu. You have to create a path using the Pen tool, and then go to the fire filter. There are lots of options for adjusting the height and characteristics of the fire. With some experimentation, you'll often be able to get some appropriate fire when you need it for a scene.

One of the most illuminating things you can do as an artist is to collaborate with another artist.

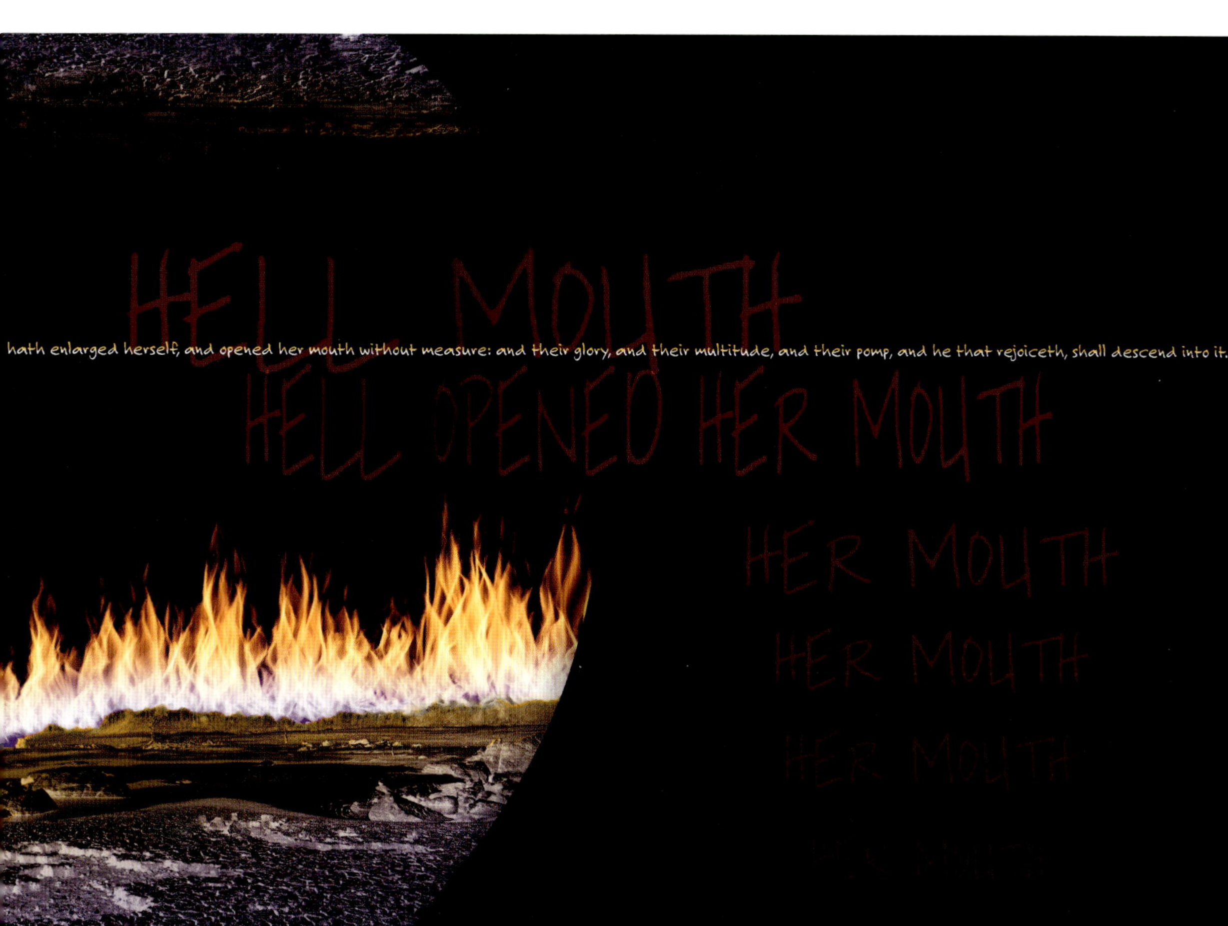

Built in Photoshop

You can built nearly any kind of tree you want, from evergreens to maples and oaks, fully leafed or bare.

This tree was also created in Photoshop. One of the other options under the Filter > Render options is a tree filter. You can build nearly any kind of tree you want, from evergreens to maples and oaks, fully leafed or bare. I was able to create exactly the right type for tree for my scene with just a little experimentation. Put the tree on its own layer and to make a reflection, copy that layer, flip it vertically (Edit > Transform > Flip Vertical) and move it into position. You can then adjust the opacity and layer blend modes, if necessary, to get the right look.

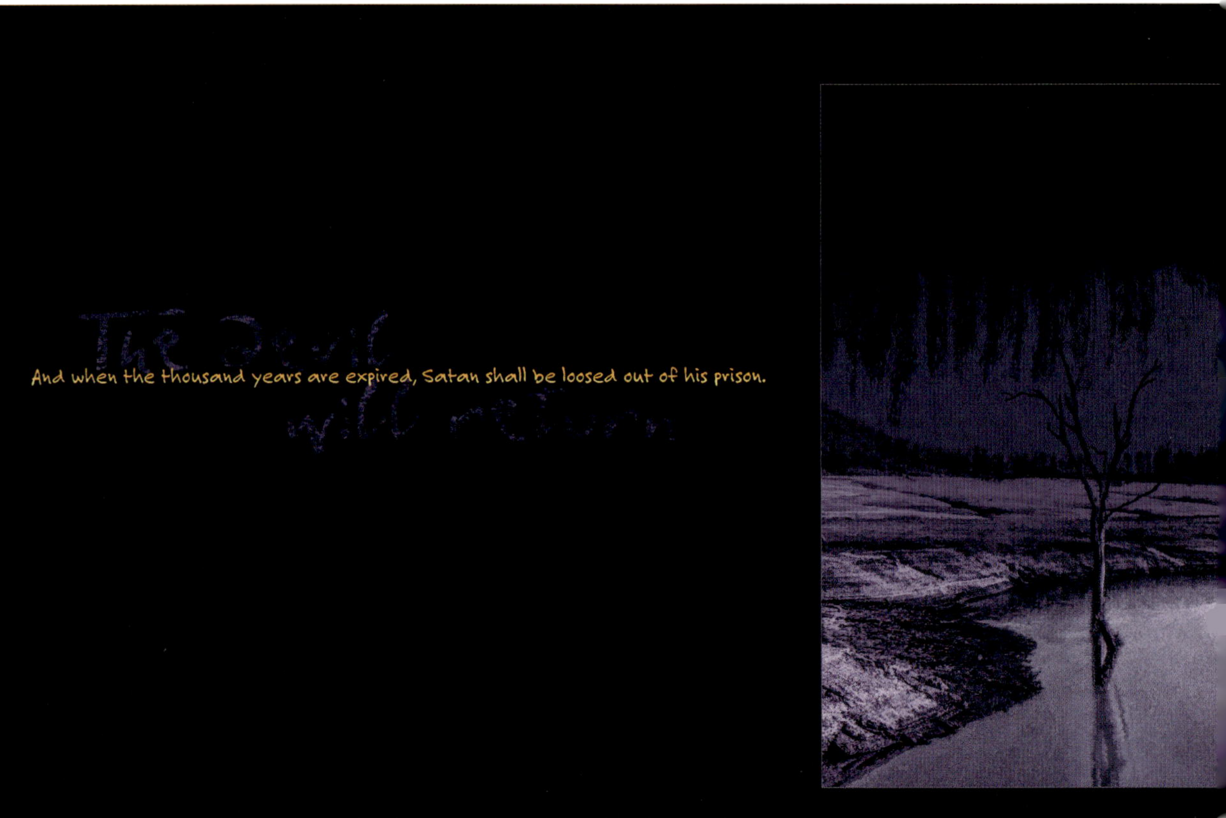

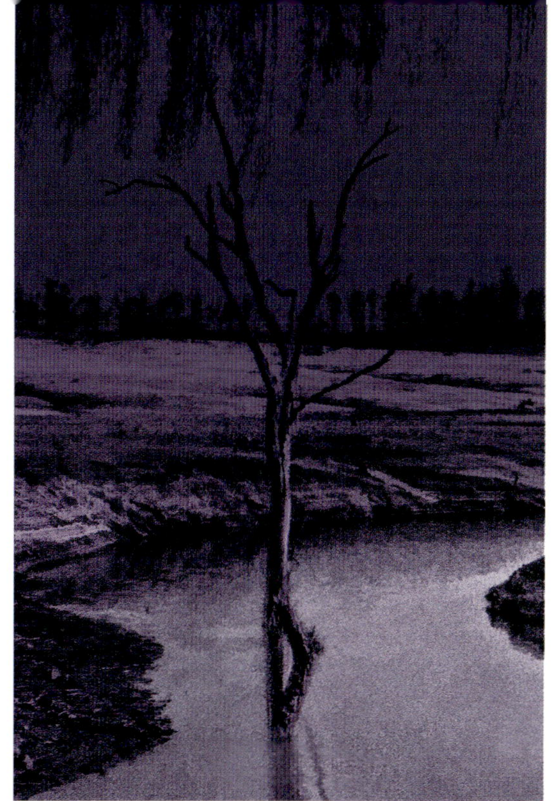

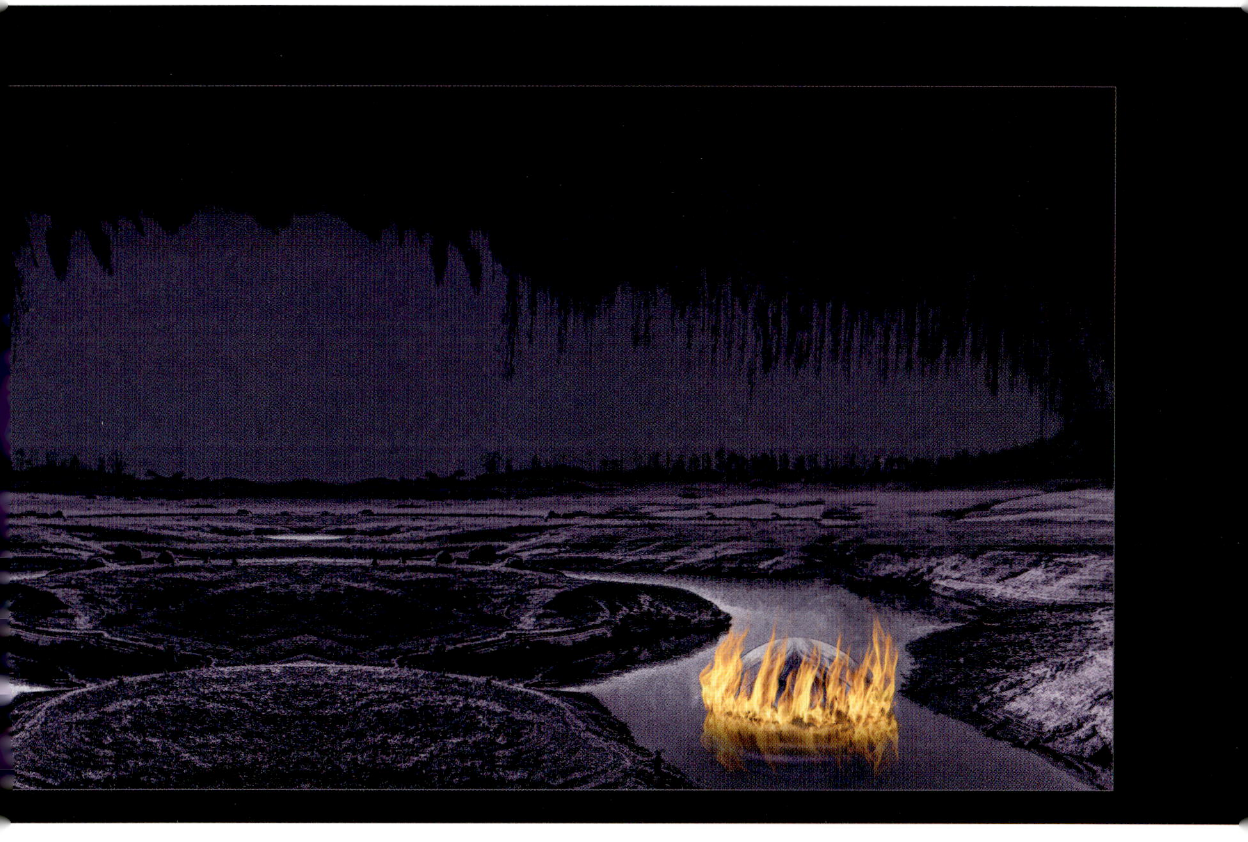

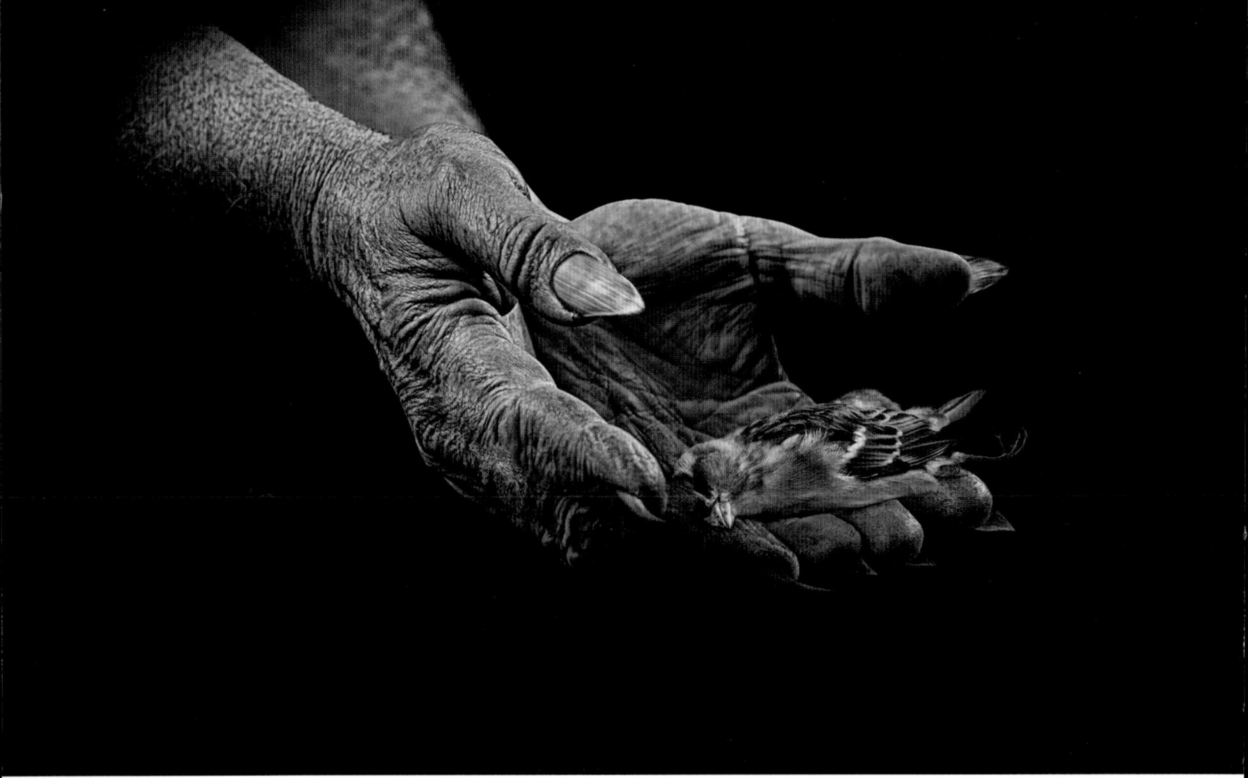

Seamless Blend

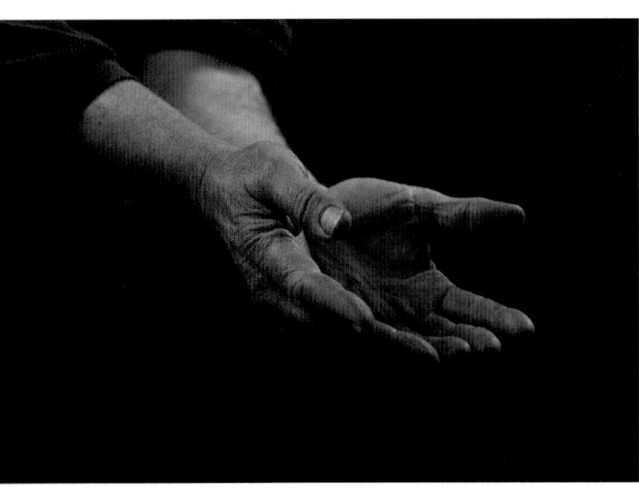

This is a very dark part of the graphic novel, and I wanted to have a distinctly creepy feel to this particular character—the villain. I photographed the hands of a man in his sixties, and to make them appear even craggier, I used Topaz Adjust to bring out the most detail in his hands, including some age spotting that was nearly invisible before. After that, I used the Burn and Dodge tools to create even more depth to the wrinkles and creases.

I photographed the man's hands in a number of positions in order to be able to use them for several pages. The bird was found after flying into a window and photographed in the studio using the same lighting in order to blend the hands and the bird together more seamlessly.

Creating Fingernails

Creating those fingernails may look daunting, but they aren't actually as difficult as they appear to be.

First make a selection of the existing fingernails. The Pen tool is very helpful in doing this, but if you use the Quick Selection tool, make the selection of the fingernail before running the Topaz Adjust plugin filter. It will be a bit easier that way. Once selected, copy the fingernail to its own layer. On this new layer, use the Transform command to lengthen the nail. Make it long enough to go well past the end of the finger. If you can use the Pen tool, then simply make the desired shape for the nail. In this case, I wanted it pointed and long to add to the very strange look. If you're not comfortable with the Pen tool, you can make a rough selection with the Lasso tool, then zoom in and erase the parts of the nail you don't need.

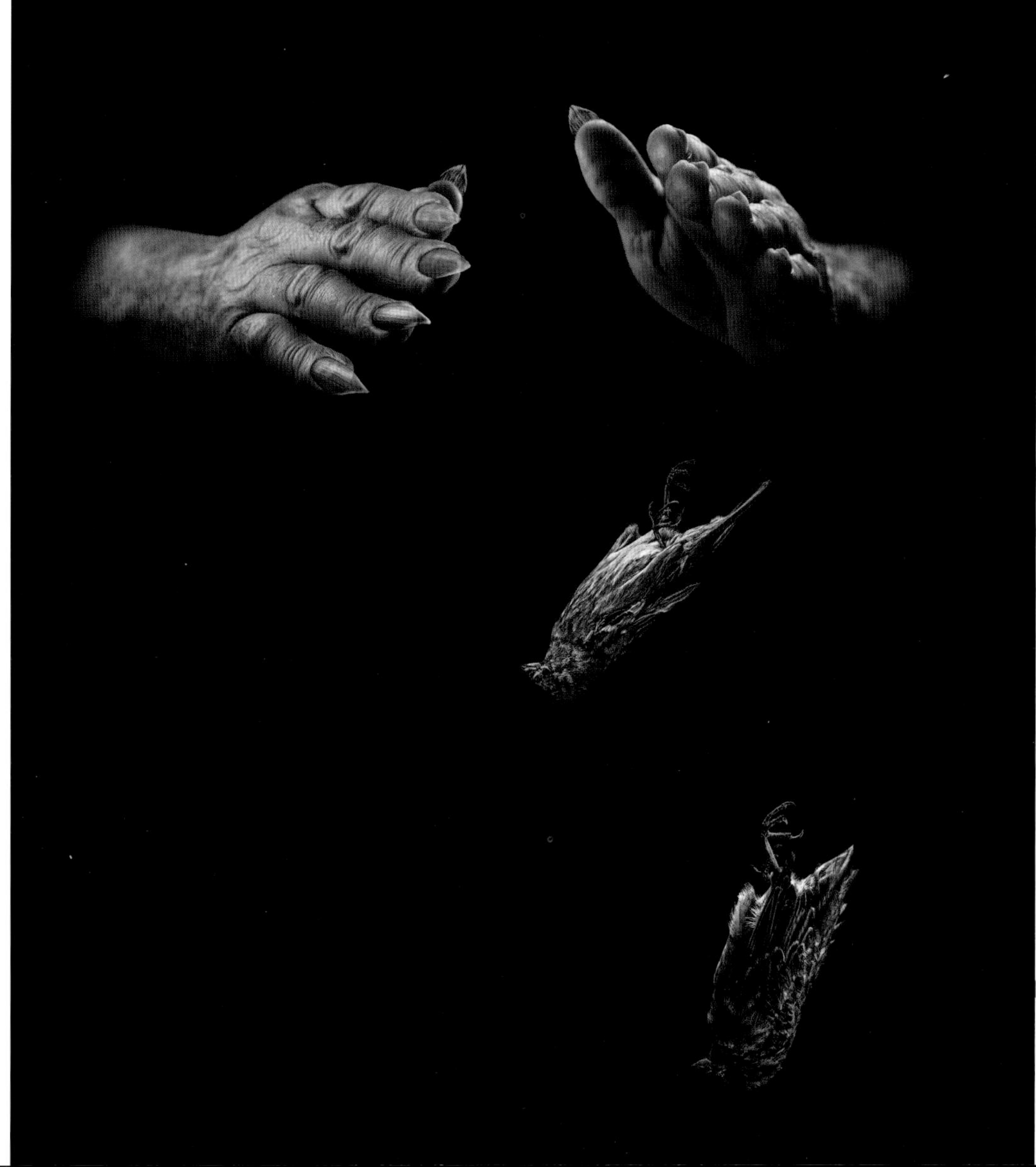

Source of Your Light

The robe this character wears is created using the same techniques used in the *Alien* and *Tea Reconsidered* series, but further enhanced. From an original photograph, a section was selected, copied and mirrored. After that, I transformed the result, pulling it into shape and bending it with the Warp tool and Liquify options in order mold it into the robe shape. Lightening and darkening areas give it dimension. Remember to keep the source of your light in mind as you do this. Your lighting needs to be consistent, even the imaginary kind, or your composition will fall apart.

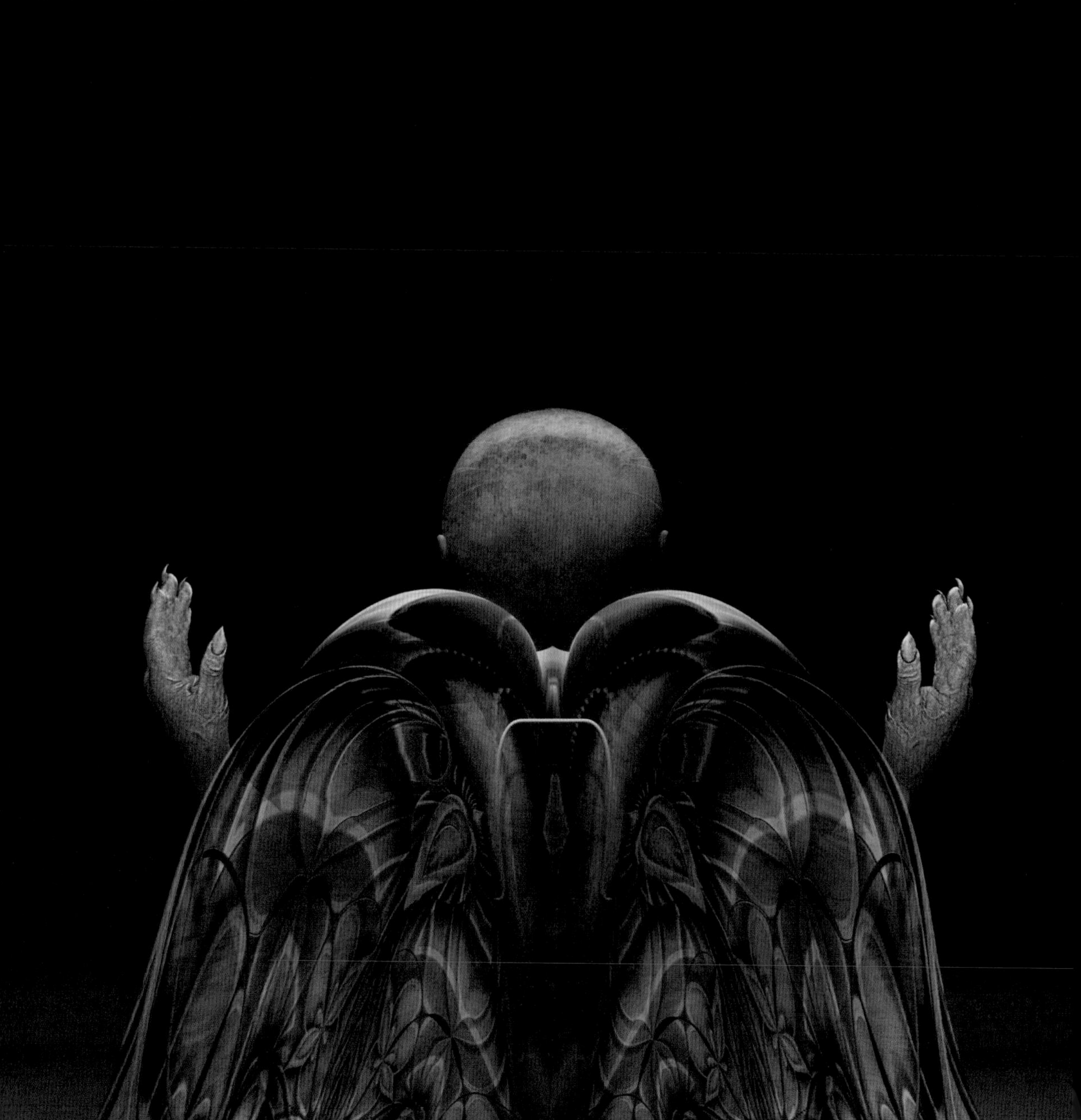

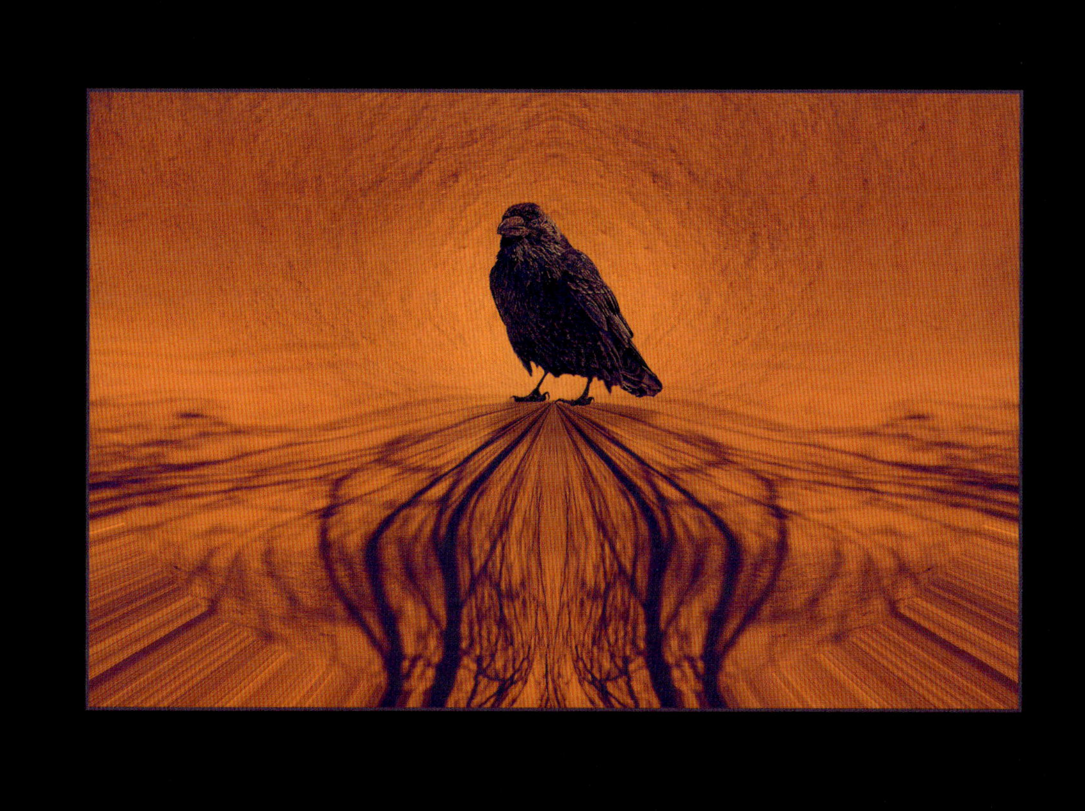

Gradient Map ▲

I photographed this black bird at Bryce Canyon, and when I was working on the graphic novel he seemed like a great addition. I selected him from the original background and ran the Topaz Adjust plugin filter to bring out detail in the feathers. The background comes from a photograph of shadows on snow. I used a gradient map to change the colors from white, off-white and gray, to the orange and dark purple colors. To do this, go to the Layer panel and choose the Gradient Map adjustment layer. You'll see a band of color—a gradient. That is the gradient that will be applied to your image. The colors to the left will be the ones mapped to the darkest colors, and the colors to the right will be mapped to the lightest colors with a range from light to dark in the middle. Click on the gradient to open up the next dialog box. Clicking just under the gradient, on the little house shapes, which are called Stops, will allow you to add colors. Once you click on a stop, or click at any spot to add a stop, go to the color box, click in it to get the color picker.

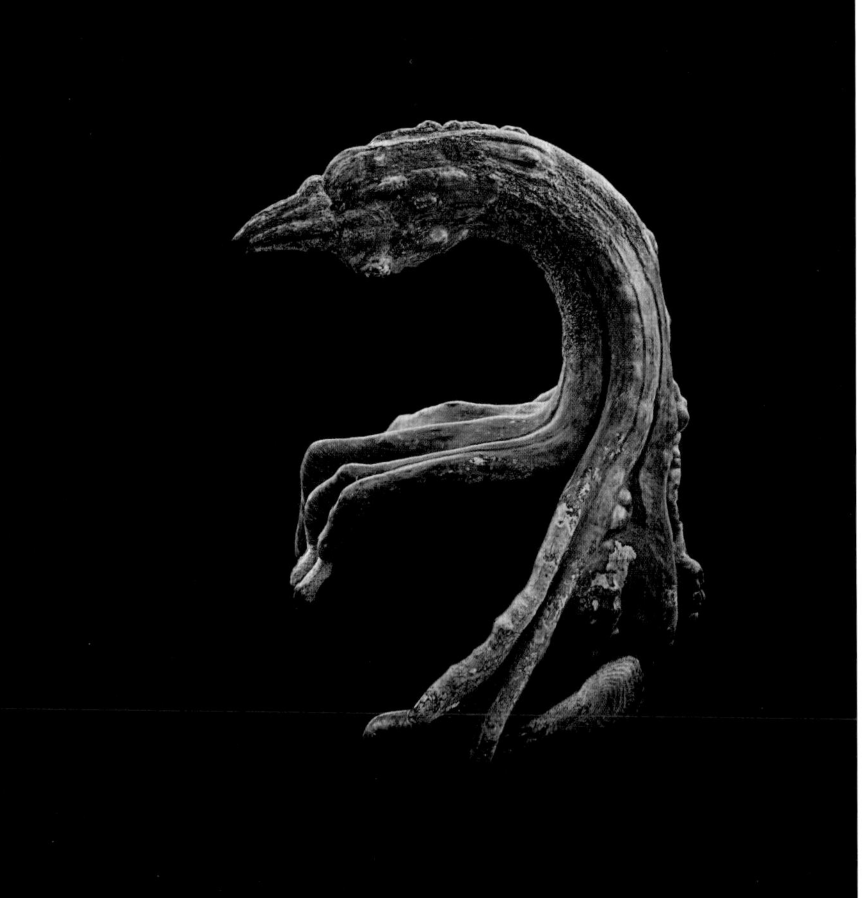

Some Kind of Creature

By taking away part of a simple gourd, in this case part of the bottom, it begins to take on different characteristics. Here, they begin to look like arms and legs, at least to me. By tapering the top end of the gourd, it enhances the look of some kind of creature.

I still love capturing something right out of the camera . . .

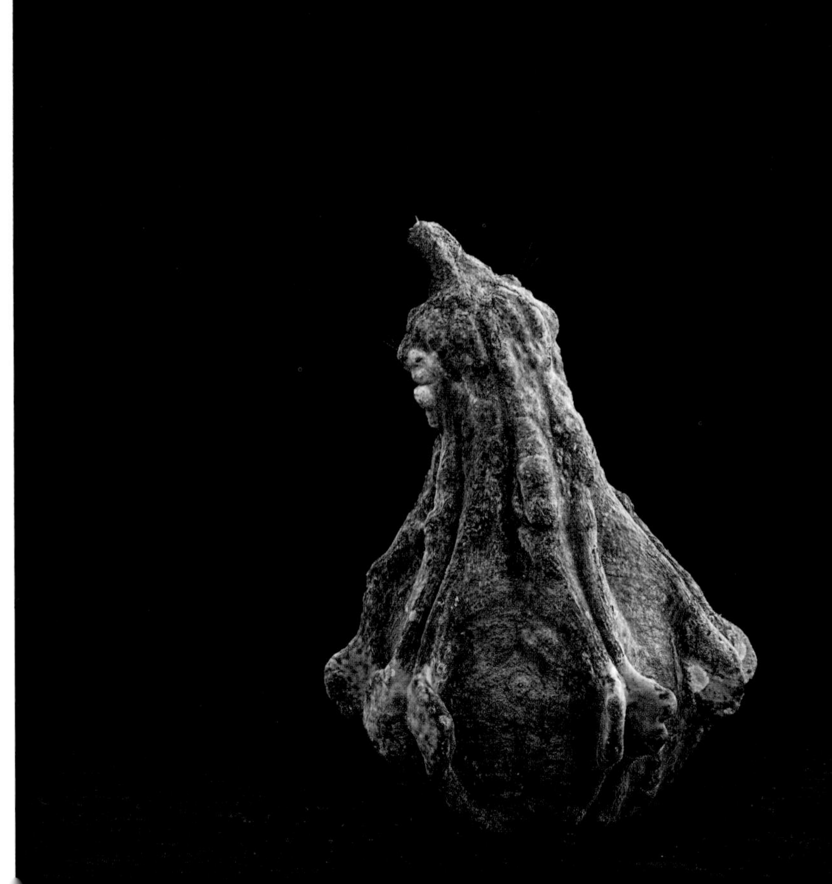

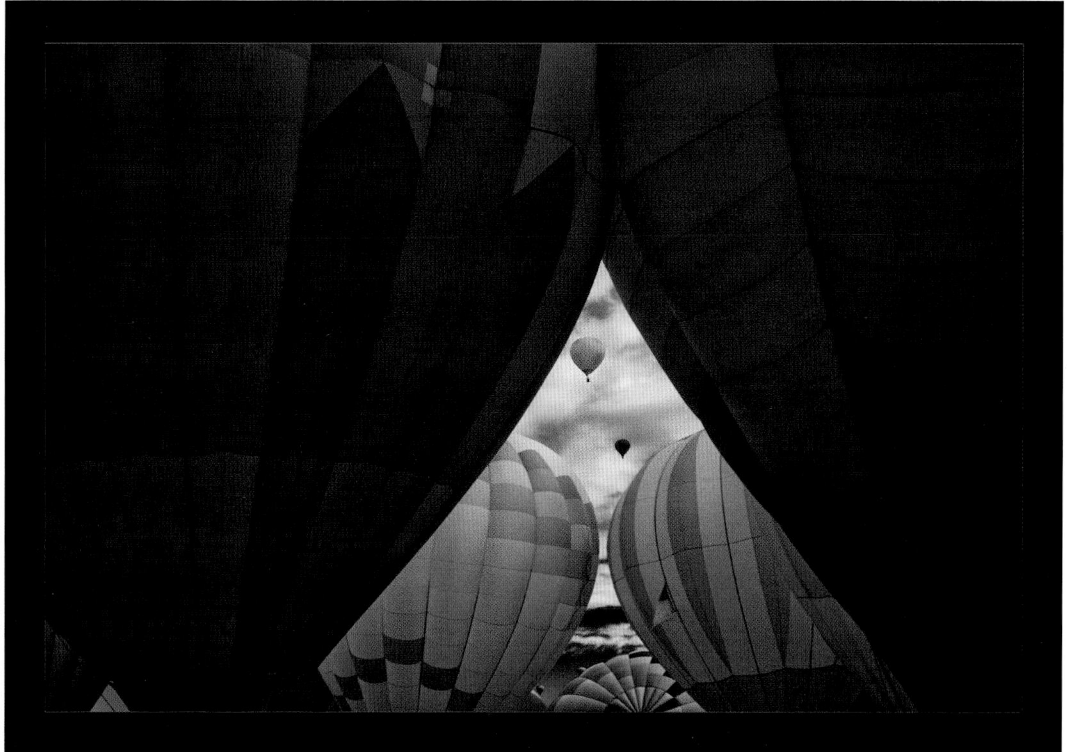

Allude to Structures ◀

All that was needed for this shot of a gourd to make it a bit more interesting was to add little whiskers on either side. Suddenly, the little bumps along the side start to allude to structures you might see in a living creature, especially considering the tilt to one side of this gourd. In really looking at the subject, often a direction becomes evident. At other times, just starting with one step will then suggest the next step.

Right Out of the Camera ▲

While I'm an avid fan of all the options available in digital imaging to manipulate images, I still love capturing something right out of the camera as well. The Albuquerque Balloon Fiesta in October is a riot of color. I'd already photographed this spectacle once before, so I approached it differently the next time I went. I brought two wide-angle lenses with me, a 24mm and a 16mm and my infrared converted camera. Albuquerque is one of the very few places left in the country where you can stand right next to the balloons as they take off, so I placed myself right between two and caught several balloons taking off for this shot.

Index